Developing and Managing a Successful Payment Cards Business

Developing and Managing a Successful Payment Cards Business

JEFF SLAWSKY and SAMEE ZAFAR

Routledge
Taylor & Francis Group
LONDON AND NEW YORK

First published 2005 by Gower Publishing

2 Park Square, Milton Park, Abingdon, Oxon OX14 4RN
711 Third Avenue, New York, NY 10017, USA

Routledge is an imprint of the Taylor & Francis Group, an informa business

First issued in paperback 2017

British Library Cataloguing in Publication Data
Slawsky, Jeff H.
Developing and managing a successful payment cards business
1. Credit cards 2. Debit cards 3. New business enterprises – Finance
I. Title II. Zafar, Samee
332.7'65'068

ISBN 978-0-566-08648-9 (hbk)
ISBN 978-1-138-24864-9 (pbk)

Library of Congress Control Number: 2005932750

Typeset by Bournemouth Colour Press, Parkstone, Poole.

Contents

List of Figures

List of Tables

CHAPTER 1

Introduction to Payment Cards

What would life be without a credit card? Unimaginably inconvenient. Credit, debit, and other payment cards are so much part of our daily lives that we take them for granted. They represent one of those necessary and indispensable things in life, like cars, computers, and light bulbs that are the 'must haves' of modern living – amazing inventions that have forever changed the way we live.

Millions of transactions are being made every day in all parts of the world with credit, debit, and charge cards – collectively called payment cards. People are using payment cards to buy groceries, clothes, shoes, household goods, books, gifts for their loved ones; paying for movie tickets or booking flights and hotels, renting cars, paying for fuel, eating at restaurants – every second of the day. Even at places where cash is predominantly being used, it is highly likely that it has been obtained from a cash machine using a payment card. It is not difficult to appreciate the extent to which we all depend on payment cards to make our lives simple and convenient.

Visa, MasterCard, and American Express are globally recognized brands that process consumer and business payments to the tune of billions and billions of dollars all across the world. Their success lies not only in offering consumers a convenient way to pay for purchases but also in enabling retailers to sell their goods and services without any credit risk.

In addition to being convenient devices for making payments, credit cards are a key source of consumer credit. This feature, within limits, works as a dynamo for economic growth. Credit cards enable customers to be billed later for purchases, usually at the end of the month. After payment of a small minimum amount, consumers can borrow the remaining outstanding balance. Admittedly, credit cards are not always the cheapest source of credit but certainly a very convenient one. Debit cards are used for immediate payment very much like checks. Payment is simply deducted from funds available in the cardholder's bank account. Charge cards, on the other hand, are in between the two. The cardholder settles the monthly bill of purchases in full at the end of the month. There is no extended credit facility. These three card types are commonly called retail or consumer card products.

Just as individual consumers use consumer card products, there are business or commercial card products for small, medium, and large business entities. Cards for small businesses are called business or small business cards while those used by employees of a company are known as corporate cards. Corporate cards are most commonly used for travel and entertainment (T&E) expenses of company employees for business purposes. There are also purchasing or procurement cards used by businesses for buying office consumables usually referred to as maintenance, repairs, and operations (MRO) items. These cards are relatively new and, except to some extent in the United States, such cards have yet to achieve widespread usage.

These cards can be used at any merchant who accepts them. Merchants display the card brands they accept. Visa and MasterCard are more widely accepted than American Express, Discover or Diners Club. There are also store cards that can only be used at one or a few selected stores. These are very similar to the original payment cards that were accepted at limited locations. Retail stores tie in promotional events and offer discounts to retain customer loyalty and encourage use of such cards. In addition there are also prepaid cards, such as gift cards, issued by banks, stores, telecommunication companies, and others that utilize a prepaid balance for spending at a specific store, location or purpose.

Technology plays an important role in the world of payment cards. Primarily, there are two forms of payment card technologies. The most prevalent is the magnetic stripe at the back of the payment card. It stores the necessary information required to process a payment transaction. The terminals – at retailers called point-of-sale (POS) terminals, or cash machines also called automated teller machines (ATM) – are devices that can read the contents of the magnetic stripe when the card is inserted or swiped. Chip or smart cards represent the next generation of payment cards. A chip card has a small embedded microprocessor that stores considerably more information than a magnetic stripe and is a lot more difficult to counterfeit.

A brief history of payment cards

Apart from the obvious pleasure of knowing unfamiliar historical trivia, there is a practical benefit to be gained from delving a little into the past history of cards. It will explain how the unique market structure of the industry developed and why some markets are very different from others.

The practice of buying things on credit is not new. It is thousands of years old. Sellers sold their goods and services on credit, maintaining customer accounts in their books often without a collateral or guarantee. Why lose a sale just because the customer does not have money to pay right at that very moment of purchase? Customers pay when they have the means to do so. Customers with regular incomes would pay up as soon as they receive their wages. Of course merchants selling on credit are more likely to extend credit to those with a regular and certain source of income and a past record of paying their debts on time.

However, credit cards developed not just because people did not have any money to pay for purchases but because people did not want to carry wads of hard cash with them all the time. It is a lot more convenient and safer to be billed later for purchases then having to carry cash in your pocket. Convenience is the primary value proposition for payment cards.

Realizing this, some establishments in the early part of the twentieth century started giving account cards to their trusted customers. This was particularly suitable for companies that had multiple and dispersed outlets such as oil companies. A motorist could purchase fuel at any station belonging to a particular oil company. The General Petroleum Corporation of California, later Mobil Oil, issued cards to employees and customers in 1914 that could only be used at the company's sales outlets. These were the first store cards.

Towards the middle of the century banks began to think of creative ways to tap this growing market. The Flatbush National Bank in New York introduced a 'Charge It' plan in 1947 and a few years later, Franklin National Bank was the first to issue credit cards. But the banking sector in general was slow in developing the new product. Other companies were quicker in realizing the immense possibilities.

Diners Club, according to company lore, was the brainchild of two visionaries Frank McNamara and Ralph Schneider. They were dining at a New York restaurant sometime in the year 1950 when to their embarrassment they discovered they did not have any cash. It is unclear how they resolved the problem but it made a lasting impression on them, and gave birth to a well-organized club of friends and colleagues. It was agreed with a selected group of hotels and restaurants to bill club members – members of the Diners Cub – on a monthly basis. It was a mutually advantageous situation. New members joined and the network of hotels and restaurants grew.

About the same time, a New York-based travel company called American Express was so impressed that it started its own club. Its merchant base also consisted mainly of restaurants, hotels, transport companies, and selected stores. In time, American Express outstripped its rival to lay the foundations of a global business that still flourishes to this day.

In the meantime, banks were gradually building up their own card businesses. By the end of the 1950s almost a million cards issued by banks were in circulation in the US. Merchants understood the positive impact on their sales but paid the fees, charged by card companies and banks, a bit reluctantly. They felt they had no choice but to pay. The charge, called the merchant service commission (MSC) or merchant service fee (MSF) or simply merchant discount, generated healthy profits for the card companies who initially proved unwilling to negotiate on these charges. This slowed down business growth in the early years.

Visionary banks understood the true potential of this new opportunity. Here was a product that was gaining consumer confidence rapidly which could be marketed to customers easily. Bank of America, a California-based bank starting in the late 1950s, successfully developed and marketed its BankAmericard throughout the state of California. After some initial hiccups, the business prospered and reached the million cards mark early in the 1960s. About this time it started licensing its card product to other banks which did not have the resources to incur the considerable set-up costs of developing their own network of merchants and cardholders. This was a watershed event in the history of the financial services industry. By the end of the decade over three thousand banks had signed up to participate in the BankAmericard franchise.

BankAmericard continued to make significant advances. Its success led to the development of rival schemes in the US. The Interbank Card Association founded in 1966 acquired the 'Master Charge' brand from the California Bank Association in 1969 later renaming it 'MasterCard' in 1979.

The BankAmericard business also evolved during this time and after such uninspirational acronym-heavy names as IBANCO and NBI, it rebranded itself as Visa – a name that was to go down in history as one of the most widespread, successful, and well-recognized global brands in the world. A lot of Visa's successes were due to its visionary leader, a charismatic banker called Dee Hock, in whose formidable presence, it is said, employees and senior bankers literally trembled in fear. But it was not fear that helped make Visa a household name but Dee Hock's dogged and relentless pursuit of his vision for the future of the credit card industry.

But his forceful leadership style, while resolute and confident, began to create friction with senior bankers particularly outside the US. His famous disagreements with Dr Eckart Van Hooven of Deutsche Bank led the German banks to develop and expand separate European payment systems delaying Visa's (and MasterCard's) growth in Europe by many years. Eurocheque was set up in 1969 and operated along with Eurocard, with the two merging in 1990s, to form Europay. Europay was acquired by MasterCard and the combined entity is now known as MasterCard Europe. In the UK, Barclays Bank acquired a license to market the BankAmericard in the mid 1960s and became the dominant Visa player. Rival banks joined to form Access which was also later acquired by MasterCard.

There are three dominant global brand names in the world today: Visa, MasterCard and American Express. Discover, Diners Club, and JCB and many other regional or product specific brand names are also prevalent. The dominant local brands in domestic markets are usually linked to either Visa or MasterCard.

In the US, till the mid 1970s, banks could be members of either Visa or MasterCard but not both. Worthen Bank and Trust, a Visa member bank, filed a lawsuit against Visa for not allowing this membership 'duality'. The case was settled out of court but Visa, perhaps expecting additional lawsuits, eliminated the 'duality' condition in 1976 for both issuing and acquiring.

Card transactions

How does a payment card work? Well, in the simplest of terms, one can say that there are two basic components of a payment card transaction. The first is transaction authorization. When a retailer swipes a card at a POS terminal, an electronic message is sent all the way to the issuer requesting it to authorize the transaction, in other words, guaranteeing payment to the merchant, so that they can deliver the goods and services to the cardholder. In the second component, the merchant submits the authorized transaction for payment which is usually received within one to three days. This process of transaction completion is called clearing and settlement. The transaction then appears in the cardholder's card or bank statement.

In the early days, authorizations were all voice based. The merchant would phone to obtain transaction authorization. Now electronic POS terminals automatically do so by dialing out, using the Internet or dedicated/leased lines on a telecommunications network. In countries where the telecommunication infrastructure is widespread, efficient, and inexpensive, all or most payment card transactions are authorized online. Other markets have developed floor limits; transactions are only authorized online if the transaction value is greater than the floor limit. Sometimes they may be authorized against data held at intermediary computers only. The key trade-off in this context is between credit/fraud risk and costs of online authorization.

Types of widely used payment cards

PAYMENT CARDS

All types of cards that are used to make payments are called payment cards. The term broadly encompasses all forms of card-based payment products irrespective of who issues, markets, or services them. These may be issued by banks, card companies, retail stores, or other private or public entities.

BANKCARDS

Bankcards are payment cards issued by banks. However, the term is quite commonly though inaccurately used to describe all forms of payment cards.
Let us review two main categories of payment cards: consumer cards and commercial cards.

CONSUMER (OR RETAIL OR PERSONAL) CARDS

Consumer cards are issued to individuals and are used for personal expenditure. The decision to issue a personal card is dependent upon the customer's financial standing with the bank evaluated using internal and external reports on financial assets, earning power, and credit history. As we will describe in a later chapter, the process for reviewing an application for a card depends on the type of card the customer wants. A credit card application requires far greater evaluation than a debit card which provides a convenient way to access one's funds with the bank and is normally issued, like a check book, as part of a bank account.

Credit/charge cards

Credit and charge cards are issued by banks, card companies, and stores for the purposes of making purchases at points of sale. They can also be used to obtain cash advances at ATMs and branch locations. They offer a convenient way to make payments by accessing a credit limit that has been assigned to them by the card issuer. Cardholders benefit from an interest-free period as they can pay for all their purchases at the end of the billing period. There is also an optional extended credit facility. After making a minimum payment, cardholders can choose to borrow the remaining outstanding balance they owe the card company. Charge cards are similar to credit cards as they offer convenience and an interest-free period but do not offer an extended credit facility. The balance must be paid back in full on due date.

Debit cards

Debit cards are issued by banks. They enable cardholders to make purchases and withdraw cash against the cardholder's funds available with the bank in the same way as checks. Because they are almost always linked to a bank account, debit cards are classified as bankcards – that is, they are issued by banks to their customers. In general, all over the world, debit card transactions are processed in the same way as credit or charge transactions. However, in the US, a slightly different terminology is used. Debit cards requiring personal identification number (PIN) entry as a part of the authorization process and owned by such networks as STAR and NYCE are called 'online' debit cards. Visa and MasterCard debit cards, known as Visa Check and MasterMoney respectively, are very similar to credit and charge cards in terms of transaction authorization, clearing, and settlement, and are called 'offline' debit cards. Both types, however, access funds in bank accounts with the card issuer.

Online debit cards usually do not offer the same additional benefits of fraud protection and insurance as credit, charge, and offline debit cards do.

ATM-only cards

Also called cash cards, these cards are used to withdraw cash from ATMs. The use of ATM-only cards is becoming less and less common but many large banks continue to issue ATM cards as part of their basic bank account package. In some instances, as in the US, these cards can be used at selected local merchants for purchases.

Retailer or store cards

These cards are issued by retailers such as department stores and specialty shops (store cards), oil companies (fuel cards), and others. They are also commonly referred to as 'private label' cards and are accepted only at the card issuer's stores or outlets. They operate as charge or credit cards.

COMMERCIAL CARDS

Commercial cards are issued to small, medium, and large business enterprises. They assist businesses to 'empower' their employees to control their purchasing activities and facilitate better expense management.

It is important to note that commercial cards can be credit, charge, or even debit cards, but most often in the marketplace they operate as charge cards. The outstanding balance is due at the end of the billing period.

Business cards

Business cards are issued to small businesses. Though there is no standard definition across markets, these are generally defined as entities with fewer than ten employees or under US $1 million in annual turnover. The card is also known as the 'small business card'. The card is generally issued based upon the personal guarantees or personal credit history of the primary business owner.

Corporate cards

Corporate cards are issued to larger businesses – usually corporations – for employees' travel and entertainment (T&E) purposes. Corporate card systems have expense reporting capabilities which are used by companies to monitor and track corporate expenses. The reporting features enable corporations to aggregate transaction and balance data by cost centers, departments, or other organizational units within the company. Corporate cards are issued based upon the company's financial standing and stability but the responsibility to repay the balance is usually the employee's.

Purchasing or procurement cards

The purchasing card is a relatively new product specifically designed to meet the needs of centralized purchasing departments of major corporations. Corporations spend significant amounts of money, often in a number of currencies, for MRO items. The traditional purchasing process requires the setting up of trading accounts with suppliers and booking the transaction within the regular accounts receivable/accounts payable systems. This process is time consuming and administratively expensive. Purchasing cards automate this process reducing the administrative costs of running purchasing operations. In addition, they enable better control over corporate expenditures by providing spending and tax information.

Card technologies

Most cards today operate on two types of technologies. The most prevalent is the magnetic-stripe technology, which is inexpensive but vulnerable to attacks by fraudsters. Smartcard technology, on the other hand, is more sophisticated and far more secure. In a later chapter, we will review smartcards and other latest leading card technologies in more detail.

The magnetic stripe is the thin stripe on the back of the card which stores important data about the customer account to which it is attached. Smartcards, or chip cards have a small computer microprocessor embedded on the face of the plastic card. The chip has significantly more memory than the ordinary magnetic stripe and also has computational functionality, allowing it to process stored information. For smartcards to work, ATMs and point-of-sale terminals must have the capability to read the information stored on the embedded microprocessors.

Lending

To millions of consumers around the world, credit cards provide a quick and effective, if not always the most economical, source of financing their purchases. Banks have traditionally offered installment lending services to their customers. The financing structure of traditional installment lending is simple. The customer requests to borrow a specified amount of money. The bank reviews the request and, subject to the customer's credit worthiness, decides whether or not to approve the request. If the request is approved, the bank then develops a schedule of repayments over the term of the loan and determines the monthly or quarterly installments to be paid, each installment containing two elements – a part repayment of the principal amount borrowed and the interest for the period. The terms and conditions for such loans are stipulated by the bank and also negotiated by the customer with the bank. Mortgages represent the most common form of installment lending.

Banks usually require some form of security or collateral to reduce their exposure in the event of a default. Secured loans are made in exchange for an 'interest' in some type of an asset owned by the customer – usually in the item being purchased such as the property being mortgaged in case of mortgages, or as funds on deposit with the bank or other tangible assets. In the event the borrower is unable to repay the loan amount, the bank holds the legal right to repossess the asset and liquidate it to satisfy the loan outstanding.

Credit and charge cards have only recently started offering installment lending on specific purchases made with the card. For example, some issuers allow cardholders to select purchases over a certain amount, such as payments for a new kitchen, household equipment items, or holidays abroad, and convert them to installment loans with flexible terms and conditions. Cardholders can treat the amount as a separate loan to be repaid in equal installments over the period of the loan.

Most credit card lending, however, is of a different type. It is called 'revolving' credit which is very different from installment credit. The key feature of revolving credit is that there is no specific outstanding loan amount. Instead, the lender grants a line of credit against which the customer can borrow and make payments multiple times during the year. In this sense the revolving credit is an open form of credit. The customer may not only make actual purchases but can draw cash against the credit line as well.

Revolving credit is most commonly, though not always, granted without any collateral or security. It is unsecured lending. The bank determines the credit line or limit decision based upon the customer's risk profile which includes consideration of his or her previous borrowing history, knowledge of the customer from other financial relationships with the bank, and other factors such as total household income and total repayment commitments. In the event the borrower does not repay the loan as agreed, the bank has no security or collateral to repossess and satisfy its debt. There is considerably more risk involved in unsecured lending than in secured lending.

The policy for managing revolving credit risk is very different from that for installment lending. In installment lending, the actual outstanding loan balance plus any unpaid charges and interest appear as receivables in the lender's books and represent the lender's total exposure. But in revolving credit, both the line of credit available to the cardholder as well as the extent to which it is actually utilized (amount borrowed) together throw light on the wisdom and success of the overall risk policy of the bank. Cardholders can, on their own, enhance or reduce the outstanding balance. These risk measures have to be reviewed continually and a careful eye has to be kept over credit-line management. An over-conservative risk policy means lower credit lines but missed revenue earning opportunities. An over-aggressive risk policy translates to higher lines of credit resulting in credit losses eroding program profitability.

So while installment lending requires the bank to make a lending decision at a single point in time based upon information available on the credit worthiness of the customer at the time of the loan, revolving credit requires the bank to monitor the customer's credit status on a continuous basis. The tools and techniques required to effectively manage the bank's risk exposure are explored in a later chapter in this book.

Business profitability

Across the world, the payment cards business has consistently produced healthy returns on investment making it one of the most profitable businesses in the financial services industry. Card companies that lost money in the past decade or so were primarily the victims of their own aggressive lending policies resulting in bankruptcies and credit write-offs. This is quite an achievement for a mature product operating in highly competitive, developed, and saturated markets.

Morgan Stanley's (see Figure 1.1) research shows that Western Europe and North America – the more developed regions of the world in terms of market penetration and credit consumption – are poised to maintain their current levels of profitability despite market saturation and severe competition among issuers. Advances in technology, strong emphasis on risk management, focus on operational cost optimization, pricing strategies that look beyond the traditional sources of revenue, and development of new products and services are some of the key factors that will help maintain healthy industry returns in the future. However, overstretched markets like the UK may see returns decline partially due to possible increases in personal bankruptcies but mainly due to expected cuts in bank interchange fees. Interchange fees are explained in a later chapter.

Profitability levels in Latin America and Asia Pacific are expected to remain stable. Overall market returns in Hong Kong and Taiwan are expected to increase due to reduction in credit losses. South Korea will generate low returns reversing the trend of substantial

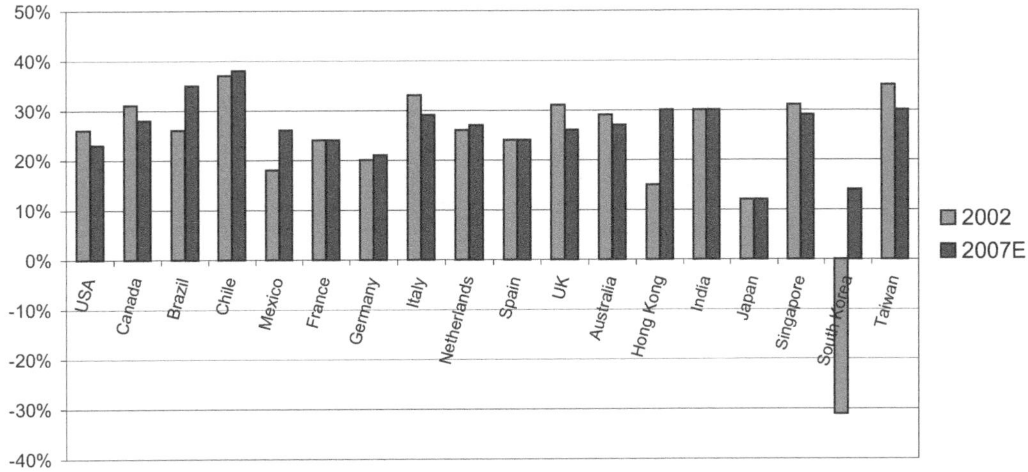

Source: Morgan Stanley Report 2003

Figure 1.1 Credit card return on equity

losses in the past. Those losses had been suffered in the wake of a bloated market for consumer credit which stood at 83 per cent of income (compared to Japan 49 per cent; USA 31 per cent; UK 17 per cent).

CHAPTER 2 How Payment Cards Work

How do payment cards work? Most of us know the basics of course. We know that when we use a payment card to make a purchase we are authorizing our bank or credit card company to pay the merchant on our behalf. Debit card purchases are deducted from funds on deposit with the bank, and credit or charge card purchases are billed to us at the end of the month.

Let's take a quick look at a card transaction. You live in London and are visiting New York. You need some cash to pay for the taxi from the airport to your hotel. You walk up to an ATM at the airport to withdraw some cash. In an instant, the ATM verifies that the card belongs to you by verifying your PIN (personal identification number). It sends a message to your bank in London to ask if you have enough money in your account. Your bank checks your account and approves the request because there are sufficient funds in your account. Cash in dollars is immediately dispensed while your account in London is debited with an equivalent amount in pounds. The exchange rate is usually better than any other you can obtain elsewhere. All this is done in a matter of a few seconds – at any hour of the day or night.

In New York during your stay, you make some purchases with your card. Just like an ATM, the merchant's POS terminal requests and obtains approval from your card issuer to complete the transaction. The merchant receives a payment guarantee and can, therefore, deliver your purchases without any risk. The store does not know you or your credit history but sells the goods to you without receiving cash. It does so because it knows once the transaction is approved, payment is guaranteed. The purchases are billed to you later in your own currency, while the merchant obtains funds in their own currency shortly afterwards. This transaction too is completed in the matter of a few seconds.

It is not difficult to see the convenience payment cards lend to the process of buying and selling. But more than anything else, payment cards enable merchants to sell goods to complete strangers without encountering any credit risk. This payment guarantee is the key feature at the heart of the payment card revolution and has a significant positive impact on retailer sales. At the same time, consumers are happy because they can make purchases in an organized and convenient way, often on credit and from a seller who does not know them at all.

No other method of payment is capable of such versatility. But what goes on behind the scenes is taken for granted. So let's briefly review how a bank transaction is completed.

Flow of a bankcard transaction

Purchase transactions made with bankcards operate in a four party payment system. Each party plays a key role in the completion of a payment transaction and together they ensure that card transactions are undertaken in a safe and satisfactory manner.

A key principle in the value proposition of payment cards is what is known as the 'honor all cards rule'. Visa and MasterCard require their merchants to accept all cards that carry their respective brands. A merchant cannot accept Visa debit cards but not Visa credit cards. Partial acceptance would cause confusion in the minds of the customers and dilute the brand's overall value.

The four parties involved in a transaction are:

- *Cardholder* – the customer of a financial institution (the card issuer) who has been issued a bankcard by that institution to withdraw cash and make purchases;
- *Merchant* – the seller of goods and services and a client of a financial institution (the merchant acquirer) who guarantees payment for authorized payment card transactions at the time of the transaction. Money is paid to the merchant shortly thereafter;
- *Card issuer (or issuer)* – the financial institution which issues the bankcard to the cardholder;
- *Merchant acquirer (or acquirer)* – the financial institution which makes the payment to the merchant for bankcard transactions.

Subject to how a particular payment market is organized, there is also a fifth party involved in a bankcard transaction: the bankcard scheme such as Visa or MasterCard facilitating the transaction directly or indirectly.

The card issuer has a direct relationship with the cardholder: debit cardholders are almost always retail banking customers whereas credit and charge customers may not have any deposit accounts with the issuer; indeed the issuer may not be a bank but a specialist credit card issuing business such as MBNA or Capital One.

The merchant acquirer is a financial institution with a business relationship with the merchant. It markets to and signs up merchants to accept bankcards. It undertakes to guarantee payment against all approved bankcard transactions.

Figure 2.1 shows the process flow for a purchase transaction. The two financial institutions – the card issuer and the merchant acquirer act as providers of payment transaction services whereas the cardholder and the merchant can be viewed as 'consumers' of payment transaction services.

Four-party payment systems – roles and responsibilities

Each participant provides a number of critical elements to the bankcard transaction process. Therefore, it is important to understand the specific roles and responsibilities each participant performs in making the process work.

CARD ISSUER

The issuing financial institution's roles and responsibilities are as follows:

- Recruit customers and enter into contract with them to provide bankcards for making purchases and withdrawing cash.
- Extend credit to and/or manage cardholder accounts (funds on deposit or credit limit).
- Bill the cardholder – preparing and delivering cardholder statements.

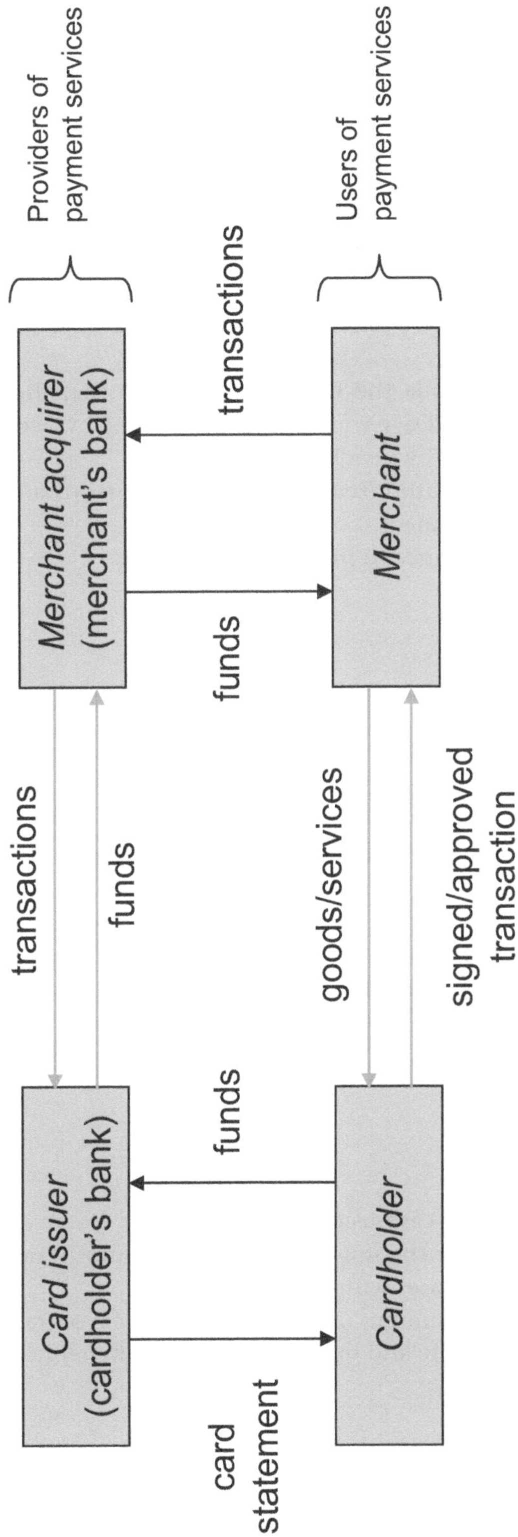

Figure 2.1 Purchase transaction process flow

- Pay the acquiring financial institution for payments made to merchants on behalf of the issuer's cardholders – directly or via a payment association such as Visa or MasterCard.
- Finance the purchase transactions as acquirer is paid immediately or within a few days whereas, in the case of credit and charge cards, funds are received from the cardholder at a later date.
- Receive interchange fee from the acquirer for transactions made by issuer's cardholders at the acquirer's merchants.

MERCHANT ACQUIRER

The acquiring financial institution's roles and responsibilities include:

- Recruit merchants and provide the necessary set-up so that the merchant is able to accept cards for payment (POS terminals can be owned by acquirers and let out to merchants or directly owned by merchants).
- Enable transactions to be authorized and processed for onward submission to card issuers for clearing and settlement.
- Providing support and assistance to merchants.
- Pay the merchants.
- Receive fees from merchants.
- Pay interchange fees to issuers.

MERCHANTS

The merchant's roles and responsibilities are:

- Capture card data from the magnetic stripe at the back of the card or from the embedded chip.
- Initiate and authorize the purchase transaction through the payment card system.
- Verify cardholder identity by checking the signature or enabling entry of PIN at the POS.
- Capture the transaction for onward submission to the merchant acquirer.
- Pay a fee called the merchant service commission (MSC) to the merchant acquirer.

CARDHOLDERS

The cardholder's role includes:

- Make purchases or withdraw cash using the card.
- Pay the full amount billed or the minimum amount requested or have sufficient funds on deposit for making purchases with a debit card.
- Pay interest and / or fees on amount unpaid as per terms of contract with the card issuer.
- Keep and use the card securely and in accordance with the terms and conditions of the contract.

Benefits of payment cards

Merchants obtain the following benefits from accepting payment cards:

- a payment guarantee
- immediate funds
- increase in sales
- reduction in cash and check handling and management costs.

Cardholder benefits for using cards include the following:

- convenience and ease of use
- availability of limited or revolving credit.

Three-party or closed-loop systems

In a four-party system two banks are involved in providing payment services. The issuing bank contracts with the cardholder who uses the card to purchase goods and services. The acquiring bank on the other hand enters into a relationship with the merchant who accepts bankcards for receiving payments. In some cases, the issuing and the acquiring bank may be the same entity. Such transactions, made by a bank's card customers at its own merchants are called 'on-us' transactions. Where issuers and acquirers are separate banks, the transactions are generally termed 'not-on-us' or interchange transactions.

In a three-party or closed-loop system (see Figure 2.2) such as American Express, the same company contracts with cardholders as well as the merchants. In other words, all the purchase transactions on Amex cards are on-us transactions. However, American Express has now started partnering with banks who issue Amex cards mainly to their affluent customer segments.

Sources of revenue

How do financial institutions make money from bankcards? Issuers collect fees from cardholders though this is becoming increasingly rare for general purpose cards. Issuers also earn interest income on unpaid or 'revolving' balances. Acquirers collect fees from merchants, which are by far the primary source of income for the acquiring banks. This fee is called the merchant service commission (MSC) or merchant service fee (MSF) or simply merchant discount.

For credit and charge transactions, the MSC is usually a percentage of the transaction amount. In many markets, especially for debit card products, the MSC is a flat fee per transaction. This structure was introduced in markets where retailers saw the debit card as a replacement for check transactions and agreed to a per-transaction charge and not one that is linked to the value of the transaction.

Acquirers pass on part of this fee to the issuers to cover issuer costs. This is called the interchange fee and represents the issuer's primary source of income. Interchange fees are applicable to four-party payment systems and therefore applicable to bankcards only (see

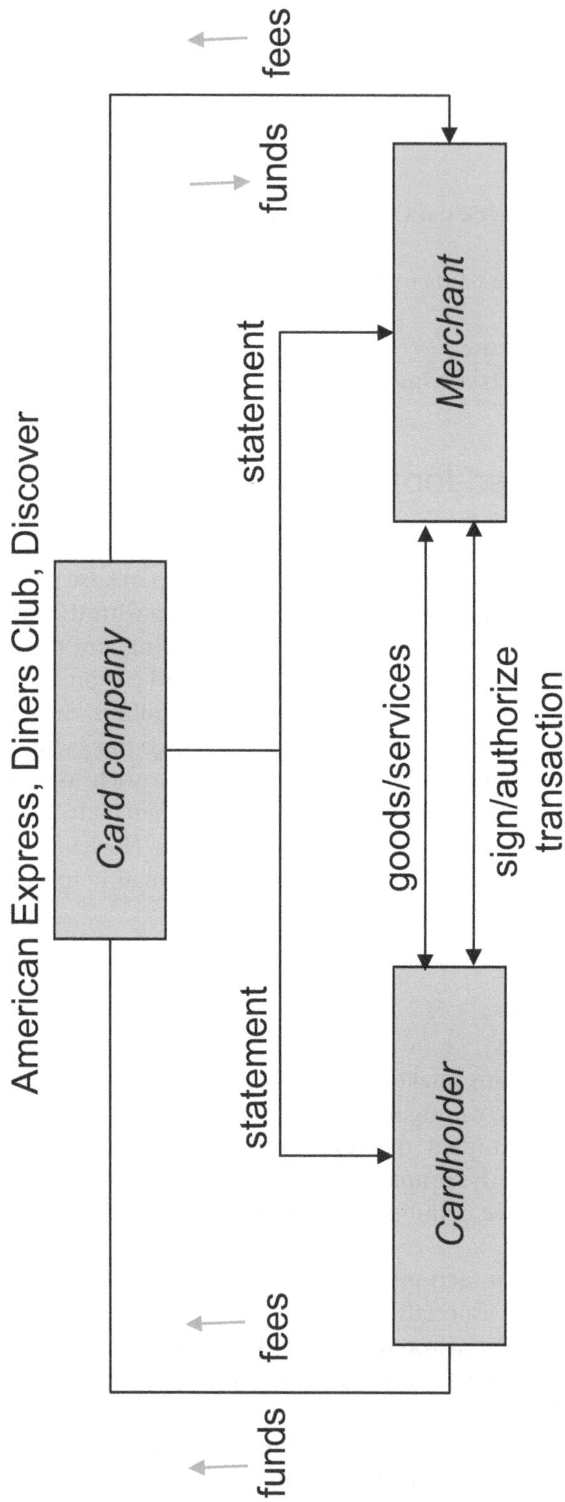

Figure 2.2 Three-party or closed-loop system

Figure 2.3). They are designed to compensate the issuer for some of its expenses and risk undertaken in supporting a bankcard transaction. For a more detailed discussion on how interchange fees are determined, please refer to the chapter on profitability.

Interchange fees are set by the card associations and vary by type, manner, and timing of the completion of the transaction. An electronic transaction that is settled in one or two days will attract a different interchange fee than a transaction processed manually and settled in five days.

As discussed before, credit card customers can borrow up to their credit limit on the card by paying a finance charge to the issuer. The different ways in which the finance charge is determined are discussed in the chapter on profitability. Finance charge is a key source of income for card issuers.

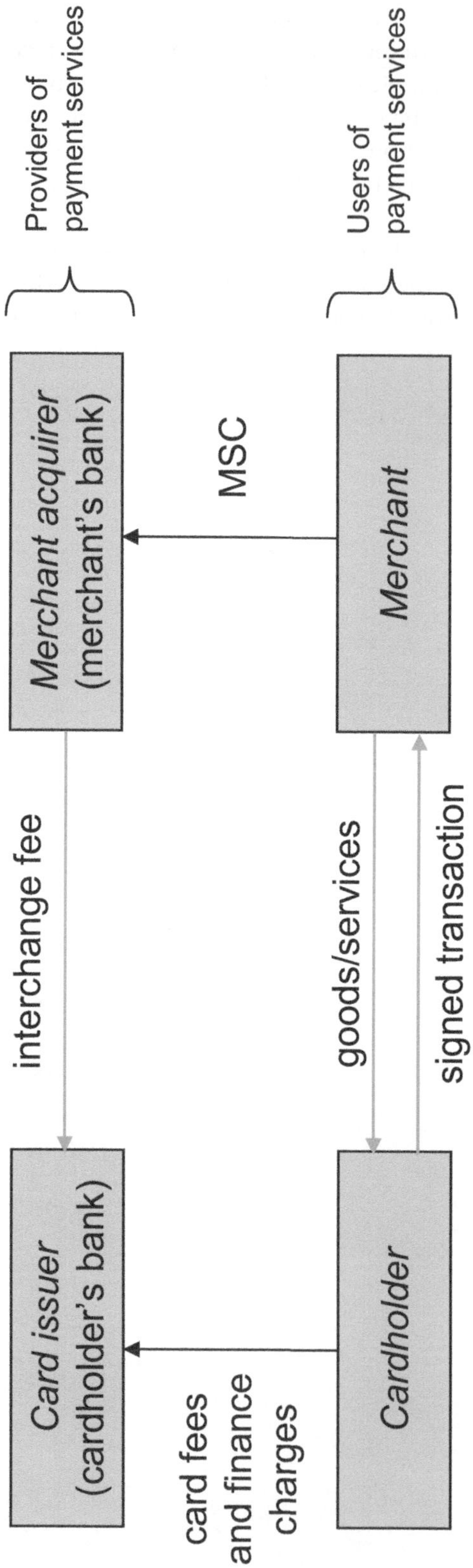

Figure 2.3 Sources of revenue

CHAPTER

3 Organizational Design

The success of a business depends on its ability to harness its human capital – in other words, how its people are organized to ensure that all tasks are managed in an efficient manner. The way an organization is structured is referred to as its organizational design. The two pillars for planning business success are business strategy and operational strategy. The foundation on which these two pillars stand is the organizational structure of the business. In this chapter we will review some of the elements of organizational design and how it can be made efficient and effective from the perspective of a card issuer.

Before designing the organizational structure, a card issuer needs to answer some key questions with regards to its core offerings: what are the products and services to be offered and, equally importantly, over what channels will they be marketed and serviced? These choices have an impact on the type, size, and design of the organizational structure.

Additionally, card issuers that offer multiple types of payment cards, such as credit, debit, and commercial, must decide how each card business will be managed – separately or all together under one corporate umbrella. A card product may be viewed as a separate profit center in its own right or as an attractive tool designed to attract, develop, and cement customer relationships so that other more profitable product packages can be offered to the cardholder.

Types of organizational structure

It is an obvious truth that for each card issuing business, the most suitable organizational structure is that which best fits its goals and objectives.

Not surprisingly, therefore, in the card issuing industry, all types of organizational structures can be found. But at a high level, one comes across two types of organizational structures at card issuing entities. These are discussed below.

SEPARATE ENTITY

Some large card issuers are managed as separate business entities. They may be fully or partly owned by another large entity such as a bank, but are managed as standalone businesses that must provide an acceptable rate of return to their investors. This trend is more prevalent in large banks that have substantial card businesses which contribute substantially to the banks' bottom lines. These entities are known for using advanced techniques in card management especially for card marketing and risk management. There are of course additional layers of administrative and legal overhead to be considered including separate capitalization for the entity, regulatory compliance requirements, and management of financing needs.

PRODUCT BASED ORGANIZATION

A majority of banks manage their credit and charge card business as separate profit centers. Commercial card businesses are also considered standalone. These profit units report directly to the CEO of the bank or sometimes to the head of consumer lending business.

Debit cards, on the other hand, are considered part of retail banking business. This is because the debit card is viewed as an access device to a bank account. Just like checks, debit card costs and revenues can only be viewed in conjunction with the overall bank account to which they are attached.

Commercial cards – business, corporate (T&E), and purchasing cards are targeted at businesses, from small businesses to large corporations. Corporate and purchasing cards are organizationally part of the corporate banking division within the bank. Non-bankcard issuers also treat commercial cards as a completely separate business than consumer cards. In banks, however, business cards, which are designed for small businesses, are normally serviced from local or regional retail banking branches. As such business cards, like debit cards, are organized within the retail banking business.

While card products may be organized within different parts of the card issuer, they may share systems infrastructure and a number of operational functions undertaken with other card or banking products. For example, the card center will usually develop, personalize, and mail cards to customers for all card products.

For debit cards, functions such as marketing, statementing, and customer service are not separately undertaken for the debit card but for the bank account as a whole. But credit risk management, fraud prevention and investigation, and especially cardholder dispute management are specialist areas as they not only involve sophisticated systems and processes but also require sound knowledge of the rules and regulations of domestic and international payment schemes. These activities are also undertaken centrally by the card center. Retail banking operations staff are less likely to have any significant knowledge of these areas and specialists in the cards center can attend to all card products regardless of how the business is organized. They are usually fully trained and conversant with compliance and operating rules.

Organizational design

So what is the best way to design a card issuing organization? The answer is that every entity is different. The organizational design should be conducive to the execution of overall corporate strategy. Whether the card business operates independently or as part of the overall corporate structure, it is built around key card issuing business processes or functions, as shown in Figure 3.1.

Some of these functions may be outsourced but the supervision and overall control of these functions are retained in-house. Support functions such as finance and analysis, information technology (IT) and human resource management (HRM) may be organized centrally where the card business operates as part of a larger corporate framework.

In many card issuing organizations, risk management, customer service, as well as IT may all be part of the operations department. Let's briefly review the primary organizational units of a typical card issuing business.

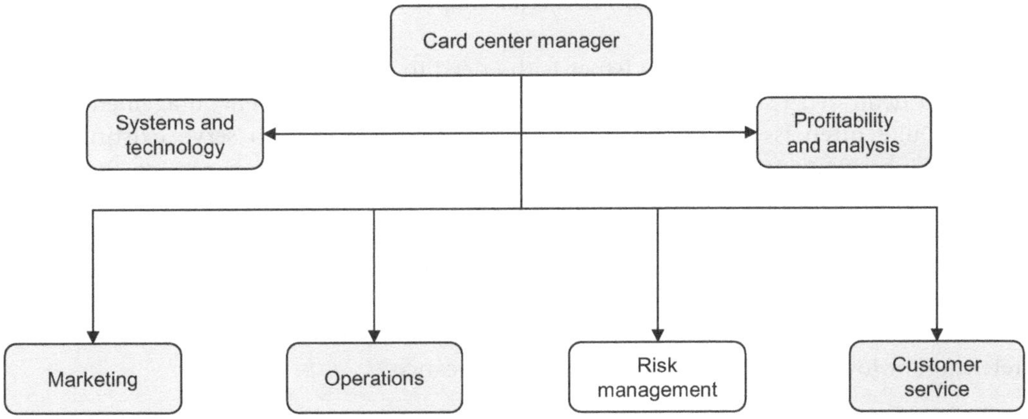

Figure 3.1 Key business processes

MARKETING

Marketing covers all activities required for soliciting new card accounts including general marketing to groups of potential cardholders over all relevant channels. It also includes more specific and focused solicitations to narrower segments of potential customers identified using consumer segment behavior data and analysis. Marketing messages are specifically tailored for these target segments for maximum take-up success.

What does the marketing team do? The marketing team is responsible for card product development and for devising strategies for soliciting potential cardholders. We can divide the tasks and activities in two key stages.

1 Planning and development

- Design card features and functionality.
- Determine product pricing options.
- Identify potential client segments that are most likely to take up the offer.

2 Marketing campaign management

The Marketing department will develop and execute the 'new account acquisition campaign' designed to acquire potential cardholders being targeted within a budgeted cost per new client limit. This economic constraint is important because too often aggressive marketing campaigns offer attractive discounts and features that quickly erode product profitability. In some cases it takes years before the card product breaks even let alone generates an acceptable return for the issuer.

The marketing campaign can involve some or all of the following solicitation channels; channel choice depends upon the selected target customer segments:

- mass-market advertisements
- promotions at branches or other physical locations
- direct mail
- outbound telephone marketing
- Internet marketing
- co-brand partnerships or affinity-based relationships.

More about new account acquisition in a later chapter in this book.

Equally important for a large card issuer is the need to retain existing cardholders. There is usually a dedicated team responsible for customer retention and encouragement of card usage. Quite often issuers do not allocate sufficient resources to serve existing clients resulting in 'account attrition'. If a card is not activated immediately on receipt, the chances of it being used by the cardholder are slim. While satisfactory customer service is a key element in a successful card issuing program, issuers must devise strategies and programs to enable cardholders to use their card more often, and where appropriate, use the cards as their prime source of borrowing. In developed markets where consumers have multiple cards in their wallets and are regularly bombarded with new card solicitations, customer retention or loyalty programs are of crucial significance.

OPERATIONS

The operations team is responsible for all the 'back-office' processes that support the card program including end-to-end transaction management. Back-office processes are discussed in detail in a later chapter. Here we will briefly review the key components of transaction management undertaken by the operations departments.

In the first place, transaction management involves setting up the systems and processes to facilitate transaction authorization in conjunction with Risk Management. Authorization parameters are set up and managed so that a purchase transaction can be authorized at the POS. The risk management department along with operations staff monitor the parameters and adjust them to ensure that the issuer's exposure to credit and fraud losses is minimized.

After a transaction has been authorized, it is 'captured' so that it can be passed to the issuer who can then bill the cardholder. This process, called clearing and settlement, is undertaken by the operations department.

Then, of course, there are transaction disputes that have to be managed and resolved. Cardholders may claim that a particular transaction was not initiated by them or is not in accordance with the terms agreed with the merchant. In the former case, a full investigation is required to identify any possible fraudulent activity. In addition to these, some other transactions may be charged back by the issuer to the acquirer for lack of compliance with rules and regulations of the card companies. Acquirers are asked to re-submit these 'chargebacks' to the issuers in accordance with these rules.

Chargebacks and disputes are usually handled by a specialist group within operations who are familiar with chargeback rules and regulations.

Cards or plastics issuance is the process associated with the design, physical production, and delivery of payment cards to cardholders. An important part of this function is called 'card personalization' that involves information about the individual cardholder being put onto the magnetic stripe or the embedded chip on the card. This information is utilized for a number of different business functions such as transaction authorization and fraud prevention.

Other operational activities include cardholder billing or statement generation or monthly billing statements. These are fairly automated to keep operational costs as low as possible and quite often outsourced to third party providers.

RISK MANAGEMENT

Risk management is a critical component of the overall card issuing organization. It ensures that risk management policies and procedures are aligned with business and operational strategies of the business. The risk management function may be a separate organizational department or may operate within the card operations department. It is responsible for developing the necessary parameters for reviewing new account applications and for setting up and managing credit limits for new and existing accounts.

The marketing department's objective is to acquire as many customers as possible from a mailing or telemarketing campaign, but the goal of the risk management team is to apply risk management criteria to new applications so that as many card applications are approved as possible without exposing the issuer to unnecessary or excessive risk. Applicants who are likely to default on their outstanding card balances in the future will be rejected. Risk procedures must be in place so that all fraudulent applications can be identified and rejected as well. The risk management group relies extensively on internal and external risk evaluation tools such as credit scores and data obtained from credit bureaus.

Credit risk is monitored and managed by the risk management unit. This involves the granting of credit limits and the timely collection of cardholder debts. Usually this function is managed by a separate team within risk management called 'collections'. Losses from bad debts can have a significant adverse impact on card program profitability. The collections unit is responsible for monitoring and identifying accounts that have a high probability of default. It also develops measures to recover overdue card balances and minimize credit losses. Collections teams work closely with third-party debt collection agencies. Early-date over-due balances are pursued by the collections team and long overdue and difficult to collect debts may be handled by specialists at the third-party agencies. Sometimes these long overdue debts are transferred to the agencies at a discount. These debts are taken off the issuer's and put on the agency's books. The agencies then use their own tools and resources to pursue the debt in place of the card issuer.

The risk management unit is also responsible for the prevention and investigation of cardholder fraud and overall card program and transaction security. It works closely with other areas across the issuer organization to devise and implement controls to prevent fraudulent use of payment cards which can arise from fraudulent card applications, unauthorized use of cardholder information, lost, stolen, or counterfeit cards. A later chapter discusses fraud risk in more detail.

CUSTOMER SERVICE

The customer services department is an integral component of the issuer business. It handles and resolves cardholder problems, queries, and complaints at branches, over the phone, by mail, or email. Its significance can be illustrated by the fact that quite often the largest team at a card center is the customer services unit. Customer service representatives (CSRs) need to be well trained and efficient, as how they work with cardholder issues has an important impact on cardholder retention. They also help in educating or familiarizing the cardholder in new products or new technologies such as Internet access to cardholder statements. They are also in a good position to be able to cross-sell other products or services based on cardholder needs. The feedback they provide internally to other areas in the card issuer organization helps improve card systems and processes. In addition to the primary departments above, there are other departments that provide support services.

FINANCE AND ANALYSIS

This area is responsible for finance, accounting, and tracking all revenues and expenses to provide insights into the performance of the card portfolio. The analytical information developed by this department is utilized by the management to analyze card segment profitability and to determine which product groups and what customer segments are not performing according to expectations.

INFORMATION TECHNOLOGY

The success of a card business is dependent on the technology and systems used to deliver the card products and services to cardholders. Technology plays a big part in completing a card transaction and in supporting all the key areas within the card issuer organization. As explained in the chapter on systems and technology, this department manages all systems (front-end systems that enable the cardholder to contact the issuer; and back-end systems where all cardholder records and information are stored and managed).

HUMAN RESOURCE MANAGEMENT

As in every organization, the human resource group looks after planning, hiring, de-hiring, and the overall skills development of employees.

CHAPTER

4 *Marketing and Strategy*

The payment card business is a big business – US $4 trillion on Visa and MasterCard credit and debit cards. That's right, trillion with a 't'! But why? Why do over 1.5 billion people in the world carry at least one Visa or MasterCard branded plastic in their wallet? Why, despite such widespread acceptance and usage of payment cards, do card issuers continue to solicit consumers for new cards at the rate of billions of pieces of direct mail offers each year? Why are credit and debit card advertisements on television, on radio, in newspapers and magazines and even over the Internet so prevalent?

The answer is twofold. First, the card product itself is an elegant solution to the consumer's need for convenience in paying for goods and services. It is portable, safe, and accepted at millions of merchants around the globe. Second, and perhaps a more telling explanation, is that card products, when managed properly, are inherently profitable for issuers. And as with any good business, issuers with profitable card portfolios want to grow them, so they are constantly enhancing and evolving their card product offerings to entice consumers to obtain their new and improved card. Consumers, in turn, continually upgrade to these new and improved card product offerings because the utility of the card is usually enhanced, thus making the new offer even more valuable and convenient than the old one it is replacing.

In Chapter 1, country profitability profiles from Morgan Stanley's 2003 research were reviewed. But it is much more than that which drives the focus given to marketing card products. These simple pieces of plastic act as the linchpin of a financial services provider's overall relationship with its customer. Bankcards serve as the gateway to accessing multiple bank products and services, so bank managers deem it critical to have customers carrying its bank's card as opposed to a competitor's. Several global banking institutions now view the credit card as the core product in establishing customer relationships, replacing the traditional view of the current account as the core banking relationship product.

The result of all this attention and focus upon payment card marketing is that sophistication in the marketing of cards has reached unprecedented heights. In today's marketplace, the development of card products and their marketing to consumers is among the most sophisticated product strategies, in terms of data-driven customer marketing, in the world. The marketing of card products has become crucial to the overall profitability of an issuer's cardholder portfolio, indeed to the profitability of the financial institution as a whole.

In this chapter we will explore the ways in which card products are marketed, from product development to new account solicitation to existing account marketing designed to encourage card activation and usage. It is important to understand these concepts because it is no exaggeration to say that marketing is the key to creating and sustaining a portfolio which will be profitable over the long term.

Perhaps the most important element to remember when it comes to payment card marketing is that the buyer of the product is a human being and, as a result, card marketing suffers from all of the vagaries that human beings bring to their endeavors. It is no stretch to say that human beings may be the most irrational of all living things on our planet. For all our intellect and ability to adapt to our surroundings, we display a remarkable aptitude for making decisions based upon the most irrational of factors. We buy cars because of their color, not their safety. We purchase clothing based upon style as opposed to comfort. And we obtain and use payment cards for a host of reasons that have little to do with the core function of a card, which is to enable purchases at the point of sale which can be converted into a loan should the customer desire to do so at some later date. The picture on the plastic card, the ability to earn points which can be redeemed for merchandise, and the perceived status of a gold or platinum card all enter into a customer's thought process when deciding which payment card to obtain and use. This would be all well and good if it weren't for yet another human trait – we as humans change our minds almost constantly with regard to what is important to us at any given moment. Today our payment card meets our needs and we earn frequent flyer miles. Tomorrow we want a card which meets our needs and creates a long-term savings mechanism to pay for our children's university education.

This is to be expected because as we progress through life, our needs and wants change. As young university students we are content to eat fast food, go to clubs, and buy lots of CDs and music downloads for our MP3 players. As young working professionals laboring in our first jobs, we need to upgrade our wardrobe, obtain our first apartment, and maybe even buy a car. Perhaps we then get married, buy a home, have children. All of these things have a profound effect upon our priorities, needs, and wants. Later in life, after our children have grown up and gone out on their own, our desires change again and we think more about traveling the world and spoiling our grandchildren. All of these changes are a normal part of the cycle of life and they have significant impacts upon the products and services we purchase and types of features we seek within those products and services.

A key factor in effective payment card marketing is to understand this type of consumer behavior, even to anticipate it, and adjust and refine the features and benefits of the card products offered accordingly. Of course, this is much easier said than done and requires a number of tools and support mechanisms to achieve. These required elements include a robust database of potential card customers as well as current cardholders and their activities on the card. Talented analysts with strong logic skills and modeling capabilities are also needed to organize and interpret the data in the database. Finally, creative individuals who can conceptualize new and unique card features and services are necessary to convert the analysis into products and promotions which can be successfully marketed to consumers.

Of course, all successful marketing derives from an effective and well-executed strategy. Strategy is the blueprint which successful card issuers utilize to ensure that they are deploying precious resources, both human and financial, in the most efficient and effective manner possible. So let's look at card marketing strategy by following the most basic of marketing frameworks – the 'four P's of marketing'.

Marketing strategy

As with any business endeavor, successful marketing begins with a clear and well-thought- out strategy. Marketing managers at card issuers must have a clear idea as to which types of consumers they wish to have as customers and why. They must also understand the role of the card product in achieving the overall goals and objectives of the financial institution. For instance, a bank may see a card product as the primary driver of the overall banking relationship, thus mandating a strategy which focuses upon bringing in new customers to the bank via the card product, then cross-selling them other retail banking products such as bank accounts, time deposits, and loan products such as mortgages and home equity lines of credit. Another bank may see its payment card product as a profit enhancement tool for existing relationships creating a strategy which focuses upon cross-selling cards to existing deposit and loan account customers. Both strategies are valid and linked to specific goals, but each requires a very different approach to the marketing of the card product across each of the four P's.

The four P's of marketing are taught in every entry-level university marketing class in the world. They are universally known and have stood the test of time. As with all products, they apply to payment cards in the same way they apply to automobiles, clothes, shoes, or any other consumer offering. What are the four P's in the context of marketing for payment card products?

- *Product* – this is the area of marketing which most directly influences the type of consumer which will be attracted to the issuer.
- *Price* – this factor directly impacts the profitability of the card issuing business.
- *Placement* – placement most directly influences the number of consumers who will be exposed to the issuer's card product offerings.
- *Promotion* – this component combines the number, type, and profitability characteristics of the consumers who obtain the issuer's card product offering.

All four of these areas must be addressed if the card issuer is to be a successful card marketer, and there is a high degree of correlation among these elements. The nature of the products offered will be a determining factor in the type of customer attracted to the bank via its card offerings. How those products are priced also plays a role in which types of consumers apply for the bank's card products as well as how many. How consumers learn of the issuer's product and price offerings directly influences which ones and how many will apply for the cards. Finally, the ways in which the benefits and features of the various card product offerings are communicated will also influence the type and number of who will apply for the card being offered.

Development of a cohesive strategy must address all the four P's, but in a manner consistent with the bank's overall strategic goals. Thus, the product strategy must be consistent with the issuer's risk tolerance, desired growth rate, and overall profitability objectives if it is to gain management support and resources required to be successful. The card product manager who recommends pursuing consumers of dubious credit quality in order to achieve a significant growth rate when the bank has a very conservative stance with regard to risk will soon be seeking employment elsewhere.

A good card marketing strategy must take into account the basic card product life cycle as shown in Figure 4.1.

Over the course of time, every card product will progress through each stage of the life cycle. Each stage of the card product life cycle requires very different marketing initiatives and successful marketing strategies take this into account. For example, the promotion discipline for a new account prospect is very different than that for an account which the issuer is trying to retain, and the communications developed must vary accordingly.

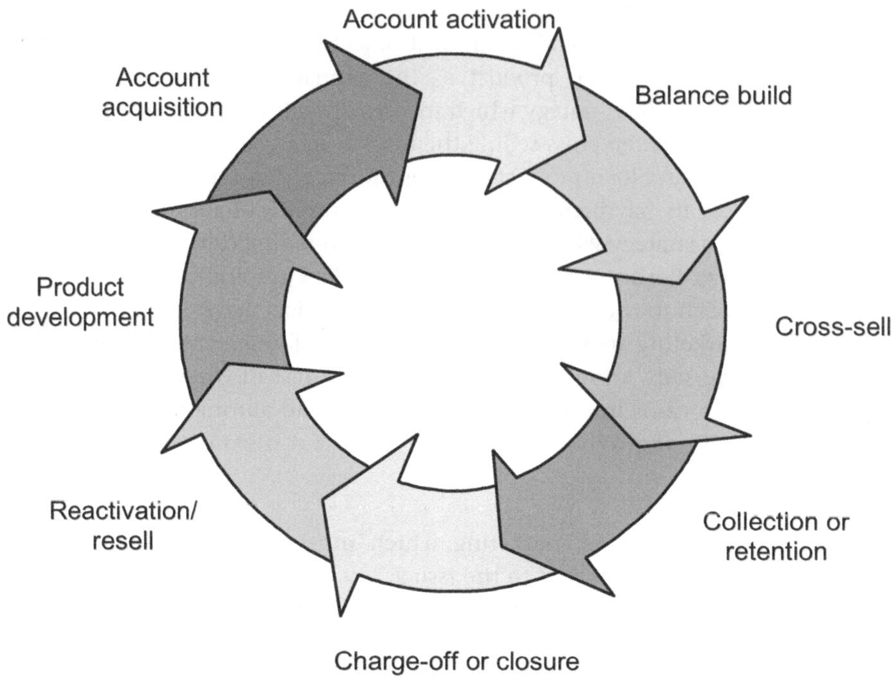

Figure 4.1 Card product life cycle

What is clear when it comes to card marketing is that success starts with a well-planned strategy consistent with the issuer's overall goals and objectives. Just as important, this strategy must be communicated throughout the organization so as to ensure that all staff members are aware of what is being done and why from a marketing perspective.

Product

While it seems an obvious statement to make that in order to build a portfolio of card accounts you must have card products, behind this thought is a tremendous amount of effort and strategy. What exactly is a card product? What features and benefits are important? Are they the same for everyone or do different people desire different features? The answers to these and many similar questions are the key to successful product development in the payment card industry.

In most markets around the world today simply offering a 'plain vanilla' or 'one-size-fits-all' product is a sure way to fail in the marketplace. Regardless of country, climate, or culture most markets today consist of reasonably savvy consumers who spend time shopping around for things they want in order to ensure the products they buy meet their needs and desires. This is the norm for consumer behavior in today's societies. Most of us desire things which meet our specific requirements, not some generic product which will suffice for me as well as millions of others. As a result, marketers need to be aware of the major needs and wants of the majority of consumers in their product area and offer multiple choices so that consumers can self-select products which best meet their specific requirements.

For payment cards, this basic tenet of consumer behavior is an absolute truth. When it comes to financial services and consumers' attitudes towards the products they choose to meet their needs, it pays to understand the thinking behind the consumer's actions. Fortunately, in financial services, a basic understanding of consumers' attitudes towards the products they use is fairly easy to acquire. If the product in question involves the consumers' money (for example, a bank account, debit card, or certificate of deposit) then the basic attitude is 'It's my money, treat it carefully.' This point can be proven based upon the fact that most consumers compare their bank deposit account statements with their own records and call the bank to question any discrepancies, no matter how small. Conversely, when the product in question involves the bank's money (for example, a credit card, a home equity loan, or a personal installment loan), the basic attitude of consumers can change dramatically to 'I am less concerned because it isn't my money and I have time to manage repayment.' Consumer purchases made with borrowed funds tend to be larger and more luxury-oriented than purchases made with the consumers' own funds. Purchase clothing; it is probably a debit transaction. Purchase a big screen television; it is probably a credit transaction. An analysis of debit card and credit card transaction volume at large banks bears out this dynamic.

Why is it important for card marketers to understand and heed this principle? Because, as noted previously, marketing payment card products is an inherently consumer behavior-oriented activity and if that behavior is misunderstood or, worse, ignored, then the likelihood of successful marketing activities diminishes dramatically.

One of the keys to successful product development within the card marketplace is to understand that different consumers will desire different product features and to offer a broad line of products designed to appeal to the greatest number of consumers as possible. In order to achieve this, card marketers must identify the features which appeal to significant numbers of consumers within any given market, then develop products which deliver those features. Proper research and analysis can identify the key features and benefits to offer in order to appeal to the greatest number of potential customers. Identifying these core benefits and designing products to suit them is known as market segmentation.

What exactly is a segment? Well, the answer to this question is one of the most appealing benefits of conducting market segmentation research in the first place. Quite simply, a segment is whatever the bank identifies it to be. There is no preconceived structure or requirement in segmentation. Rather, research and analyses should yield basic consumers' desires and behaviors which can then be translated into products and services. For example, if a market is analyzed and researched and the indication is that all consumers in this particular market over the age of forty-five drive four-door sedans and play golf, then that is a segment, and designing a card product around these consumers and their behaviors makes sense.

Of course there are problems if segments are defined too broadly (for example, men, women, homeowners, city dwellers). Too broad a spectrum of consumers lumped into a single segment makes the creation of a product difficult as there are likely to be more than one or two common characteristics desired by the population of the segment. Too narrow a definition (for example, women aged thirty-one to thirty-two and a half who own condominiums and sport utility vehicles and earn in excess of US $50 000 annually) also causes problems as these segments may be so small as to preclude the development of a card product designed exclusively for them due to cost considerations.

There exist some tried and true segmentation techniques which card issuers may wish to consider prior to developing their own more sophisticated segmentation schemes:

SEGMENTATION BY STATUS

Segmenting by perceived status has proven to be an effective technique. This is why there are products such as classic, gold, platinum, and black. Most issuers use income or net worth as a measure for status and usually add extra product features to the card such as loyalty schemes and concierge services the higher up the status chain the cardholder goes.

SEGMENTATION BY CREDITWORTHINESS

Many issuers have developed segmentation schemes across the risk spectrum. Riskier cardholders, often referred to as 'sub-prime', are offered higher-priced, lower-credit-limit products while the best cardholders, referred to as super-prime receive the lowest-priced, most enhanced card offerings featuring many of the same benefits as the status-oriented card products.

SEGMENTATION BY ENDORSED PROGRAMS

Globally, one of the most popular forms of segmentation has been via what are called endorsed programs, commonly referred to as 'co-branded' and 'affinity' card programs. Co-branding involves a third party such as an airline or retail store and the card product incorporates the ability to accrue some sort of value via use of the card which is redeemable at the third-party outlets. Affinity programs revolve around membership groups and/or causes, are generally affiliated with not-for-profit entities and usually involve financial contributions being made to the sponsoring group or cause, based upon the usage associated with the cards issued.

Regardless of the type of segmentation, it is crucial for issuers to utilize segmentation techniques if they are to be successful over time in the card issuing business. This is quite simply because most payment cards are now primarily perceived as commodities. The existence of Visa and MasterCard schemes has created a circumstance whereby all credit and debit cards operate on the same global interchange system thus making them provide the same core functionality. In terms of the ability to use a payment card at a point of sale, most cards work in almost exactly the same manner. Segmentation enables issuers to differentiate themselves by adding unique features and benefits to this core functionality – the features which are designed to appeal to a specific group of customers. So, for example, individuals who are known to travel frequently, such as members of an airline frequent flyer program, will prefer a card which enables them to add to their accumulation of frequent flyer miles. An issuer interested in such customers could partner with an airline and offer a co-branded card which enables the accumulation of miles based upon card usage thus capturing a significant number of these types of consumers due to the attractiveness of the benefits offered via the card. Such card products are now very common in most mature markets.

Today, there are card products designed to appeal to every type of consumer from frequent travelers to Elvis Presley fans to supermarket shopping addicts. The unique nature of the core operating platform for payment cards enables an almost limitless number of features and functions to be added to the card offering which can be customized to meet the needs of a particular group of customers.

Card issuers are merely following the well-established practice of segmenting a saturated, commodity market seen in markets as diverse as those for writing instruments or bottled water. What is the difference between a line written with a $0.99 Bic pen and a $300 Mont Blanc? Visually, if there is a difference, it is imperceptible to the human eye. But emotionally it is clear that to a large number of consumers it is important to have a writing instrument which conveys class, elegance, and timelessness – a segment Mont Blanc is only too happy to serve. Water is the same. Nothing is more of a commodity than water. After all, it's all H_2O! But millions upon millions of consumers are willing to pay anywhere from $1.00 to $3.50 a bottle for twelve ounces of water. Why? Consumers will list a variety of reasons from quality to taste to purity. Yet consistently in blind taste tests, consumers prefer tap water to various bottled waters. So, the reality of all water basically tasting the same is much less important than the perception that certain bottled waters offer better quality, taste, purity, or some other attribute consumers are willing to pay for.

Card products offer consumers the same opportunity to differentiate themselves based upon customers' perceived notions of what makes one card 'better' than another. Price, benefits, credit line, whatever – customers' perceptions of what is important are what card issuers must identify, develop, and market if they are to enjoy success in the marketplace.

Segmentation is so critical because it enables issuers to compete along dimensions other than price and allows for the creation of perceived value at the customer level. These elements are extremely important in building long-lasting relationships with customers. In addition, segmentation enables issuers to treat customers as individuals based upon the information and analysis they review in order to develop their products. Most people like to be treated as individuals, so this is a key element in developing long-lasting customer relationships.

But segmenting the potential cardholder universe is only half of the equation. Once that is accomplished, you have to decide what type of products to offer your segments. This begs the question what is a product?

Different people will have different answers to this question, but in the world of payment cards the answer is really quite simple. A card product is nothing more than a 'set of entitlements'. The card issuer simply allows the customer to access the various features and benefits which it attaches to the card. What does this mean? Consider the listing in Table 4.1 as entitlements for a credit card product.

The first thing to understand about successful generation of new accounts in competitive markets is that it is not merely a question of lowering the price below your competitor's. In fact, in the US marketplace, the most successful marketing campaigns are not based on low priced solicitations at all. In fact, just the opposite is true as some of the most successful offers have relatively high interest rates and fees. How can this be? Quite simply because the successful offers provide entitlements which consumers find appealing and of value, thus they are willing to pay for them.

Table 4.1 Entitlements

Access	*Convenience*	*Affordability*
• Credit line	• Global acceptance	• Rates and fees
• Bank deposits	• 24/7 availability	• Enhancements
• Retailers	• Goes anywhere	• Loyalty schemes
• Cash (ATMs)	• Monthly record	• Repayment terms

What are these benefits which offer value to consumers? Surprisingly, in a mature market, they are less likely to be the traditional airline miles or points-based loyalty schemes which have served credit card issuers so well in the past. Rather, they are of a new generation of value offerings with a much more practical and immediate, benefit to cardholders. The three most successful offerings in terms of new accounts take-up in the United States in early 2004 were one providing a 1 per cent rebate which is paid directly to the cardholder's mortgage lender to reduce the principal balance of the loan; another offering a 1 per cent rebate which cardholders can accumulate and then apply to their credit card account to pay a fee, reduce their interest rate, or even make their minimum payment; and the most unusual offering whereby cardholders received a free laptop computer in exchange for a significant balance transfer which must remain outstanding at a moderate interest rate for eighteen months.

What did these three offerings have in common? They were all value based as opposed to price based. All three products had interest rates at or above the current average in the marketplace. All three offered balance transfers, but not at 0 per cent. In fact, the laptop computer offer, which required a balance transfer, was priced at 9.9 per cent and had to remain outstanding for eighteen months, well above the price of most other balance transfer options available. Clearly it was not the price, but rather the entitlement, which in this case was a free brand-name computer, that consumers are finding appealing.

Other card products with above industry average response rates include a card with a 1 per cent overall cash rebate, higher within specifically targeted merchant categories, whereby the rebate is invested in a tax-deferred educational savings account for future use in paying children's college tuition costs. Again, the interest rate and account fees associated with this offer are above the industry average in the marketplace.

Why would consumers pay more for a commodity product such as a credit card? After all, don't all credit cards work in the same manner? Does a 1 per cent rebate which reduces your mortgage principal balance really amount to a significant saving for consumers?

In fact, a 1 per cent rebate reducing the principal balance on a mortgage is not a particularly beneficial feature considering the average mortgage in the US is over $140 000 and the average amount spent on a credit card in a one-year period is about $4500, meaning the annual rebate is just $45. But that isn't what matters. What matters is that a large cross section of the market perceives that the 1 per cent rebate applied towards their mortgage is more valuable than a 0 per cent balance transfer or a points program which requires significant accumulations to receive an item of questionable value. It is not the value, but rather the perception of value which is important.

These successful credit card offerings point out the key to generating new accounts in a highly competitive marketplace, taking into account the unpredictable nature of consumer behavior. Creativity and uniqueness are critical to breaking out of the me-too mode of most competitors in active markets. What these successful product offerings have in common is that they are not 0 per cent balance transfer offers. They are not another no-annual-fee-low-rate card. They are not the same as everything else in the market and they offer something of real and practical value for some segment of the population. But that does not mean that issuers should stop offering the me-too card products. Many me-too features have wide appeal and are essential to the core offering. But for competitive advantage, the winning features that distinguish products with moderate success from those that are highly successful, are developed by issuers that test and experiment with various offers which focus on benefits, not price, and on customer segments that are particularly responsive to such benefits. In highly competitive marketplaces, growth and success comes at the margins, not in the center. Multiple product offerings targeted at different segments of the marketplace and unique and creative offerings which will appeal to different types of consumers are the key to successful new account growth.

But being different for the sake of being different is a mistake. The unique offerings issuers develop must be practical and appealing to a large section of consumers so that it is viable, from a business profitability perspective, to develop and support them. This means issuers must test new offerings carefully before committing to rolling them out on a large scale. The 1 per cent mortgage rebate and college savings cards were tested multiple times over a six-month period before they were rolled out across the entire US market, both in terms of focus group studies to refine the concept and live market test mailings to gauge their ultimate appeal. This testing revealed, for example, that the 1 per cent mortgage rebate card was much more appealing when applied to principal balance as opposed to interest reduction because consumers liked the idea of generating equity in their homes faster. From a financial perspective, there is no difference to the issuer where the 1 per cent rebate is applied, but from the consumers' point of view, there is a great deal of difference and that perceived difference directly impacts their ultimate acceptance of the product.

So new account growth in a highly competitive market requires that issuers develop well-tested, value-based card offerings which are unique and appealing and which stand out from the crowd in terms of other offerings available. In other words, issuers must develop new and creative entitlements which will appeal to different segments of the marketplace. Can it be done? Obviously the answer is yes as the examples demonstrate.

There exists an almost endless number of entitlements which can be assigned to a card product. The key is to attach the ones which will appeal most to a given segment based upon the information and analysis the issuer has conducted and reviewed. Even this needs to be done in a structured way as illustrated in Table 4.2.

The table provides a simple example of some basic product features, or entitlements, based upon a simple segmentation scheme utilizing income, creditworthiness, home ownership, card usage, and affiliations. This sets the tone for the core product to be offered (debit or credit card; classic, gold or platinum).

Table 4.2 Potential product matrix

	Age	*Income*	*Creditworthiness*	*Deposits*	*Home Ownership*	*ATM Usage*
High		Platinum/Gold credit card		Charge card	Best-priced platinum credit card	
Medium	Classic credit card		Classic/Gold credit card – low price			Gold debit card
Low	Debit/ATM card		Debit card only		ATM card	

As shown in Figure 4.2, further product definition stems from the core features decided upon such as brand and card type. It is this 'funneled' approach to selecting product features and benefits based upon the segment characteristics of the customer group selected that is crucial to effective product development.

Price

Let's now turn our attention to the second of the four P's: Price.

Being the lowest-priced product in the marketplace is not a successful long-term strategy. Right pricing a product is essential. In a competitive cards market, a crucial element of product packaging is pricing. One must ensure that products are priced properly, both from an internal profit and external market point of view. Set the price too low, and the issuer could end up with a large number of cardholders which are unprofitable and costly to service. Set the price too high, and the issuer could end up attracting too many poor credit risks and not enough good ones, a phenomenon known as 'adverse selection'. This leads to credit loss rates that are too high and an unprofitable portfolio.

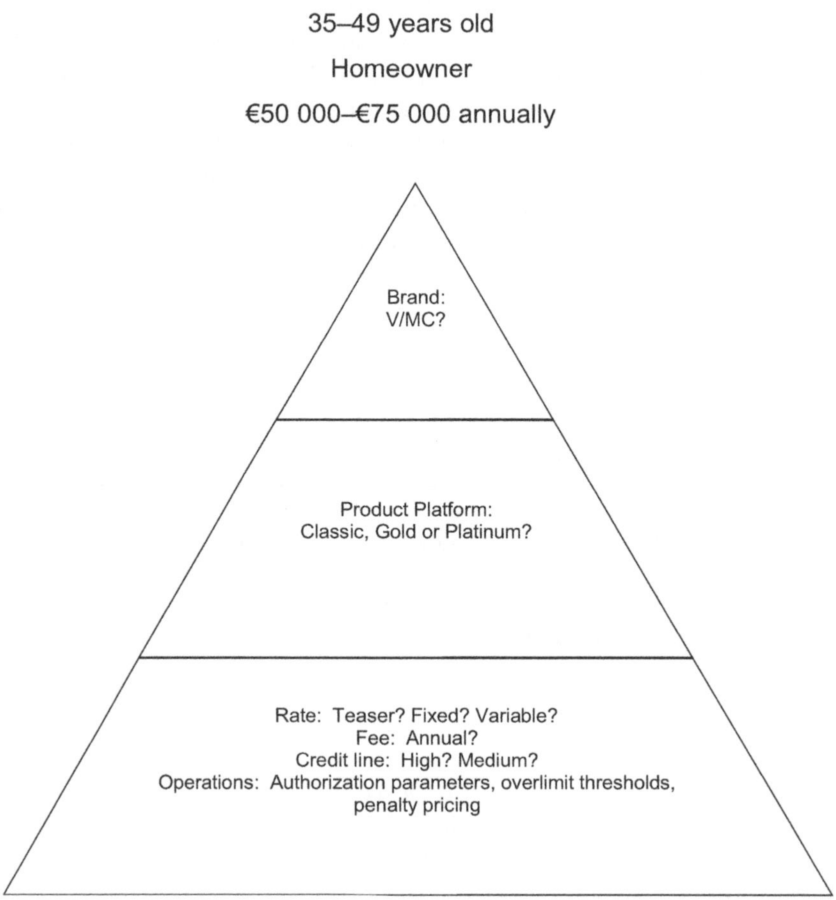

Figure 4.2 Potential product definition

But just what are the critical elements of pricing? Are they the same from the bank's and the customer's point of view? To answer these questions, we must first understand three fundamental observations about payment card pricing based on our many years' experience working in markets across the globe:

- Pricing cannot motivate a specific behavior. Revolvers will revolve (that is, carry a balance from one month to the next and incur finance charges) and transactors will transact (that is, charge throughout the month and then pay the balance in full when due, thus incurring no finance charges). Offering a transaction a low interest rate in order to try and get them to revolve is wasteful.
- Price, in and of itself, is not a sustainable competitive advantage. Just because your bank has the lowest-priced offer in the market today does not mean a competitor will not undercut your price tomorrow. Price leadership in any given market is, at best, a temporary advantage.
- There is a lot more to pricing in the mind of the cardholder than just rate and fee. There are other factors involved as well such as minimum payment, due dates, and similar price-related notions.

With these three pricing observations in mind, let's review the basic elements of payment card pricing.

INTEREST RATES

Fixed vs. variable

The interest rate is the rate charged on balances which the cardholder does not pay in full by the payment due date shown on their monthly billing statement. Issuers must decide between a fixed rate, one which does not change based upon market conditions, or a variable interest rate, which changes periodically based upon a market index such as LIBOR (London Interbank Offered Rate), Prime, or Government Bond rates. In many markets, interest income is the largest source of card issuer revenue, so the rate and its movement are critical to overall card profitability.

Purchases vs. cash advances

Often, issuers will assess one interest rate for purchase transactions made at retail outlets and another, usually higher rate, for cash advances obtained at bank branches or ATMs via the card. This is based upon issuer experience that customers who utilize the card for cash tend to be more risky and have higher loss rates than those that do not use their cards for cash advances.

Floors and ceilings

If an issuer applies a variable rate of interest, then it must decide if it wants to limit or cap how high the rate can go (the ceiling) or how low it can fall (the floor) based upon the market index rate it has chosen. For example, the interest rate could be the market prime rate + 10 per cent, but in no event will the rate go above 20 per cent or below 12 per cent.

Penalty interest rate

In many markets, issuers assess a penalty interest rate, or default rate, on balances which are delinquent for more than some predetermined timeframe such as thirty or sixty days. This rate is higher than the normal rate on the account and usually remains in force until the cardholder has made several on-time payments, usually between four and six. The theory behind default pricing is that the higher interest rate will motivate the cardholder to repay their monthly bill in a timely manner. There is some debate within the industry as to whether or not this theory is, in fact, correct. Another school of thought is that the unusually high penalty rates charged today in many markets, often times as much as 10 per cent or more above the original interest rate on the credit card, cause ill-feeling between the customers and the card issuer. Customers lose hope that they will ever be able to repay the amount owed as it accumulates interest at the higher rate; so many choose to simply not even try. There have been no significant studies as of yet which attempt to quantify this concept, but overall delinquency and loss rates in mature markets around the world do lend some credence to this theory. In 2003, the industry loss rate for credit cards in the US was near 6 per cent, quite high for a country whose economy, while not robust, was certainly not in recession at that time. This compares to loss rates below 3 per cent in the UK in 2003, a market similar in many ways to the US. Many observers have expressed the opinion that perhaps some of this stubbornly high loss rate may be attributable to the high default rates issuers charge on delinquent balances.

Promotional rates

Many issuers offer so called 'teaser' rates on new accounts, or on existing balances cardholders transfer from other competitor accounts. These rates are lower than the normal rate on the account and usually expire in six to twelve months from the offer date. There are a number of ways card issuers utilize promotional rates and, as a result, there are quite a few variations on this pricing mechanism. Some issuers charge a fee in the amount of 0.5 per cent to 1.5 per cent of the balance amount being transferred. Still other issuers will offer a promotional rate which is not for a limited period of time, but rather stays in effect until the amount of the balance transferred under the promotional rate is paid off in full. This is more beneficial to the customer than a limited time promotional rate offer in most instances, but is more costly for the card issuer.

Finance charge calculation

In most markets, there are a number of ways card issuers can calculate the amount of interest a cardholder is required to pay on outstanding balances. Needless to say, these different ways can have a significantly different result in terms of the amount of interest a cardholder pays. These options can range from simple interest to the more common average daily balance plus new purchases methodology. It is important for card marketers to understand all of their options and to monitor closely what competitors in the marketplace are doing. Finance charge calculations are discussed in more detail in the chapter on profitability.

FEES

Annual fee

In more mature markets, this type of yearly fee is hard to apply. In markets such as the UK and US, most cards are offered with no annual fee. Only those products which offer a high perceived value to the customer such as airline frequent flier cards and co-branded retailer cards are able to charge an annual fee.

Late payment fee

This fee is charged if a cardholder fails to pay their account minimum payment by the due date as shown on their monthly billing statement.

Overlimit fee

A fee charged each month when a cardholder exceeds their account credit limit.

Cash advance fee

A fee charged each time a cardholder utilizes the bankcard for a cash advance. Usually expressed as a percentage of the cash advance amount with a floor and a ceiling such as 3 per cent of the cash advance amount, but no less than $2.00 and no greater than $25.00.

Other nuisance fees

Many banks charge cardholders an assortment of other fees, ranging from fees for sending copies of billing statements to fees for payment checks which are returned to the issuer due to insufficient funds on deposit.

OTHER PRICE COMPONENTS

Some other factors need also to be considered when formulating a pricing strategy:

- *Grace period*: This is the amount of time a cardholder has to pay their monthly bill in full and not incur finance charges. While a very valuable feature of a credit card product to the consumer, this is quite costly to the bank as it requires the bank to fund the charges its cardholders have made until payment is received.
- *Minimum payment calculation*: This is the methodology utilized by the bank to determine the minimum amount a cardholder must repay each month based upon their card account balance. Like finance charge calculations, there are numerous options here for card issuers. The two most commonly used are discussed in the chapter on profitability.
- *Minimum finance charge*: This is the minimum amount of finance charge a credit card issuer will assess in a given month, regardless of the balance owed which is accruing interest. This is a tool which enables issuers to avoid having to send billing statements to cardholders who owe very small amounts as the minimum finance charge (usually $0.50 to $2.00) encourages the payoff of such small balance accounts.

From the card issuer's perspective, the ability to charge the highest interest rates and fees in order to drive as much revenue as possible is desirable. From the customer's viewpoint, lower rates and fees are desirable. So how can card products be priced so that everyone gets what they desire? The answer lies in balancing product features and the pricing required to support those features. This is where proper segmentation makes life easier.

By grouping consumers with similar wants and desires together, card issuers can design products which will appeal to that group of potential cardholders. Knowing the basic features the group desires enables the issuer to price to the level the market will bear. For example, a group of high risk consumers who have had past credit troubles will attach a high value to obtaining a credit card. Accordingly, the issuer can charge a high rate of interest and a large annual fee because the segment targeted will understand the value of the credit they are receiving relative to the price they are paying. For revolvers, this 'pricing to value' concept may mean a willingness to pay an annual fee in exchange for a lower interest rate. For transactors, this may mean offering a rewards program tied to sales volume, thus incentivizing cardholders to charge more to the card. Careful analysis of market data will enable payment card issuers to maximize their revenues from pricing options while minimizing cardholder dissatisfaction with price so long as the product features are seen as valuable by the segment in question.

Placement

So far we have reviewed how to strategize, how to target and design our products and what to think about when it comes to pricing. But we still haven't promoted anything to potential cardholders! Let's now take a look at our distribution channel options, or 'placement' as it is referred to in the four P's of marketing.

How accounts are acquired can have just as big an impact upon profitability as how a product is designed, priced, and targeted. Most card issuers utilize multiple channels for acquiring new cardholders, but each offers its own advantages and disadvantages:

DIRECT MAIL

In mature markets, this is the most prevalent method of new account acquisition because it is easy to develop and execute. In addition, it is extremely cost-effective and, from the Management Information Systems (MIS)/analysis viewpoint, direct mail provides prompt feedback in terms of response rates regarding how well a product is designed and priced. Finally, a significant advantage direct mail has over other distribution channels is that it allows the issuer to target appropriate consumers, thus making segmentation of the marketplace much easier to accomplish. In general, there are two primary forms of direct mail solicitations, pre-approved and non pre-approved. Pre-approved solicitations are utilized in markets where there is good credit bureau data or in instances where the card issuer has good internal data from which to render a credit approval decision before soliciting a prospect. Non pre-approved solicitations are utilized when the card issuer does not have access to information which will enable it to make a credit decision prior to soliciting a prospect, or when the issuer simply chooses to solicit a list without first qualifying the prospects which it contains in order to reach the maximum number of potential cardholders.

The pre-approved direct mail process involves the following steps:

- prepare consumer list
- credit bureau or issuer database screen
- undertake mail solicitation
- review mail responses and back-end credit check.

In this process, the issuer accumulates a list of potential cardholders from internal sources or purchases a list from outside the bank, then screens it against its own creditworthiness criteria (before customer response), narrowing the list down to the names it wishes to mail. The direct mail solicitation offering is then designed, produced, and mailed. Responses are received and reviewed on the 'back-end', meaning after the response by the consumer, to ensure that the cardholder meets the creditworthiness criteria established by the bank at the beginning of the process.

The non pre-approved mail process is similar:

- prepare consumer list
- undertake mail solicitation
- review mail responses and back-end credit review.

In this process, no pre-screening is conducted upon the list on the front-end of the process. Rather, all names are mailed and the creditworthiness of the responders is determined once their application is received in response to the solicitation.

Direct mail new account acquisition marketing is by far the most prevalent form of generating new accounts in mature markets. This is due to several factors. First, even with today's mature market response rates of less than one percent, direct mail is still quite cost-effective relative to other forms of new account generation. In the US, efficient card issuers can usually develop, screen, and mail offerings for less than $0.45 each. This makes mailing offers inexpensive, thus lowering the response required to be cost-effective in terms of cost per new account acquired.

Second, direct mail enables issuers to design and implement campaigns relatively quickly. Large card issuers can usually implement the entire direct mail process, from product concept to mail at the post office, in five to six weeks. This ability to bring offerings quickly to the marketplace is almost a prerequisite for successful participation in the mature and saturated markets. In the card world, there is usually no substitute for being first to market with a new product idea because if imitation is the sincerest form of flattery, then the card business is rife with flattery!

Third, and perhaps most importantly, card issuers receive almost immediate feedback to their marketing ideas when utilizing direct mail as a distribution channel. Responses to a solicitation begin trickling in within just a few days of the mail delivery. Issuers can quickly discern if a mailing is being well received or not, based upon the daily rate of responses received (known as the response curve), and then comparing the current mailing's response curve with previous mailings. This enables issuers to begin thinking about enhancements, new features and other product entitlements to test while the original mailing is still in the marketplace. This immediate feedback is quite useful to card issuers who are continually innovating and testing, and it enables them to bring new products to market faster and with a greater likelihood of success.

TELEMARKETING

In many ways, telemarketing is similar to direct mail in that it is cost-effective, simple to put together and provides for almost immediate marketplace feedback. In addition, it offers the added advantage of being able to be geared up or down quickly based upon results while the telemarketing campaign is in progress. It also provides an alternative medium for soliciting prospects that are unresponsive to other channels.

Telemarketing, however, has a significant drawback in that, unlike direct mail, it is an intrusive medium which can be perceived by consumers as disruptive and annoying. As a result, telemarketing campaigns must be monitored constantly for negative customer feedback. One of the side effects of the intrusive nature of telemarketing is that potential cardholders will often say yes to an offer on the phone just to end the call, then cancel the account later or simply not activate it once the card is received. This results in less profitable, less active accounts for the card issuer.

In the US, telemarketing has become such an overused distribution channel that in 2003 the US government passed a law enabling consumers to place their name and telephone number on a list which telemarketers are not allowed to contact. This so called 'do not call' list received 24 million registrations the first day it became available in July of 2003, thus demonstrating consumers' frustrations with the intrusive nature of this medium.

Telemarketing takes two different forms. The first, whereby telemarketers obtain customer lists with phone number attached and then call the prospects directly to offer card products, is known as 'outbound telemarketing'. The second approach involves a two step process whereby prospects are sent a mailing of some kind offering the card product and they are encouraged to call a toll-free telephone number to accept the offer. This is known as 'inbound telemarketing'.

INTERNET

While still a relatively new distribution channel for payment cards, the Internet holds significant promise. As with many other web-based applications, soliciting applications for cards via the Internet is extremely cost-effective. In addition, the web can be used both proactively via e-mail campaigns and reactively via the issuer's acceptance of applications for card products on its own website. In addition, applications can be generated via partnerships with well-established web destination sites.

Card issuers must decide how they wish to utilize the Internet as a source for new account applications. Some accept and process applications entirely via the Internet and approve or decline electronically such that the process takes only a few minutes. Others use it simply as a source for prospects, which are then translated to a paper-based application process utilizing existing operations and infrastructure. Both approaches can be effective. Which one an issuer utilizes will depend upon its overall product and distribution strategy.

The biggest unknown regarding the Internet is what type of consumer does it attract? As a relatively new distribution channel, there is little history relating to performance over time of card accounts generated over the Internet. Early indications suggest that, in general, the population of consumers who favor the net as a tool for seeking credit cards exhibit a riskier profile than others. This could be because the Internet attracts younger, less credit experienced consumers or it could be simply the result of the channel being so new there has not been sufficient time for all consumers to learn of its existence for applying for payment cards. Regardless of the cause, caution is warranted when leveraging this channel.

But there are signs in the marketplace that internet-based applicants for credit and charge cards are a unique and potentially profitable segment of the consumer population. Interestingly, issuers have observed that cardholders who applied for and were approved for a card via the Internet tend to be more active card users and are also more loyal to the brand.

BANK BRANCHES

The other end of the distribution channel spectrum from the Internet is the bank branch or any other physical location. This is the oldest, most established source for new card customers. Branches remain a vibrant source for new accounts and should be cultivated accordingly. The keys to successful branch generation of new card account customers is to ensure that the branch personnel have the proper training regarding the card product offerings and features and that they are rewarded via incentives to sell the product.

The most significant risk associated with the bank branch as a distribution channel is the fact that many customers utilize online banking products and ATMs, thus reducing their need to visit the branch office. Less traffic in the branch, while more cost-effective for the bank, means fewer prospects to solicit for a payment card account. In addition, the type of customer who does visit the branch office may not, in fact, be the type of customer the bank wishes to have as a card customer. In many markets, branch office visitors tend to be older customers who are unlikely to be particularly profitable bankcard users. This fact tends to minimize the effectiveness of the branch as a source for new accounts.

MASS MEDIA

Many card issuers utilize television, radio and newspaper advertising to sell their bankcard offerings to non-bank customers. This is a quick way to reach many prospects, but it can be costly with a tendency to generate applications from less creditworthy consumers than most banks would like. Due to its non-targeted nature, mass media tends to attract anyone looking for a bankcard, not necessarily prospects for which a given institution's offerings are suitable.

In today's mature markets, issuers use television and newspaper advertising to establish an image for their bankcard products and services. In the US, Capital One is a consistent advertiser with its well-known tag line 'What's In Your Wallet?'. Leveraging its market presence, Capital One adjusts its advertising to focus consumers' attention upon card product entitlements where it can create a perceived advantage. Currently it is focused on card products which allow cardholders to accumulate frequent flier mileage. It emphasizes its card which offers no limit dates for redeeming miles and no seat restrictions, meaning that free seats are not limited on any given flight, thus creating a significant perceived advantage over other bankcards offering mileage benefits.

Mass media can be utilized effectively in the manner of Capital One, but it is quite costly to do so and requires issuers to have significant size and scale to justify the investment.

EVENTS

Many issuers have had success soliciting bankcard applications at events such as concerts, sporting activities, local festivals, and similar venues. This approach requires having a table staffed with trained personnel who actively solicit the event attendees entering the facility for a card account. Often, there is an incentive to apply, such as offering a T-shirt or hat. This can be a cost-effective way to generate accounts, but as it is untargeted, it suffers from risk issues similar to mass-media-generated applications. It faces activation and usage issues similar to those from telemarketing-generated applications. Many times people will apply for a card simply to obtain the free premium being offered, and then never activate the card.

Now that we have reviewed all the necessary components to acquire accounts, let's see what's involved in putting an acquisition program together.

Promotion

The fourth and final 'P' is for promotion which combines product, price and placement into actions for the development of marketing activities designed to acquire new card customers. Promotion strategy is also applied to existing customers. But more about that later.

Effective promotion involves card issuers taking all of their skills in market segmentation, product design, pricing strategy, and distribution channel utilization and combining them with clear and compelling communications targeted towards specific types of consumers in the marketplace in order to elicit a specific behavior. In the case of a new account promotion program, the desired behavior is the prospects' applying for a bankcard. In the case of an existing bankcard account customer, the desired behavior is increased usage of the card.

For now, let's focus the discussion regarding promotion on new account acquisition. As with all bankcard management areas, the key to successful new account acquisition promotions is effective use of all available data and information, both in the initial promotion development efforts as well as on an ongoing basis. This is accomplished by the creation and continuous maintenance of a promotion testing and tracking infrastructure. By meticulously testing all aspects of each new account promotion and tracking the corresponding results of each initiative, bankcard issuers develop an ever-increasing base of knowledge of what is effective in the marketplace and can utilize this knowledge in each subsequent effort. This disciplined process is represented in Figure 4.3.

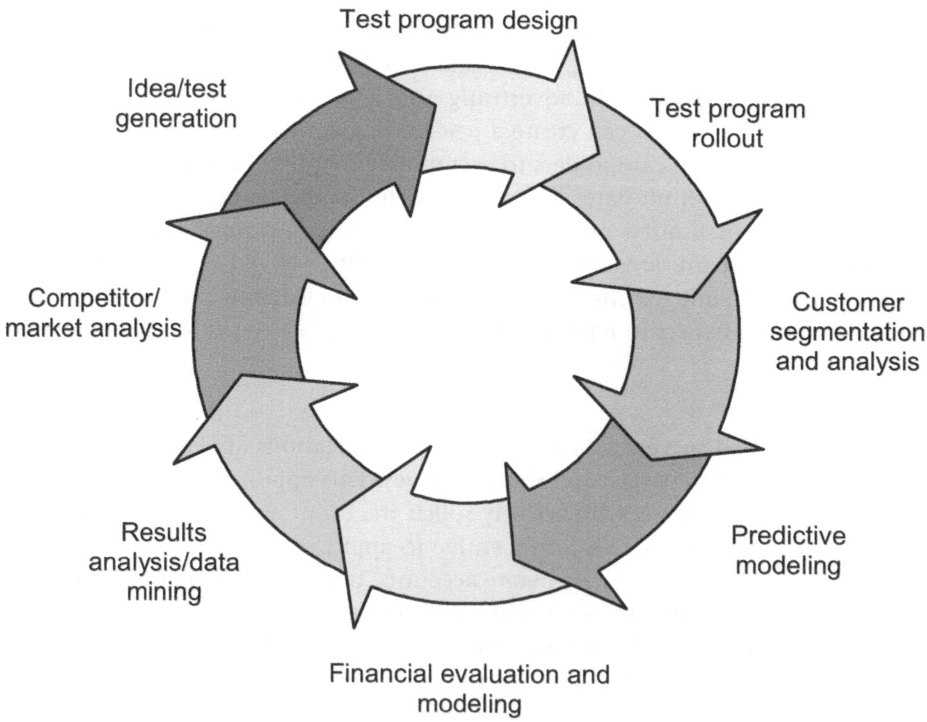

Figure 4.3 The data discipline

Effective new account acquisition involves following this discipline so that there is a constant learning process in place. This discipline is commonly known as 'information management' (IM).

INFORMATION MANAGEMENT

First coined as a phrase by Capital One Financial in its public share offering prospectus in the US in the early 1990s, IM is the rigorous and disciplined collection, storage, retrieval, and analysis of any and all available data for the purpose of designing and implementing profitable card portfolio initiatives. Implemented properly, IM yields insights into all areas of portfolio management, including product design, pricing, market segmentation, operations, risk management, and policy and procedure development.

The single most valuable thing IM does is to minimize management intuition and guesswork and replace it with statistically valid insights which, when implemented, yield predictable and quantifiable results. In short, it replaces 'guess' with 'know'. By analyzing portfolio trends and data elements, then testing well-founded hypotheses, IM creates specific actions, policies, and procedures which translate into specific improvements such as higher response rates to direct mail offerings, lower delinquencies in a targeted segment of the portfolio, increased activation in a specific group of accounts and other specific goals and objectives. IM effectively translates the trends and flows of a market and related card portfolio into specific actions designed to yield specific results.

Effective IM, through the use of disciplined analysis and testing, breaks down a portfolio's trends into minute and discernible sequences which yield 'cause and effect' conclusions. Thus, statements such as 'delinquent accounts are on the rise' are broken down into distinguishable subsets such as 'which specific accounts have rising delinquencies' and 'how and when were these specific accounts generated' to yield more precise and actionable statements such as 'delinquencies in our October 2000 direct mail solicitation are rising due to a recent repricing initiative'. Once cause and effect are known, IM generates a number of possible actions designed to create a specifically desired outcome such as a reduction in the number of delinquent accounts in the October 2000 direct mail solicitation vintage. These potential actions are then prioritized and tested, results are quantified and a recommended ongoing strategy emerges from the process.

Investment areas

There are three primary investment areas required to implement a successful IM strategy.

TECHNOLOGY

IM necessitates a data storage repository of some type such as a data warehouse dedicated to credit card accounts with sufficient capacity to hold anywhere between 150 and 300 static data elements from name, address, account number, and credit score to a rolling thirteen-month history of variable data such as transactions, customer service inquiries, outside data element updates such as credit bureau scores and variables, demographic variable appends and similar data elements as well as ongoing test results. In addition, desktop tools and software which enable analysts to access stored data in a timely fashion are also required. Given the ever-declining costs of computer hardware and data storage technology, a very efficient system can be developed and implemented which can support up to two million cardholder accounts for less than a million dollars.

PEOPLE

The key to a successful IM strategy is the analytic talent which is given access to the technology and data. A few talented analysts can generate revenue streams or cost savings on an order of magnitude which is 10, 20, or even 100 times greater than their annual remuneration. Qualified analysts must be hired if adoption of an IM approach to managing the card business is to succeed. Common characteristics among talented analysts include an educational background in disciplines such as statistics, physics, economics, and engineering, no previous consumer lending background and a work experience which includes 2–5 years in an unrelated industry to consumer lending. To attract qualified candidates, a base salary plus an incentive package tied to the economic results of programs recommended by the analyst is required. In the US, a good analyst earns around US $200 000 annually.

TESTING AND TRACKING INFRASTRUCTURE

The third investment required to implement a successful IM strategy is the testing and tracking infrastructure previously discussed which enables the timely implementation of tests in the marketplace to measure the potential of ideas generated by the analysts. This requires a sufficient budget for customer communications including direct mail, statement inserts, and similar promotional activities as well as either internal capabilities or external partnerships designed to translate test ideas into marketplace realities in a quick and efficient manner. Core competencies must include copy writing, creative design, operational skills, and communications execution capabilities.

Simply stated, in any marketplace where there is competition and consumers enjoy choices, IM is the difference between sustained success and a slow, painful erosion of the business. It is an irrefutable truth that competition creates educated consumers and that educated consumers, in turn, place greater demands upon the suppliers of the goods and services they consume. IM enables issuers to anticipate and deliver the solutions those consumers will demand, usually at the expense of competitors unwilling or unable to adopt the IM approach to the marketplace. In mature markets, IM is no longer a luxury, it is the cost to play in the credit card industry of 2005 and beyond in almost any geographic location in the world. The implications of a successful IM strategy are hard to overstate. They include sustainable growth in market share, improved profit margins, reduced operating expenses and, most importantly, a dynamic understanding of the shifting markets in which the strategy is applied. IM could very well mean the difference between success and failure for all issuers going forward.

Implementation

There are six critical steps in the successful implementation of an IM strategy.

GATHERING DATA

The key here is to gather data from both internal and external sources and store it in a common repository with integrity and controls. This ensures that the definitions and uses of the data are consistent throughout the organization.

ANALYZING DATA

This is where a group of mathematically oriented analysts pores over the data in a structured way to identify patterns of behavior which are interesting and profitable. These observations are then categorized by type and a determination is made as to whether or not the behavior observed constitutes a segment of customers which can be targeted for product design testing.

DEVELOPING STRATEGIES

This is the process whereby products are designed, and anticipated results forecasted based upon the analysis conducted in step 2. Forecasting results is critical because the forecast acts as the benchmark against which results will be measured in order to determine if the test was successful or not. In addition to the forecast, sensitivity analysis of key variables should also be conducted to ensure that if the forecast is wrong in the worst way possible, the business will still be viable. For example, if a given product is anticipated to achieve a credit loss rate of 2 per cent, what is the impact if losses come in at 4 per cent, 6 per cent, or even 10 per cent? It is important to understand the downside of any new product ideas in order to determine if they are worth testing from a risk/reward trade-off point of view.

TESTING PRODUCT STRATEGIES

This is where the new product is offered to the segment targeted via the distribution channels chosen for the offer. The key element in this step is to ensure that the test is constructed in such a way as to ensure that results will be statistically valid and can be used with confidence to predict future results.

ANALYZING TEST RESULTS

Here is where the results of the test are reviewed and compared to the forecast to see which elements performed as anticipated and which did not. Each test is reviewed and tracked with results updated on a periodic basis to see the performance of the accounts generated via that particular test over time. This is a crucial step in being able to develop predictive models for use with future product tests.

REFINING STRATEGIES

Finally, the results of the test are reviewed and the implications of the results are used to create new product tests for the segment being targeted. Almost all tests will contain elements which worked as anticipated and elements which did not. These will be analyzed and new test ideas will be generated, at which point the entire process will be repeated.

Let's apply the Information Management Discipline to an example shown in Figure 4.4.

Here we have a segment defined in the profile box and we are testing three different products as detailed in the boxes marked Test 1, Test 2, and Test 3. We plan to mail like quantities of each offer, thus making direct mail our distribution channel of choice. We have forecasted that Test 2 will have the highest response rate and be the most profitable group of accounts over time.

Customer Profile:

- Income: $20 000 – $30 000 annually
- Credit history: Fair, some delinquency
- 2 other existing bank cards
- 3 existing retailer cards
- $7500 in existing card balances

	Test 1	*Test 2*	*Test 3*
Product	Classic Visa	Classic Visa	Visa Gold
Rate	Low 6-month teaser rate	Lower 6-month teaser rate	Low 6-month teaser rate
Fee	No annual fee	No annual fee	$30 annual fee
Credit line	$3000	$3000	$5000

Track:

- Response rate
- Approval rate
- Activation rate
- Utilization rate
- Revolve rate
- Delinquency and loss
- Profitability

Figure 4.4 New account acquisition test

Once mailed, the tracking begins, with response rate being the first measure we can obtain. Let's suppose the results were as shown in Table 4.3.

Our forecast proves to be correct as our lowest teaser rate offer did, indeed, have the best response rate. It was, in fact, statistically higher than Test 1. Test 3, on the other hand, was the lowest response rate and was statistically lower than Test 1. The statistical significance test means that we are sure if we did this same offer again, we would achieve the same results.

Table 4.3 New account acquisition initial tracking results

Test	*Offer*	*Response*	*Test 1*	*Test 2*	*Test 3*
1	Classic/no fee/low teaser	1.47%		Sig –	Sig +
2	Classic/no fee/lower teaser	2.23%	Sig +		Sig +
3	Gold/fee/low teaser	0.76%	Sig –	Sig –	

The results of this test indicate that consumers matching our segment profile are more interested in a low interest rate than in the status of Gold when it comes to their credit card product. This makes intuitive sense as our segment targeted individuals with at least three other credit cards and existing account balances in excess of US $7500. It is reasonable to assume these types of customers would be interested in a low rate as they are most likely to revolve and pay interest. However, looking only at response rates does not tell us how each product will perform over time. For that, we need to periodically track a number of other elements such as activation rate, revolve rate, attrition rate, losses, and the like.

Table 4.4 reflects the results of account performance in each test one year after being booked. Look at all of the interesting things it is telling us:

- Once again, our forecast was right. Test 2 is the most profitable test on a net present value (NPV) per account basis.
- Test 3 exhibits symptoms of having created some 'adverse selection'. It had a lower response rate and a lower average credit score (or Beacon, the brand name of the particular credit score model utilized) per booked account. Higher activation rates and utilization rates indicate a credit-needy population, as does the lower attrition rate and higher credit loss rate. Knowing this offer was sent to people with the same profile as Test 1 and Test 2, we can be reasonably sure that our product was priced too high for this group, thus creating the adverse selection characteristics we are seeing.
- Surprisingly, however, Test 3 also indicates a very high profit margin per account, almost as strong as Test 2, despite the higher risk profile of the respondents to the Test 3 offer. This shows that there are many factors which determine profitability and the right combination of them in any given population can make for a profitable portfolio.

These highlights are just a sampling of what the ongoing tracking and analysis inherent in the information management approach to acquiring accounts reveals. Periodic updating of the table will provide ongoing insights and new test ideas for use in generating more accounts from the segment targeted.

Table 4.4 Ongoing bankcard account performance tracking

Package Description	*Fee/ Teaser Go To*	*Net resp rate*	*Back-end credit score*	*Avg. credit line*	*Activ-ation rate*	*Utili-zation rate*	*Re-volve rate*	*Annual-ized attrition*	*Acq. cost acc. book'd*	*Trend loss rate*	*NPV account*	*Total NPV*
Test 1	*0 fee Teaser $3000*	*1.47%*	*681*	*$3113*	*94.7%*	*61.4%*	*98.3%*	*13.6%*	*$55.09*	*3.9%*	*$104.35*	*$1 045 908*
Test 2	*0 fee Lower Teaser*	*2.23%*	*683*	*$3345*	*96.8%*	*70.1%*	*99.5%*	*15.1%*	*$41.56*	*3.6%*	*$123.78*	*$587 493*
Test 3	*$30 fee Teaser $5000*	*0.76%*	*667*	*$2324*	*96.2%*	*85.6%*	*99.1%*	*7.9%*	*$84.23*	*4.4%*	*$115.93*	*$94 256*

CHAPTER

5 Existing Account Marketing

Let's turn our attention now away from acquiring new accounts to marketing to existing customers. One of the most important things to remember when it comes to card marketing is that, unlike most financial products or services, convincing a consumer to acquire the card is not the end of the sales process, but merely the beginning. Once an issuer acquires a new bankcard account they have all of the expenses invested in generating that sale, but no revenues. So, focusing marketing efforts upon existing cardholders makes a lot of sense for several reasons:

- Revenues, and ultimately profits, come from cardholder activity such as purchase and cash advance transactions and borrowings, not number of accounts.
- Bankcard issuers understand a lot more about cardholders once they are acquired and can use that knowledge to personalize the card's features to meet the needs of the cardholder as demonstrated by their card activity behavior.
- Bankcard issuers have more ways to communicate with existing cardholders, thus reducing expenses.

Card issuers are realizing that investing in marketing campaigns targeted at existing cardholders can have significant positive impacts upon a portfolio's overall profitability as well as a much greater internal rate of return on that investment when compared to new account acquisition programs. As a result, in the US, issuers have significantly raised their marketing investments in existing account marketing.

Desired cardholder behavior

There are three key elements card issuers try to stimulate when it comes to marketing to existing accounts:

ACTIVATION

All potential revenues and profits to be derived from a card account begin with getting the customer to use the card for the first time. This is called activating the card. Simply having a cardholder accept the plastic is not enough. In fact, account acquisition represents nothing but expense to card issuers. Card issuers must incentivize the cardholder to use the card before profits can be generated.

USAGE

Once activated, card issuers must be active in providing cardholders with reasons to continue to use the card. Continual reminders of the card's features and benefits coupled with occasional promotions tied to specific events in the card's lifecycle are required to maintain a steady flow of card transactions.

RETENTION

Finally, card issuers must be both proactive and reactive in their efforts to keep cardholders satisfied. Cardholders close their card accounts when the features offered no longer meet their needs. Carefully monitoring card usage and reacting when behavior patterns change can help issuers to minimize cardholder attrition.

Communicating with the cardholder

Marketing to existing cardholders begins with the initial fulfilment of the new account and continues via numerous communications opportunities that the operational nature of the bankcard business presents.

Instead of inundating cardholders with offers every time a communication is required, issuers would be better served by building up to making offers within customer letters over time. After all, it's not as though issuers don't have multiple reasons, and multiple ways, to communicate with their cardholders. Why inundate them with promotions right from the beginning? Instead, why not show customers how much they are valued first, and then try to cross-sell other products and services later on. This is called establishing trust and it is critical to the development of long-term customer relationships.

How can this be achieved? Let's take a look at the basic communications opportunities issuers have once a new account has been approved.

- *Card mailer*. This is the package which issuers send out the newly approved card along with appropriate legal disclosures, enhancement rules and regulations, credit line assignment, and other card-related matters. Often, this is also used as a platform to cross-sell such items as credit life insurance, travel or discount purchasing clubs and the like.
- *Welcome kit*. Many issuers send a separate mailing to newly approved cardholders outlining the benefits of their new card and providing all of the necessary paperwork for such items as travel accident insurance, extended warranty protection, lost or stolen card registration service, and other card benefits.
- *Call-to-activate*. Many issuers issue cards to new accounts which require a telephone call to be activated. Often, when the cardholder calls to activate the card, they are put on hold while the cardholder's record is retrieved and a recording which attempts to cross-sell some product or service is played.
- *Security mailer*. Most issuers send this communication to cardholders a week or two after new cards have been sent to ensure that the cardholder received the plastic. This mailer is often used to cross-sell insurance or other enhancements.

- *First billing statement.* The first statement, which usually contains the annual fee billing if the card carries such a charge, is also a time when issuers attempt to cross-sell insurance and card enhancements such as credit card registration services.

The communications events listed above occur within the first thirty days of a new account's lifecycle. Let's look at how these channels of communication, along with a couple of others, can be modified slightly to create the trust between customer and issuer which is so critical to the development of long-term customer loyalty.

- *Card mailer.* Send all of the required legal disclosures and so on, but do not attempt to cross-sell any other product or service. Instead, use the card mailer to reinforce the reason the customer took the card to begin with. Emphasize the key product features or entitlements, be they interest rate, low or no fee, or loyalty points and make the cardholder feel good about the decision they made to apply for this card in the first place.
- *Welcome kit.* Provide all the necessary forms, disclosures and so on for features and enhancements already offered as part of the card and, in addition, provide a brochure listing all of the available services customers may purchase. The focus of the communication should be a brief description of each service such as card registration, credit life insurance, travel clubs, shopping services, and extended warranty programs along with reasons it may be desirable for the cardholder to sign up for the service and the price for doing so. Providing a response mechanism for signing up for each service such as a telephone number, website address, or form to fill out is also necessary.
- *Call to activate.* This customer initiated call is another opportunity to re-emphasize the benefits of the card product the customer recently acquired and can also serve as a data-gathering tool. Instead of playing a message trying to cross-sell an additional service (a tactic which has demonstrated very low response rates), have cardholders answer a short survey of no more than three or four questions regarding their preferences for additional product or service features they would like to see offered as a part of their card product. Innovative issuers in the US market have taken this approach. The information gathered is then followed up with separate promotional offerings. These follow-up efforts have demonstrated higher response rates and, of course, help to lower costs as only cardholders who have expressed an interest in a product or service receive the follow-up material.
- *Welcome call.* This is an additional contact opportunity which issuers around the globe have found to be useful in driving new card activation. Calling a new cardholder shortly after the card mailer and welcome kit have been sent simply to see if both items have been received and to answer any questions cardholders may have helps customers trust that the issuer has their best interest at heart. Under no circumstances should the welcome call be used to actively cross-sell any products or services. Instead, answering any cardholder questions regarding the new account or the features available is the goal of the call.
- *Security mailer.* This becomes unnecessary if a welcome call is introduced. If no welcome call is conducted, then the security mailer can be used to offer additional enhancements to new cardholders as long as a response mechanism like a telephone number or website address is included.
- *First transaction letter.* Another new communication, utilized by some card issuers is a brief letter to new cardholders when the first debit transaction on the new account is

posted. The letter is a thank you and reinforces the main benefits of the card product. It is especially useful for products with a loyalty scheme attached. The fact that loyalty points have now begun accruing can be pointed out in the letter. No cross-sell attempt is made as part of this type of communication.
- *First billing statement.* This is a good time to include an insert re-emphasizing the core features of the card and to cross-sell enhancements such as insurance now that there is a balance to protect should the cardholder become ill, die, or lose their job.

As you can see, the differences between the first and second approaches to these routine cardholder communications opportunities are subtle, but they can be quite effective. Simply by softening the cross-sell efforts and by introducing some communications which are designed to help new customers, banks have driven better cross-sell results and helped to foster a spirit of caring and concern for their customers which is crucial in creating long-term customer loyalty.

The modified approach to new customer communication does cost a little more, but it has proven to be more effective in driving cross-sell results and lowering attrition rates over time, thus making it a good investment. It may take some convincing on the part of the card issuer marketing team to convince senior management of the value in a softer communications style, but it is an effort worth making and one which cardholders will appreciate and reward the bank for over time.

Account development goals

Beyond the initial communications opportunities issuers enjoy when a new account is developed, marketing to existing accounts over time should be designed to accomplish three things:

- improve profitability
- reduce risk
- increase cardholder loyalty.

Each of these three goals is important in its own right as shown in Table 5.1.

Table 5.1 Existing account marketing objectives

Profits	*Risk*	*Customer loyalty*
• Fuel for growth • Measured/projected • Readily available • Meet bank goals	• Drives funds availability • Changes over time • Continuously monitored • Management credibility	• Only with best customers • Will be driven by customer needs • Product must meet needs • Changes as cutomer needs change

Unlike the account lifecycle associated with new account acquisition, existing account marketing is tied to specific actions, or events, in the life of an account because each specific event represents a precise behavior by the customer and this specific behavior warrants an action by the card issuer which can be effective in modifying the customer's behavior into a more desirable one. This is depicted in Table 5.2.

Similar to Newton's Third Law (every action creates an equal and opposite reaction) every cardholder event creates data which the issuer can use to determine an appropriate response. The compilation and analysis of this relevant data on a continuous basis enables issuers to deliver the right incentive to the right cardholder at the right time based upon the cardholders' actions as shown in Table 5.3.

Table 5.2 The 'event-based' marketing concept

Cardholder Events	*Action (data)*	*Reaction*
• New account opening	• Card not activated	• Letter with usage incentive
• Annual fee billing	• Account closure	• Re-opening offer (balance transfer)
• Rate change	• Usage decline	• Volume incentive
• First transaction	• First statement	• Thank you statement message
• Balance transfer in	• Less availability	• Credit line increase
• Balance transfer out	• Paydown	• Aggressive re-price downward
• Overlimit	• High usage	• Credit line increase
• Card reissue	• Usage decline	• Benefits reminder/balance transfer offer

Table 5.3 Using 'event' data to match offer to customer behavior

Activation	*Utilization*	*Cross Sales*	*Retention*	*Spread Mgmt.*
• Benefits reminder sent with card • Welcome call • Call to activate • Incentive loyalty scheme • 'Spend and get' offer	• Loyalty scheme • Balance transfer offer • Additional card • Line increase	• Other bank products • Insurance • Buying club • Travel club • Extended warranty • Statement inserts	• Customer survey • Repricing • Thank you programs • Line increases • Closed account resolicitation	• Risk-based pricing • Behavior-based pricing • Change in terms notice • Negotiated terms

Similar to new account acquisition, the key to effective existing account marketing is information management. Tracking cardholder behavior patterns over time provides the information required for the targeted promotions and actions which drive the achievement of the three goals of existing account marketing.

The quickest way to improved profitability within an existing card portfolio is to identify specific cardholder behaviors which are profitable, then design products and promotions designed to produce more of that profitable behavior. What are these profitable cardholder behaviors? Well, while somewhat influenced by individual card issuer expense dynamics, in general, these are as follows:

- *Revolvers*. No surprise here as interest income, in general, makes around two-thirds of total issuer revenue in some markets such as the US. Cardholders who utilize their credit card product as a loan source tend to be the most profitable customers, but they are also the most volatile in terms of credit risk.
- *High volume transactors*. These customers pose little credit risk and generate significant transaction-based income as well as fee income as they tend to be attracted to products which can charge an annual fee due to their value such as airline mileage cards, point-based loyalty schemes, and similar offerings.
- *'Episodic' revolvers*. These are unique customers who transact most of the year, but revolve balance for two or three months once or twice a year, usually after an unusually high volume period of transactions. Identifying these customers can be tricky, but they are highly profitable cardholders as they generate significant levels of interest income with less credit risk than continuous revolvers.

The key to improving overall portfolio profitability is the ability to identify the cardholders within an issuer's portfolio exhibiting these behaviors, then crafting specific promotions designed to create more of their existing behavior pattern.

Identifying cardholders with profitable behaviors

In order to target offers to cardholders exhibiting profitable behavior patterns, issuers first must be able to identify such behaviors within their portfolio. This requires some data mining and analytical skill. The critical element in identifying profitable behaviors is at the transaction level. Issuers must track transactions at the account level for a rolling thirteen-month timeframe in order to stratify cardholders into the behavior categories mentioned previously. Thirteen months is the ideal timeframe for such stratification as it enables issuers to compare the current month's activity to the same month one year prior and displays the activity in the period between the endpoints which accounts for the change in behavior, if any. This requires a database into which is deposited the monthly transaction files and related data from the billing statements such as interest paid, delinquency status, and repayment amount. These elements can be analyzed by staff members with the appropriate skills in order to sort out which cardholders exhibit which behaviors. It is important to have the rolling thirteen months of data to analyze so that true revolvers, transactors and, most importantly, episodic revolvers can be properly identified. Shorter timeframes can lead to erroneous conclusions and wasted marketing efforts as a result. In general, cardholders will fall into a behavioral category based upon the following definitions:

- *Revolver*. Carried a balance and paid interest in at least ten of the thirteen months analyzed.
- *High volume transactor*. Had at least twice the portfolio transaction volume in half or more of the thirteen months analyzed and paid no finance charges in any month.
- *Episodic revolver*. Carried a balance and paid interest in three to nine of the thirteen months analyzed with at least two of the three months in which finance charges were paid being consecutive.

Note that these definitions will not result in every cardholder falling into one of the three categories. This is to be expected because not every cardholder utilizes credit cards in a manner profitable for the issuer. By categorizing the behavior of cardholders, issuers will not only learn which ones are profitable, but also which ones are not profitable and require attention as well. For now, let's focus on what to do with the customers who fall into one of the three profitable behavior categories.

TARGETING OFFERS BASED UPON BEHAVIOR

Profitable behavior

Remembering that the goal is to get more of the behavior already being exhibited, not to change it, here are some potential offers for each behavior category:

- *Revolvers*. The key here is to create larger revolving balances while minimizing the associated credit risk. Accordingly, cardholders who fall into this category should first be stratified by risk profile utilizing tools such as credit score and behavior score (assuming they are available) and offers should be made only to those cardholders who exhibit acceptable risk characteristics. Once this is done, offers should focus upon two key elements: price and ease of moving balances from higher-priced loans to the credit card. Balance transfer offers are the standard here and usually take the form of a low rate for a limited period of time ranging anywhere from six to eighteen months, or sometimes even for the life of the transferred balance, after which the rate on the transferred balance reverts to the card's standard interest charge. In addition, issuers make transferring a balance easy by providing a simple form for the customer to complete, directing the card issuer as to which balances are to be moved or, in some cases, by providing a check for the cardholder to write directly to pay off another balance and which will debit the credit card account at the appropriate rate. Many card issuers also offer transfers via telephone or their website. In many markets, issuers charge a small fee for this lower rate, usually 0.5 per cent to 1.5 per cent of the balance transferred up to a maximum of $25 to $30. This helps to improve the profitability of the overall offer. From a communications viewpoint there are a couple of critical elements to convey in order to ensure a successful promotion. First, the text of the promotional offer should provide numerous examples of which balances to transfer to the credit card, from other credit cards, retail store cards, small personal installment loans, automobile loans, and appliance finance contracts. Second, an illustration of the potential cost savings should also be provided so that cardholders can easily translate the lower interest rate into dollars saved. This is usually accomplished via a chart showing the interest savings on a transferred balance at the promotional rate versus typical credit card rates.

- *High volume transactors*. Offers to this group of cardholders center upon loyalty schemes. If the cardholder is already enrolled in a program, then crafting an offer which rewards incremental volume with higher point rewards than normal is a proven initiative. If the cardholder is not enrolled in a points-based program, then offering one with short-term incentives for incremental volume has proven to be effective. In many markets, these loyalty schemes can be offered with an annual fee for participation – another profitability enhancement. The goal with any offer is to have the cardholder spend above their current level on the card, so setting the thresholds for receiving the rewards at the appropriate levels is critical to profitability. The primary driver of profitability is incremental interchange income, so issuers must use caution when setting up their incentives in order to ensure that the cost of the incentive does not exceed the value of the incremental interchange income generated.

  Loyalty schemes can be very useful here, but they require a tremendous amount of effort and commitment on the part of the bankcard issuer. Most successful loyalty programs involve significant investments in people, capital and systems support. In addition, loyalty schemes must be continually updated and enhanced in order to keep the cardholders' attention and interest in continuing to accumulate points towards the rewards offered. This requires periodic refreshment of the program in terms of ways to earn points and ways to redeem them. If this organizational commitment is present and the continuous innovation of the program is achieved, loyalty schemes can greatly enhance sales volume and positively influence customer retention.
- *Episodic Revolvers*. This is perhaps the trickiest group to leverage because the cause of their revolving 'episodes' is usually not known. It can be assumed that the higher balance levels which lead to the revolving behavior for a month or two are driven by an event such as an automotive emergency or moving into a new home. Knowing this, however, does not necessarily help in designing a promotion because predicting the next event is near impossible. Accordingly, promotions targeted at this group should focus upon a lower interest rate which the cardholder can trigger when needed. How can this be achieved? Some issuers have had success with these types of cardholders by offering them a special check which they can write for large purchases and which will post to the credit card account at a lower rate than normal. These checks are usually issued for a limited period of time such as six months and require a minimum amount, usually $500 or so, for the special interest rate to apply. This type of promotion has the added benefit of keeping the revolving balance on the books for a longer time period as cardholders take advantage of the lower rate.

While the specifics of the promotional offerings will vary, the key to success is to match the offer to the current behavior and simply provide the cardholder with an incentive to do more of what they are already doing.

Unprofitable behavior

But what can be done to stimulate profitable activity from cardholders who do not exhibit behavior which is already inherently profitable? While presenting a more difficult marketing challenge, there are a number of tools and techniques which issuers have tested over the years and which seem to have some positive effect. Let's first define the categories of behavior and then look at some potential programs.

- *Inactives*. These are cardholders who have had no balance and no transactions on their bankcards for anywhere from one to three months. While cardholders may exhibit longer periods of inactivity, issuers would be well advised to ignore customers who have been inactive for longer than three months because experience shows they are highly unlikely to re-activate regardless of the offer made.
- *Low volume transactors*. These are cardholders who have very low activity on their cards each month, perhaps just one or two transactions totaling $100 or less and who pay their bill in full at the end of each month generating no interest income for the issuer.
- *Pay downs*. These are customers who carry a revolving balance, but who do not make any new charges on their account and are simply 'paying down' their balance until they can pay off the entire account.

These are indeed difficult cardholder behaviors to turn into profitable accounts, but it must be remembered that individuals indicating these types of activities usually have more than one bankcard and are probably exhibiting profitable behavior on one of their other cards. The key to marketing success in these instances is to transfer that profitable behavior from a competitor's card. Here are some existing account promotions which have proven successful in doing just that:

- *Inactives*. Cash rebate offers for a limited time have shown some success in this category. A typical program would offer cardholders a cash rebate from 3 per cent to 5 per cent of transactions charged to the card for a limited period of time, usually three to five months. The rebate, commonly referred to as a cashback offer, appears as a credit to the customer's bankcard account each month. The key is to have the cashback amount be meaningful, meaning more than 1 per cent, and to limit the time period in which the customer can obtain the rebate, thus imparting a sense of urgency to activate and use the card.
- *Low volume transactors*. Cashback offerings can be utilized here as well as with inactives. Another proven tactic is called a 'spend and get', which is a variation on the cashback offering. In the case of a spend and get, low volume transactors are offered a specific spending threshold to achieve in the next one or two months which, if met, results in a fixed credit amount being credited to their bankcard monthly bill. For example, spend $500 or more in the next month and receive a $10 credit on your next statement. As with Cashback, the key to success is for the credit to be meaningful, at least $10 if not more, and for the volume threshold to be an increase over current activity, but a reasonable one. Experience shows these programs to work quite well and, in fact, that most customers who take advantage of the offer tend to spend more than the required threshold in the period incentivized.

  In addition to cashback or spend and get offers, low volume transactors sometimes react favorably to enrolment in a loyalty program where they can earn points redeemable for merchandise, free travel and other benefits.
- *Pay downs*. Perhaps the most difficult customer behavior to alter, pay downs usually have made up their minds to close the bankcard account they are paying off and, in most instances, have already obtained a replacement card. That said, aggressively priced balance transfer offers or cashback programs have shown some success in turning around this type of consumer behavior.

TRACKING ACCOUNT BEHAVIOR

Detailed tracking of account activity via an effective IM strategy provides information which can be utilized to drive more than just marketing activities. What is learned can be used to develop segmented strategies for all aspects of the bankcard operation, from customer service to risk management to product enhancements. How? Consider the following in Table 5.4.

Table 5.4 Individual cardholder profitability groupings

% of customers	*Variable profit contribution*
Top 25%	80%
Next best 25%	10%
Next best 25%	10%
Lowest 25%	(Negative)

Once an issuer knows which customers create the most value, it is a simple step to utilize that information to initiate different operating strategies for each group of cardholders as shown in Table 5.5.

As demonstrated in this table, segmenting a portfolio of existing card accounts by profitability enables issuers to design and target specific actions towards precise subsets of customers that will ultimately result in 'personalizing' the card product of each cardholder based upon their own activities.

Table 5.5 Customer management strategies based on profit contribution

Customer	*Line mgmt.*	*Retention*	*Cross sales*	*Customer svc.*
Top 25%	• Aggressive increases	• Proactive • Lowest priced offers	• Investments • Deposits • Insurance • Preferred rates	• Dedicated unit • Personalized • Human touch
Next 25%	• Selected increases	• Reactive offers	• Deposits • Insurance • Extended warranty	• Automated • Easy opt out for CSR
Next 25%	• Maintain and monitor	• Non-price offers	• Travel, shopping clubs • Credit insurance	• Automated
Lowest 25%	• Decreases and closures	• No offers	• Travel, shopping clubs • Credit insurance	• Automated

The ongoing tracking and analysis of customer actions and behaviors provide a road map for issuers to utilize in determining what steps might best be taken to improve card activation, transaction levels and customer loyalty. Consider the following examples:

- *Cardholder has only a few transactions and never revolves a balance.* This is a customer who is likely to be a pure transaction and who uses the bankcard strictly for convenience. Since the only opportunity for additional revenue is more interchange income, issuers must persuade the customer to use the card more for payment at the point of sale. This implies some type of reward program which enables the cardholder to accrue value for increasing transaction activity as well as possibly an educational communication which advises the cardholder of other, non-traditional ways to use the bankcard as a payment device, such as for recurring monthly payments for household utility bills, magazine subscriptions, insurance premiums, and similar bills.
- *Cardholder has a very high level of monthly purchase volume.* In this instance, it is likely that the card issued occupies the cherished 'top of wallet' position and is perceived by the customer to be the best card they have. This is potentially a very loyal and profitable cardholder, so the card issuer wants to reward and thank this customer by offering some type of product enhancement or rewards program to encourage continued use of the card. This type of cardholder is one which the issuer wants to keep, so retention of the relationship is the primary goal.
- *Cardholder has a small balance which revolves, pays the minimum each month, with no new sales activity on the card.* These are the signs of a customer paying off their account, which means they are highly likely to close once the balance reaches zero. Since the issuer knows this cardholder utilizes the card for borrowing, they may want to incentivize a transfer of a balance from another card by offering a special interest rate.

This section shows how important it is for card issuers to understand and track the account behavior of each cardholder within its portfolio. This type of tracking, coupled with effective analysis and promotion testing, enables issuers to motivate cardholders to exhibit behaviors which are more profitable, thus providing the capital required by issuers to continually invest in enhancing and improving their card issuing business.

There remains an important element of card marketing yet to be discussed, and it is appropriate to raise it here because it is closely tied to issuers understanding the behavior of their customers. This last element of bankcard marketing is the development of the communications to be utilized in conveying offers to customers.

Developing an effective cardholder communications plan

The development and implementation of advertisements, direct mail offerings and telemarketing scripts is where the understanding of consumer activity ascertained via effective information management techniques runs head on into the vagaries of human nature. Most of us enjoy those times when companies with which we do business treat us as individuals and make us feel as if they are designing products and services just for our specific needs. Just as true, however, is the fact that most of us do not like the feeling that our privacy has been invaded in some of type of 'big brother' fashion. Cardholder communications thus have to straddle this fine line between customization and customer intrusion. Failure to do so almost invariably results in swift and negative retribution by cardholders.

There are a few key principles with respect to customer communications which bankcard issuers must keep in mind in order to ensure that this fine line is never crossed:

- *Less is more.* Remember the KISS principle – Keep It Simple, Stupid! If a letter or advertisement offering cardholders a special deal is busy and complicated, it is likely that the message will be lost upon the typical consumer. Simple and direct communications are always the most effective because they tell a story and lead the reader where the writer wants them to go.
- *Familiarity breeds contempt.* Shakespeare was right. If cardholders perceive that their bankcard issuer is getting too personal with regard to monitoring their card behavior and too specific with how it is being used, the reaction will be swift and definitive – and not favorable to the issuer.
- *'Nothing will kill a bad product faster than good advertising.'* David Ogilvy was also right. If an issuer convinces a cardholder that the card product is going to deliver a valued service, and then fails to deliver upon that promise, it will end up with a dissatisfied cardholder who is likely to close their account and, even worse, tell all of their friends about their terrible experience with that bank. Card issuers have to deliver what they sell.

A little common sense goes a long way when it comes to cardholder communications. Consider the following example:

> A cardholder has recently purchased an expensive new kitchen appliance on a given issuer's payment card, which the bank knows because it is tracking behavior at the transaction level. The bank's cross-sales group offers an extended warranty service which they would like to sell to this cardholder. Which of the following communications should be initiated?
>
> Dear Cardholder,
>
> Recently you purchased an expensive new household item for your kitchen. Our Extended Warranty Plan is the perfect thing to protect your new purchase from expensive replacement or service work.
>
> Dear Cardholder,
>
> If you've recently made a major purchase, you know how expensive replacing household items can be. Our Extended Warranty Plan can help save you from the expense of replacing household items unexpectedly, regardless of the reason for the replacement required.

Both communications are selling the same thing, but the second approach is much more customer friendly and less imposing than the first. Remember, it is perfectly appropriate for issuers to know a lot of things about their customers, but they must take extreme care to not tell them all they know every time they communicate with them lest they violate the trust between themselves and the cardholder. It is this ongoing trust between the issuer and the customer which ultimately determines the profits the bank will earn from the relationship.

Other marketing considerations

There are some other elements it is important to note when it comes to bankcard marketing.

RISK/REVENUE CONUNDRUM

As is the case with most things involving risk and reward, there exists a direct correlation in the card business between risk and revenue. In other words, the riskier the cardholder, the more likely they are to respond to offers and to create revenue. Of course, due to their higher risk, they are also more likely to not pay back their borrowings and result in credit losses for the issuer. Card marketers need to balance this risk and reward relationship through appropriate targeting of offers to each segment of the card portfolio and pricing which reflects the inherent risks associated with the segment being solicited.

REGULATORY ISSUES

There exist in almost every market in the world various governmental agencies which oversee banking activities. Whether it is the country's central bank or some other agency, card marketers must be aware of the regulatory requirements involved in all marketing activities, from pricing to cardholder communications. In general, card marketing is impacted by three distinct areas of regulation.

Banking oversight regulatory agencies

This group generally regulates the pricing and terms of bankcard accounts which are acceptable in the market.

Commerce regulatory agencies

This group generally regulates the terms under which business commerce can be transacted within the country. This may include electronic commerce transactions, of which payment cards constitute a large number. This area is of particular importance when it comes to customer relations as most consumer protection regulations are usually found within this regulatory body.

Advertising regulatory agencies

Most countries have laws regarding 'truth in lending', or what must be disclosed to customers prior to entering into a loan agreement with them. Payment card marketers are most directly affected by this group.

Organizational structure

How do card issuing organizations effectively manage all of the various aspects required to successfully market card products?

Successful marketing of card products begins with the staffing of an organization which places resources and emphasis upon the keys to effective marketing:

- products and pricing
- promotion
- distribution
- data and information management.

By organizing around these critical marketing elements, successful card marketers ensure that appropriate levels of attention and thought are being given to the areas most likely to create success.

Utilizing these key elements, a typical card marketing organization is organized as shown in Figure 5.1.

In this typical organizational structure, each of the four key elements is addressed and staffed appropriately:

- *Product and pricing* is addressed by the new account acquisition and existing account marketing areas based upon detailed profitability analysis provided by the MIS/analysis area.
- *Promotion* is addressed by production and execution, which is the area tasked with designing and implementing all advertising, direct mail, and other promotional campaigns.
- *Distribution* is addressed by the production and execution area as well, ensuring that all relevant product distribution channels are utilized effectively.
- *Data and information* is managed via the MIS/analysis group, the area responsible for correlating existing customer and product usage data with potential new cardholder groups in the general marketplace. The importance of this area can not be overstated as it is the rigorous analysis of promotional campaigns, ongoing card account performance, and cost and revenue drivers which leads to the continuous innovation required to be successful in marketing bankcard products.

Each area within the marketing organization has specific tasks and responsibilities in order to ensure that the profitability of the bankcard portfolio is maximized:

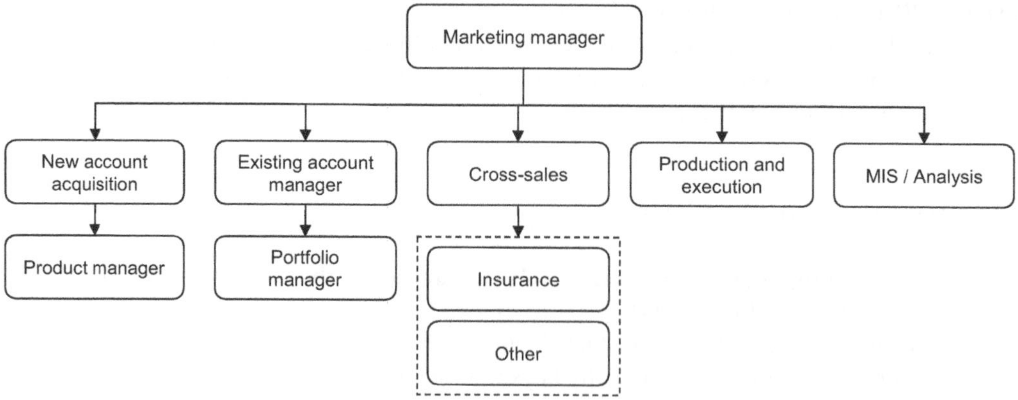

Figure 5.1 Marketing organization structure

- *New account acquisition* is tasked with the design and targeting of new product offers to selected segments of the general population as well as to existing customers utilizing other bank products and services.
- *Existing account marketing* is responsible for creating promotional offerings targeted at selected areas of the portfolio to drive improvement in cardholder activation rates and card usage.
- *Cross-sales*, often overlooked, is responsible for selling additional bankcard-related products and services to the existing card base as well as other bank products such as checking and savings accounts.
- *Production and execution* is the group which takes all of the new account acquisition and existing account marketing promotional designs and translates them into an actual advertising campaign. This can be done within the group or via outside advertising agencies, direct mail production houses, and similar service providers.
- *MIS/analysis*, a critical group, is charged with monitoring portfolio trends and identifying behaviors which are profitable and which can be used to segment the portfolio into groups for targeted promotional efforts as well as for new account acquisition initiatives.

So now you know how card issuers acquire and activate new accounts, but as you might suspect, there is a lot more to making a payment card work than just marketing. The operational support and risk management skills required to support the types of card product and marketing strategies reviewed in this chapter are every bit as critical to success as the payment card products themselves.

CHAPTER

6 Customer Management

The dynamic nature of the payment card business makes the management of ongoing customer relationships the most challenging aspect of the business. Cardholders enjoy an almost limitless number of choices with regard to card products for their use in many markets around the world and the ease with which customers can obtain a new card and move balances from their previous one makes switching costs almost zero. As a result, holding onto customers in the card business is extremely difficult and one of the fundamental challenges to maintaining profitability over time.

Why is retaining customers so difficult? There are a number of reasons, but the primary ones fall into the following categories:

- *Consumer Behavior*. Human beings are notoriously inconsistent relative to other living species when it comes to their behavior. While it is true that most of us strive for consistency and routine in our daily activities, it is fundamentally true that we humans are quite comfortable changing our living patterns at a moment's notice. It is also quite true that most societies in the modern world offer people a tremendous amount of choice and flexibility in their daily living environments. As a result, people tend to alter their lifestyles and activities on an almost regular basis throughout their lifetimes. This basic human behavior manifests itself in the bankcard business as an almost continually changing drive on the part of cardholders to obtain the best card for themselves. Of course what is deemed 'best' will change as the consumers' needs and desires change.

  Consider the basic changes most people go through in life in western societies as previously noted in Chapter 4. Many start their adult lives as university students. What are their needs and wants, from a consumption point of view, at this time? They are simple: primarily entertainment oriented in nature with things such as restaurants, bars, and CDs/MP3 music downloads. Upon graduation, these needs change to include business attire, outfitting a first apartment, and perhaps more upmarket restaurants. The mid-twenties to mid-thirties bring a host of changes as people marry, start families and purchase first homes. These changes lead to dramatic increases in consumption as the need for furniture, curtains, children's toys and supplies, and other needs rises. As the forties and fifties are reached, consumption needs change again as college tuition bills come and go and then personal activities such as travel and hobbies come to the fore. Then, as the sixties and beyond approach, human needs and wants change again as travel and hobbies still are important, but so are grandchildren and their needs.

  Why is this continual changing of consumer desires so important in the bankcard business? Quite simply because, as consumers' needs change, so does their use of card products and services as well as what they expect to receive for using one bankcard rather than another. Younger consumers are content simply to receive credit and are very cost ambivalent. As they mature, consumers not only expect credit at a lower cost, they also come to expect incentives and rewards for using one card rather than another. If the bankcard they currently have does not keep pace with their changing desires, they simply obtain another one that does.

- *Consumer choice.* The changing behavior of consumers is difficult enough for issuers to contend with, but the fact that there are so many card issuers in many markets compounds the problem. As card issuers strive to gain competitive advantage in a marketplace, they continually attempt to innovate and develop new and more intricate card offerings. They market these new offerings aggressively through advertising and promotional campaigns, thus providing consumers with a continually changing array of card products from which to choose. As a result, the ability to find a product which better fits their changing needs and wants is never more than a newspaper ad or direct mail offering away. This results in the rather predictable fact that consumers often change their credit or charge cards, or obtain multiple cards as they are exposed to new and unique opportunities.

  Consider all of the benefits consumers can obtain from bankcard products in most mature markets around the globe. Low rates, no annual fees, frequent flier mileage, points redeemable for free brand-name merchandise, cash rebates, free gasoline, reduced utility bills, customized plastic and many, many more are readily available today. As the needs of consumers change, their ability to find a bankcard product to satisfy their new needs is never more than a phone call away.
- *Consumer knowledge.* It is an inevitable result of the many choices available to consumers that they have become quite knowledgeable and savvy purchasers of card product offerings. In fact, consumers usually acquire and use several different bankcard products at any one time depending upon which of their multiple needs they are satisfying.

  Consider, for example, a married couple with young children who have recently purchased their first home. They may, and probably do, have several credit cards, each with a specific purpose. They have one with the lowest interest rate they can find and this is the card they use to make large household purchases, which they then repay over time to help them manage their monthly cash flow. They have another card which earns them some type of reward which is important to them, be it free travel, gasoline, merchandise or whatever, and they use this card for daily purchases and transactions which they plan to pay in full each month when the bill arrives. They may even have a third card which carries a substantial credit line, but which they do not use and instead hold in reserve in the event of an emergency expense such as an automobile breakdown.

  This type of behavior is quite commonplace in many markets and is also quite savvy from a consumer point of view. By categorizing their purchasing behavior and taking advantage of the choices available in the marketplace, knowledgeable consumers are able to maximize the value of their bankcard transacting activities; good, even rational, for them, but difficult for card issuers.

So how do card issuers deal with these difficulties and retain customer relationships? There are two critical components issuers must focus upon in order to retain their best cardholder relationships. The first is the development, maintenance, and use of a customer database which integrates information from the credit, risk, marketing, back-office and collections areas and the second is the more traditional customer service function within the bankcard issuing organization. Combined, these two elements are called customer management. Let's look at each component individually.

Customer database

The bankcard product is unique in the breadth and depth of information it provides regarding customers who use it, whether sporadically or on a regular basis. Just think of all of the data issuers obtain:

- customer name and address
- telephone numbers
- e-mail addresses
- employment and income data
- other loan and bank account information
- purchase activity
  - location
  - amount
  - date
  - type of merchandise
  - how often
- payment history
  - minimum/full/in between
  - on time/late
  - electronic/in person/via mail/via transfer
- service requests.

This is just a partial listing, but it hopefully makes the point that sophisticated card issuers have the ability to know an awful lot about their customers if they take the time to capture, organize, analyze, and act upon the data available to them. But how to do this? Again, let's break the challenge down into its component parts.

There are essentially three key components to the effective use of all of the data bankcard customers create for issuers:

- the database
- analysts
- program tracking and development.

THE DATABASE

The customer database is at the core of effective customer management. It provides the raw material for the testing of programs designed to maximize the value of every customer relationship and serves as the repository of all information which may assist in this endeavor.

Most customer databases utilized within the payment card industry contain three key functions:

The database hardware and software

This is the heart of an effective customer management strategy. The servers and database software utilized to establish and run the database are the primary drivers of this component.

There are an almost limitless number of choices when it comes to establishing a database from a hardware and software viewpoint, but a few basic rules apply. First, regardless of the brand and type of server utilized, they must allow for expansion over time as both the number of accounts warehoused and the number of individual data elements stored per account will inevitably increase.

Second, the brand of database software utilized, or the structure of the database software developed internally by the card issuer should they decide to go that route, should be relational in terms of its structure. This means that each individual database element is its own little database and can be cross-tabulated with any other element within the entire database structure. This is necessary in order to provide analysts with the greatest degree of flexibility in conducting their analyses. The standards within the industry in terms of purchased database software packages are Oracle and IBM DB4, but there are many other alternatives as well. Most issuers license a core database software platform from an established brand name supplier, then enhance and modify it according to their particular approach to data management.

Regardless of the hardware and software configuration, there are still a couple of critical elements required for the successful development and maintenance of any database. The first is the establishment of a data dictionary. In any database, the data dictionary is the keeper of the definition and location of each element contained within the database. This is a task whose value cannot be overstated.

The data dictionary defines each individual data element warehoused within the database. Each element may have one, and only one, definition which all parties who will be accessing the database must agree upon in advance of the structuring of the database. While this sounds completely logical and necessary, which indeed it is, it can be horribly difficult to achieve. The reason is that there are so many ways to define some common customer card activities. For example, here is a partial listing of how card issuers define the phrase 'active account':

- any account with a balance;
- any account statemented this month;
- any account with a debit transaction this month;
- any account with a debit transaction this quarter;
- any account which made a payment this month.

There are many more to choose from, but the point is made that there can be only one when it comes to a database and its corresponding data dictionary. That is not to say that a given issuer may not wish to have multiple data elements surrounding the same activity such as customer account usage. It simply means each specific usage pattern must be assigned a separate and distinct definition within the database. Thus, continuing our example, it may be prudent to create several data elements within the database regarding customer account activity as follows:

- active account – account with a balance at statement date;
- debit active account – account with one or more debit transactions at statement date;
- payment active account – account where payment was received by due date.

All of these customer activities are important and have the potential to yield useful and usable information. By creating a data element for each activity, the issuer maintains the integrity of the data dictionary while allowing for a number of unique customer usage patterns to be tracked and analyzed.

The second key element is the integrity of the process for the updating and maintenance of the data elements contained within the database. So called 'data cleansing' is a critical function if quality analyses are to be developed from the data warehouse. Once the data dictionary is established, it then becomes necessary to update the data elements each month and store them in a time series format so that future analysis can look back at how each data element performed over time. Most issuers utilize a rolling thirteen to eighteen months of data for analysis, meaning they will store the same data element within the database thirteen to eighteen times in the active portion of the data warehouse so that analysts can write a query which can retrieve and display the trends in each data element over the period of time for which it is stored.

Filling up to eighteen months of the same data element within a database is not particularly difficult, but ensuring that the data being stored each month is defined consistently and sourced from the same place can be a challenge. Most card databases gather data elements from a number of different sources and systems within as well as external from the issuer. This means that there are multiple opportunities for data to be corrupted or redefined without the issuer's knowledge unless they have a disciplined and well-defined database updating process which compares sources and definitions for each data element each month to ensure consistency.

The database update process usually falls within the information technology (IT) group of the card issuer (as opposed to the management information systems, or MIS group, which tracks and analyzes the stored data) and adheres to a strict verification process before any data element is added to the database. Source and data element definition are verified and compared to previous sources and definitions contained within the database for that particular data element. Once verified that they are consistent, the new data will be added to the database in the time series chain for that particular data element.

Desktop access tools for analysts

Of course having great data which is well defined and well organized is of no value in and of itself. Value is created by turning data into insightful and useful information. This is the job of the analytic staff. In order to do this job effectively, analysts require access to the database and its contents on an ad hoc basis, thus enabling them to create tables and analyses which match various components of the database in ways which yield insights into what the data is telling them. To accomplish this, analysts must be able to query the database from their intelligent workstations and create subsets of the data from which they can test their various hypotheses. This requires software which enables remote access while preserving the integrity of the database.

There are a variety of remote access software packages available in the marketplace today and a number of card issuers license these packages to accomplish this required remote access task. Other issuers prefer to develop their own database access tools in order to feel more secure in the knowledge that their database is protected from outside access, viruses, and the like.

Analytical software

The third critical element for the customer database is the analytical software tools provided for the analysts to utilize in their probing of the data. There is no shortage of software available in the marketplace for this task and many bankcard issuers purchase several packages as well as develop some custom modeling software on their own to aid in the transformation process of data into information.

Within the card industry, SPSS is still the standard analysis tool utilized by issuers globally. While older and more difficult to work with than some of the newer software tools, many bankcard issuers still prefer SPSS as it remains the standard analytical software utilized by major universities for students majoring in such disciplines as engineering, economics, statistics, and software development. As these types of educational backgrounds lend themselves to good analysis, bankcard issuers tend to hire a number of analysts who majored in these disciplines. Providing them with tools with which they are familiar simply shortens the learning curve required to make analysts more productive in a more timely fashion.

ANALYSTS

Once the database is established and all of the necessary software support tools are in place, bankcard issuers must then create and staff a unit of analysts whose job is to utilize the database to turn the myriad sources of data inherent within the card issuing business into meaningful and usable information. The primary goal of this unit is to determine the cause of cardholder behaviors and the effect of specific actions taken by the issuer related to the card product in response to those behaviors.

What this means in practical terms is creating a unit whose function is to determine how best to motivate cardholders to use their cards in a manner that is profitable to the issuer. This is a much more complicated task than it might first appear because consumers are loath to change their behavior with respect to anything, let alone card usage, unless they have a change in their needs or wants.

So how does an issuer succeed in identifying behaviors in need of change if profitability is to be established? Through insightful analysis conducted by talented analysts. The bankcard business is perhaps the most statistically oriented business within commercial banking given the large amounts of data the cards' use generates. This data can be a rich source of information for the sophisticated issuer, but the insights contained within the data are not easily discerned if the right tools are not employed.

The first tool necessary to turn data into information is a staff of qualified and capable analysts. What are the qualifications of a good analyst? Let's start with educational backgrounds. Disciplines such as statistics, mathematics, economics, engineering, and software development tend to provide an education and thought process conducive to insightful analysis. Why these disciplines? Why not accounting, business, literature, psychology, or a thousand others? At their core, the disciplines which tend to generate good analysts are based in logic, and logical thinking is the key to good analysis. After all, remember the goal of the analytic staff is to determine cause and effect. This requires an absence of preconceived notions and an ability to track a logical progression of events and eliminate correlations from causes. Good analysts are extremely logical thinkers and are very adept at constructing a chain of events which, when viewed as a whole, can be determined to be the cause behind a specific behavior or action on the part of a group of cardholders. Logical thinking also eliminates extraneous activity from analysis as the powerful process of logical thought quickly enables the good analyst to eliminate uncorrelated or unrelated data and actions from the analysis at hand.

Good analysts are also extremely self-motivated and are naturally curious on an intellectual basis. Given good data and efficient access tools, analysts will contemplate a given issue or problem almost non-stop until a cause and list of potential solutions can be determined. This is quite useful in operating a bankcard issuing business because there are always many, many cardholders who are not utilizing their cards in a profitable manner at any point in time. Analysts will evaluate past behaviors, study current profitable behaviors, and postulate several actions which may make the unprofitable ones alter their behavior such that they move closer to ongoing profitability.

There are several factors which combine to provide issuers with the analytic capabilities required to successfully manage a card issuing business on an ongoing basis. First and foremost, senior management of the bank must commit to an information-based approach to the business which relies upon detailed analysis of the data and information available on an ongoing basis. Second, management must hire sufficient numbers of qualified analysts to conduct the analysis required within each functional area of the operation including marketing, credit, collections, risk management, back-office, and finance. The key word here is 'qualified'. Banks must gain a comfort level with empowering relatively young and inexperienced individuals, but well educated in the right disciplines, to make decisions regarding all key aspects of the card issuing business, from pricing to credit decisioning to collections strategies. This means management must believe in data and analytics as much as it believes in experience. Management must also then have the conviction to stand by the recommendations these empowered analysts make and test the concepts they develop to determine their validity. Finally, the entire decisioning process of the bankcard issuing organization must be fact based and driven by data and analysis, not tradition and previous structures and policies. This may be the most difficult aspect of all for banks to adopt and follow. Information management relies upon detailed analysis of all aspects of bankcard issuance and depends upon small discoveries and insights into all aspects of the business which, when viewed as a whole, result in a more profitable operation. It does not seek to discover the next 'big thing' which the bank can then spend millions of dollars upon to promote. The key to successful IM is the empowerment of good analysts to test concepts derived from fact-based analysis on an ongoing basis and to implement the concepts which prove to work in testing.

PROGRAM TRACKING AND DEVELOPMENT

The third component of a successful IM strategy is the development and implementation of an ongoing program testing and tracking infrastructure. This effectively entails the integration of the database and analysis group into a day-to-day testing and decisioning process within the organization which is designed to address four key elements:

- an information-centric approach to managing the business;
- an iterative process drawing upon a disciplined approach to testing, analyzing, and continuous learning;
- migration to mass customization based upon successful test results (*right offer* to the *right customer* at the *right time*);
- maximization of net present value (NPV) at the individual account level.

The key is the continuous learning which the program testing and tracking infrastructure creates. The basic process is displayed in Figure 6.1.

Collect market intelligence, past campaign success, and failures to refine test strategies and develop new strategies.

Use behavioral, demographic and profitability information to develop test strategies.

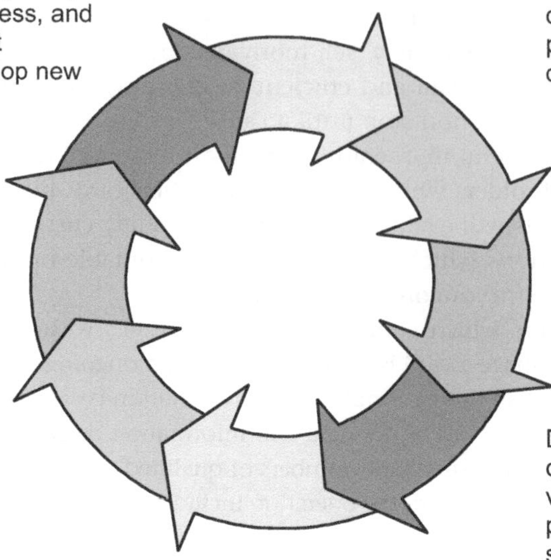

Assess results on a continuous basis. Evaluate success against expected outcomes.

Design valid champion challenger tests for various consumer, product, and channel segments.

Figure 6.1 Information management continuous learning process

But how to begin an iterative process of continuous learning? It starts with the gathering and organization of the data from all areas of the card issuing operation. Each operating area must be reviewed and key elements of account performance from each are then deposited into the database on a regular basis. Only then can the analysts access the data required to develop insights into each area as depicted in Figure 6.2.

By using all of the available data in a rigorous and disciplined manner, issuers can dramatically increase the likelihood of making successful changes in product, pricing, risk management, and operational decisions. This is accomplished by precisely defining the issue to be analyzed, combing through the appropriate data and information streams, then developing a series of hypotheses to be tested and a set of goals or expectations to be achieved.

Consider the example in Table 6.1. There are several segments of the bankcard portfolio being evaluated from a risk and profitability perspective. Each segment, as defined by the current credit score of the account, has current as well as desired profitability measurements displayed. In particular, the segment of accounts with credit scores below 650 is highly unprofitable. A bankcard issuer with this particular set of performance metrics may wish to optimize the dynamic between increased revenues and account attrition through a series of repricing tests with an overall goal of reducing the current negative return on assets of the accounts below a credit score of 650 by 2 per cent overall (thus the Target ROA of –8.1 per cent in the table versus the current –10.1 per cent). The process an IM-based issuer might pursue would look as follows:

The program is tested and implemented over several phases:

- Phase I:
  - Test rate increase on random subset of eligible population.
  - Hold out controls, and include price swap tests.

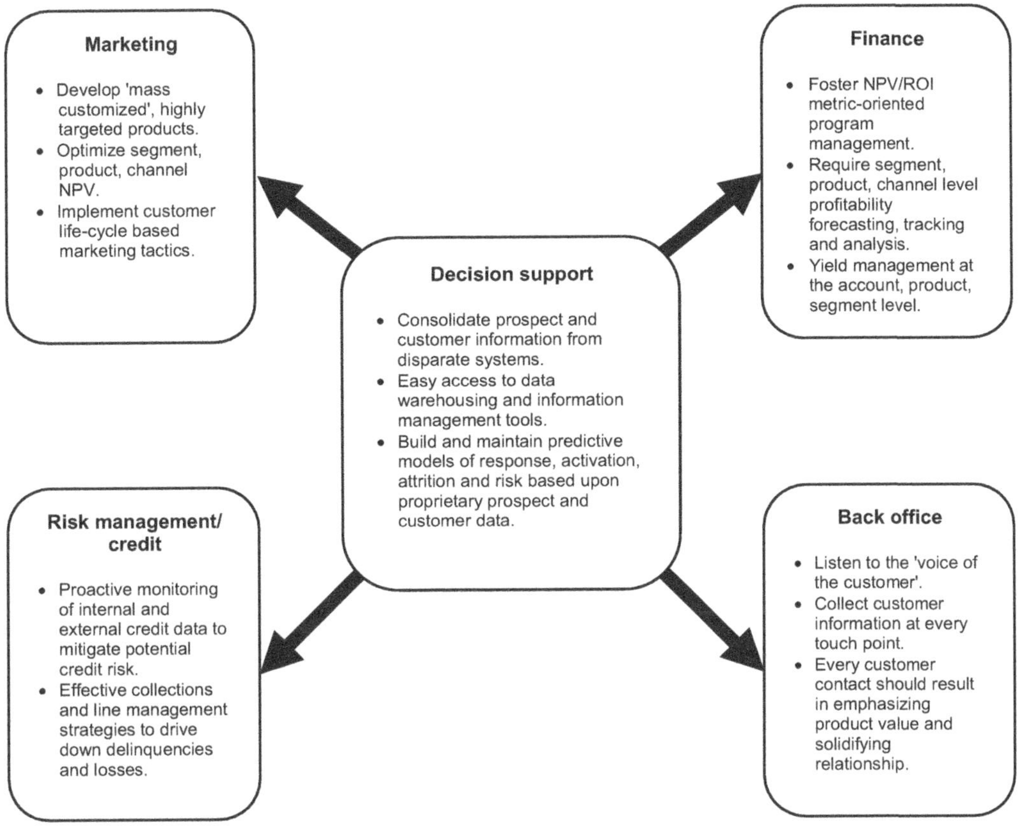

Figure 6.2 The IM decision process

Table 6.1 Yield management example

Current score	*< 650*	*650–679*	*680–719*	*720 +*	*TOTAL*
% of portfolio	15.2%	22.0%	30.7%	32.1%	100.0%
Interest margin	10.0%	8.1%	7.0%	5.3%	7.2%
Fee income	5.8%	5.0%	3.6%	2.9%	4.0%
Credit losses	(21.8%)	(9.6%)	(4.2%)	(1.6%)	(7.2%)
RAS[1]	**(6.1%)**	**3.4%**	**6.4%**	**6.6%**	**3.9%**
Operating expenses	4.0%	3.0%	2.6%	2.5%	2.9%
ROA[2]	**(10.1%)**	**0.5%**	**3.8%**	**4.1%**	**1.1%**
Target ROA	**(8.1%)**	**1.7%**	**4.3%**	**4.1%**	**1.8%**
Tactic	**• Reprice**	**• Reprice** **• Usage**	**• Usage** **• Retain**	**• Usage** **• Retain**	

Note: [1] Risk adjusted spread
[2] Return on assets

- Phase II:
  - Analyze results from Phase I.
  - Conduct segmentation analysis to isolate subsegments where program objective is achieved.
- Include new price tests to measure price sensitivities, and collect data for building predictive balance attrition models for subsequent phases of implementation of the program.

The specifics of the subsets of accounts, tests, and swap sets might look as shown in Table 6.2.

Now the issuer implements the tests and mails the repricing notifications to the affected cardholders. Responses are tracked and individual customer behavioral changes are monitored over time to determine the impact of the repricing upon account usage and cardholder attrition. Results are captured for future analysis each month. The results at the end of month three might look as Table 6.3.

The Phase I results indicate that, in general, the tests achieved the desired results as the increase in revenue from the balances repriced more than offset the revenues lost as a result of balance attrition due to account closures. The net result was a lower loss per account than prior to the test program's implementation. Armed with the results from Phase I, the issuer might now add additional levels of data and analysis to structure a Phase II effort. These additional data elements might include behavior scores and additional credit bureau data such as the number of other bankcards the customer owns to further segment the account population which can then be tested to determine if further gains in profitability might be achievable.

By following the continuous learning process inherent in an IM strategy to manage the bankcard issuing business, the bank depicted in this example would embark upon further

Table 6.2 Repricing test plan

Selection criteria	• RISK: – Current bureau score < 650 • LEGAL: – Score decline from acquisition score > 15 points – More than 3 months off introductory interest rate • EXCLUSIONS: – In-market accounts – Accounts already repriced due to delinquency
Program Specifics	• Test: accounts – 17 892, balances – \$33.1M • Control: accounts – 3157, balances – \$5.8M • Rates tested: 19.9%, 21.9% (with price swap tests) • Avg. increase in interest rate ~ 3.2%
Operations issues	• Rate change notification via solo direct mail in adverse action format

Table 6.3 Phase I repricing test results after three months

	Control	*Test*	*Variance*
Avg. balances 2 ($M)	$24.4	$22.9	($1.5)
Vol. balance attrition (annualized)	6.8%	18.0%	11.2%
Interest margin	9.6%	12.8%	3.2%
Fee income	5.9%	5.5%	(0.4%)
Credit losses	(19.7%)	(20.9%)	(1.2%)
RAS	(4.2%)	(2.6%)	1.6%
Operating expenses	4.0%	4.0%	0.0%
ROA	(8.2%)	(6.6%)	1.6%
Pre-tax net income ($M)	($2.0)	($1.5)	($0.5)
Pre-tax net income / beg. account	($112)	($85)	$27

Notes Program results for 3 months after rate change are presented on annualized basis. Program performance was tracked for a year to validate projections. Minor differences observed did not change inference.
Control beginning balances have been normalized to test beginning balances for comparative purposes.

and further subsegmenting of the population tested in Phase I so that it developed a series of ongoing repricing initiatives targeted at specific types of cardholder behavior. The bank would do this because, based upon its rigorous testing and tracking of repricing initiatives, it would have a high degree of confidence in the results it is likely to achieve via the repricing programs.

Each test and the corresponding results are retained in the database so that future analysis can take into account the results of programs already tried and their impact upon the customers targeted for the offer. Thus, the database becomes the repository for not only customer data, but also for individual program and testing results. This ensures that future analysis will be able to build upon past results, thus furthering the continual learning process.

So, as demonstrated in these past few pages, having a robust database, strong analytic talent, and a disciplined program testing and tracking infrastructure are key elements in managing customers on an ongoing basis. These tools form the core of all product modification, repricing, and risk management programs offered to cardholders. But they are only half of the customer management equation. The other half is the more traditional function of customer service, but it is anything but traditional when applied to the bankcard issuing business.

Customer service

It is a testament to the acceptance of the bankcard product by consumers on a global basis that the fact that the card will work whenever called upon is simply assumed. Card issuers worldwide and the reliability of the global interchange system operated by the card associations drive this consumer assumption. Stated simply, it is a fact that the bankcard product does function as intended over 99 per cent of the time, making it a reliable part of consumers' payment plans worldwide.

However, what happens the other 1 per cent of the time when things do not go as planned? How do consumers resolve their problems and regain their confidence in the bankcard product after it fails to perform as anticipated? The customer service department fulfils this role because it is their responsibility to resolve bankcard-related problems for clients and reassure clients that the card will always work properly.

Customer service is a critical link in the bankcard product delivery chain. For many consumers, this is the only area within a financial institution with which they interact because they may not visit branch offices regularly. Accordingly, how problems are handled and resolved goes a long way in determining how the cardholder will feel about the issuer of their bankcard. This is important because, in most markets, clients have many choices with respect to obtaining a bankcard.

If a problem arises with one issuer and is not resolved to the cardholder's satisfaction, they can simply close that account and open another with a different issuer – a phenomenon known as attrition, which is a major issue for most bankcard issuers. The cost of replacing cardholders who leave due to unsatisfactorily resolved service issues is significant, consequently making effective and efficient customer service a key part of ongoing customer management.

Customer service entails many different functions, all of which must be handled seamlessly. From receipt of an issue from the cardholder, which may come via telephone, mail, or the Internet to the research and resolution of the problem, customer service requires the timely orchestration of a number of diverse processes. And it cannot operate in a vacuum, as customer service issues may have a direct impact upon other aspects of the bankcard account, from credit to risk to collections. Therefore it is imperative that the customer service function be integrated into the overall bankcard operational support process.

How these different processes are integrated ultimately determines the effectiveness of the customer service experienced by the cardholder.

ORGANIZATIONAL STRUCTURE

Similar to back-office functions, most customer service organizations are structured around the processes that must be accomplished. In general, these functions can be grouped as follows:

- *Cardholder inquiry* – a function that involves receiving the notice from the cardholder that there is an issue requiring attention. The inquiry can be received via telephone, mail, branch office, or the Internet.
- *Research* – an area that conducts all of the necessary investigation required to determine if the client inquiry is correct and, if so, identifies the steps required to resolve the issue.
- *Non-monetary adjustments* – the area that makes all of the required system adjustments to a cardholder's account resulting from an inquiry which do not involve money such as an address change or new card request.
- *Monetary adjustments* – a function that makes all of the necessary system adjustments involving money such as a fee waiver, interest charge adjustment, or purchase amount adjustment.
- *Cardholder retention* – a dedicated group of specially trained customer service representatives within the telephone customer inquiry unit who work to retain cardholders who have indicated they wish to close their account via the use of price and non-price incentives.

Depending upon the customer service strategy employed by a given card issuer, these general functions may be grouped differently. Overall, however, the customer service organization looks something like the structure in Figure 6.3.

This structure organizes the required customer service functions into logical groups that make the management of them simpler and easier to accomplish. In addition, the presence of a separate quality control group ensures the consistent delivery of quality customer service. Separating the inquiry function from the research and adjustment functions enables each area to develop the specific skills required to perform their task quickly and efficiently. From a service delivery standpoint, however, this may not necessarily be the best approach and that determination is ultimately driven by the strategy adopted by the financial institution for its customer service delivery.

STRATEGY

How a financial institution defines its customer service strategy is critical to organizing and delivering service acceptable to financial institution management and cardholders alike. Contrary to popular belief, it is not necessarily a requirement that financial institutions provide the absolute highest level of customer service to every cardholder in order to be successful. In fact, adopting such a strategy would lead to a cost base that would dwarf the potential profits from the business.

The key to providing effective customer service is to adopt a strategy that will meet the needs of the cardholders being served. Different segments of cardholders use bankcards to meet different needs and this implies that each segment of customers has different expectations with regard to customer service.

Different segments of cardholders have differing needs when it comes to resolving issues

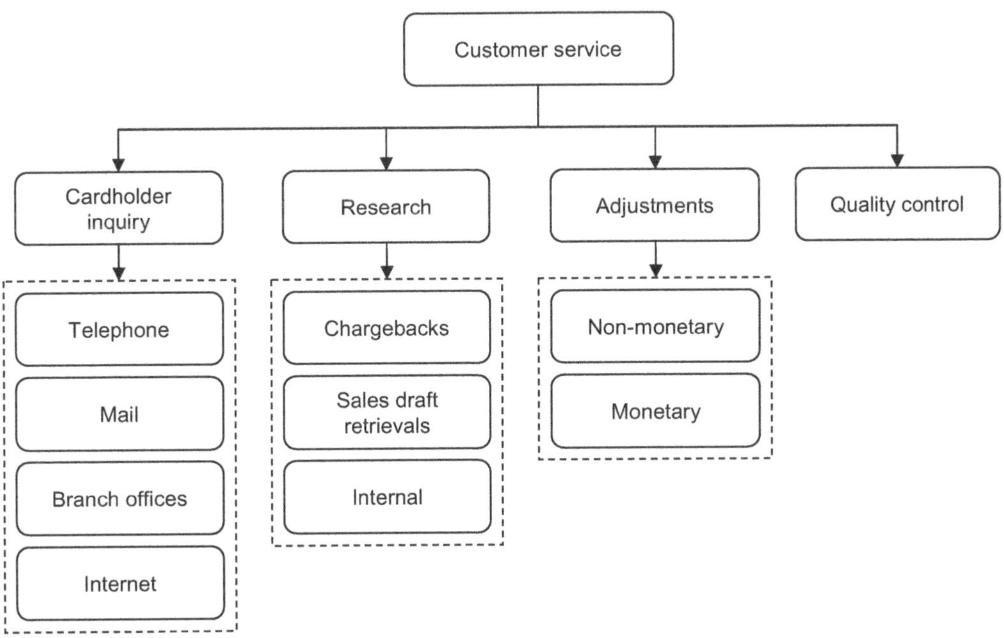

Figure 6.3 Customer service organizational structure

that arise while utilizing their card. In addition, as with other operational aspects of the bankcard issuing business, card issuers are faced with the 'efficiency versus effectiveness' dilemma.

Customer service strategy starts with an overall objective which the financial institution is trying to achieve such as mandating all customer service issues be resolved with only one call or letter from the cardholder. It may be the issuer desires cardholders to service themselves as much as possible via automated telephone menus and online capabilities. It may even be the financial institution wishes to solve all client issues within twenty-four hours' notice of the problem. Each of these examples requires very different structures and technology to achieve, therefore reinforcing the point that quality customer service begins with an overriding goal or objective set by the financial institution.

Not to oversimplify what can be a complex and critical issue within the bankcard issuing business, but the vast majority of customer service strategies fall into two primary categories:

Cost minimization

Bankcard issuers utilizing this strategy focus upon the expenses associated with the delivery of customer service and seek to reduce them as much as possible while still delivering the minimum level of customer service required to remain competitive. Customer service is indeed one of the costliest components within the bankcard issuing process. The reason is simple. Customer service is very people intensive, and people are quite costly.

To reduce costs, issuers following a cost reduction customer service strategy utilize technology wherever possible to reduce expenses and displace people with less costly computers. Expanding the bank's online servicing capabilities so that customers can service themselves for many routine inquiries such as payment date, credit availability, initiating a dispute regarding a transaction and similar inquires is also a key component in a cost reduction strategy.

An example is how a cost minimization customer service strategy handles the activation of a new cardholder account. Most issuers, as a fraud prevention technique, send plastic to new cardholders which are inactive until the customer calls a special telephone number to activate the account. This process ensures that the cards reach the individual for whom they are intended. In a cost minimization strategy, the process of handling the account activation when the customer calls the special telephone number will be entirely automated and processed by a special computer called a voice response unit (VRU). Cardholders will call, respond to the prompts relayed by the VRU by using the touch pad on their touchtone telephones or, in some cases, by speaking to a VRU with voice recognition software and have their account activated without ever speaking to a live human being. This reduces the expense associated with the process of activating new accounts.

The cost minimization strategy relies upon providing service which is adequate, but not outstanding. The goal is to be as efficient as possible by automating as many routine customer service functions as possible.

Revenue generation

A revenue generation customer service strategy, on the other hand, is focused upon cross-sales and service quality and less on cost. Instead of minimizing costs, this strategy relies upon well-trained staff and a different use of technology to resolve cardholder issues while simultaneously attempting to cross-sell them additional products and services at every opportunity to increase the amount of revenue each customer generates for the bank.

Utilizing the new account call to activate process again, a revenue generation customer service strategy views this rather mundane process as a sales opportunity and structures the activation process accordingly. If a VRU is utilized, the customer may be asked to wait on the line while their account information is retrieved and verified. During this 'retrieval' process, a pre-recorded message offering additional products and services will be played and customers can follow the prompts offered to take advantage of any offers made. Some issuers focused upon revenue generation as a customer service strategy go so far as to have live operators answer the activation calls and attempt to cross-sell additional services on a more personal basis. This is obviously a more costly customer service strategy, but the goal is to increase revenues more than the expenses associated with the strategy. Issuers pursuing a revenue generation strategy believe each customer contact is a cross-sales opportunity and structure their processes accordingly.

Once the customer service strategy is established, the rest of the pieces fall into place in order to achieve the goal. Organizational structures are put in place based upon the goal, such as more staff in the telephone inquiry group if the goal is to resolve all problems in only one call. Technology is utilized in support of the goal, such as automated call distributors and voice response units in telephone inquiry areas to increase the speed of the call process. The degree to which front line customer service representatives (CSRs) are empowered to make decisions is also determined by the goal of the service organization. In short, almost every aspect of how customer service is to be delivered is driven by the goals the organization sets for itself in this area.

Once the goal is established and the organization is deployed to achieve that goal, the last piece of the quality customer service puzzle requiring attention is the quality control process. Establishing the goal and organizing around it is not enough. Issuers must also create a monitoring and measuring function to ensure that the goals set are achieved. It is true what they say, 'what gets measured gets done.'

However, just what are the functions that need to be performed in the customer service area for the organization's goal to be achieved?

CUSTOMER SERVICE FUNCTIONS

Effective customer service is both an art and a science. It requires the effective use of all resources, both technical and human, to achieve success. More than any other aspect of the bankcard issuing business, people determine the ultimate effectiveness of the customer service function because it is the one area of the issuing process where the financial institution interacts directly with the cardholder. There is no way to avoid client interaction in the customer service area, consequently the importance of people in delivering quality service.

All of the functions performed within the customer service unit revolve around three basic objectives as follows:

- *Timeliness.* Regardless of the nature of the issue being addressed, all clients want their problems resolved as quickly as possible, preferably before they hang up the telephone. Creating an environment within customer service where this can be accomplished is crucial.
- *Interaction.* As noted earlier, customer service is the one area where direct interaction with cardholders is unavoidable. As a result, it is imperative that the interaction be made as pleasant and efficient as possible for the client using technology and properly trained

CSRs. Solving a cardholder's problem is not enough. It must be done in such a way that the client is pleased with the experience as well as the result.
- *Closure*. Finally, good customer service requires that resolved issues be documented and communicated appropriately, both internally and with the cardholder. This includes all required financial adjustments to cardholder accounts (such as reversed late fees or interest adjustments) and follow-up items (such as production and mailing of a new plastic or implementation of an agreed-upon credit line increase).

With these objectives in mind, we will now examine the major functions performed within the customer service area.

Client inquiry – telephone

The most common form of interaction with cardholders in customer service is via the telephone. For most consumers, picking up the telephone and calling to report an issue is the simplest way for them to make their card issuer aware of a problem and to get it resolved.

Cardholders call customer service for a number of reasons including:

- check current balance and credit availability;
- check to see if last payment was posted;
- check to see the date and amount of the next payment due;
- dispute a transaction the cardholder does not recognize on their statement;
- order a new plastic;
- change name or address;
- question a declined authorization;
- request a copy of a previous statement.

Regardless of the reason for the call, cardholders all have one thing in common when calling: they want their issue resolved fast and with no further action on their part. To respond to this cardholder goal, issuers must utilize a combination of staff training and application of appropriate technology.

Staff training involves educating the telephone CSRs in two very diverse areas including:

PRODUCT AND TECHNICAL KNOWLEDGE

CSRs must have a good working knowledge of all of the financial institution's card products and the features offered with each different one. In addition, they must also be able to access and navigate the various computer systems utilized within the bankcard issuing group such as the core accounting system, the application processing system, and the collections system in order to answer client inquiries.

Since the financial institution's product offerings and systems functionality change periodically, staff training in customer service is not a one-time event, but rather one that requires continuous refresher training over time.

Most bankcard issuers have a basic customer service training course for new CSRs that can run from one to three weeks. After completion, the new trainees are placed on the phones under the supervision of a more experienced CSR for a probationary period from two to four weeks to ensure that the new trainee has absorbed all of the training and can effectively handle client inquiries.

TELEPHONE AND CLIENT MANAGEMENT SKILLS

Beyond technical training, however, CSRs also require some education in basic telephone communications and client management techniques. It is an unfortunate fact of life in the bankcard industry that clients do not call the financial institution to express their gratitude for their bankcard and its 99 per cent + efficiency. Rather, clients call when things are not working as anticipated, and they are usually not happy at the time of the call.

Handling an upset client requires calm and patience as well as the ability to extract the information necessary to identify and resolve the problem. This training teaches these types of communications skills that are critical to a CSR's ability to be successful in their position.

Once trained, CSRs must then put their skills to work in resolving cardholder inquiries as quickly and efficiently as possible, which can be accomplished in several ways. The first is via the use of some basic technology whereby calls can be diverted and issues resolved without ever reaching a CSR. This requires two basic technologies such as:

- *Automated Call Distributor (ACD).* An ACD is a computer which routes incoming customer service telephone calls to the next available CSR or to a VRU depending upon the strategy of the card issuer. It is an invaluable tool in terms of its ability to maximize the distribution of incoming calls to CSRs available to handle them, therefore increasing the efficiency of the overall customer service unit.
- *Voice Response Unit (VRU).* VRUs, sometimes called automated, or audio response units (ARU) or interactive voice response (IVR), utilize touch tones from the telephone and computerized human voice technology to set up pre-established menus of common client inquiries which can then be resolved in an automated fashion by the clients themselves.

  VRUs have the ability to be available 24 hours a day, seven days a week and enable cardholders to obtain basic information about their bankcard account via a touch-tone telephone. Common inquiries such as current balance, credit availability, or date and amount of next payment are made available on a pre-established menu of options, such as press 1 for balances, press 2 for date and amount of next payment due, and so on. Cardholders select the option they desire, enter some account and security information to identify themselves, then receive the information via a computerized voice.

  VRUs improve the efficiency of the overall service unit greatly by enabling fewer staff members to handle more non-routine calls per hour. Issuers pursuing a cost minimization strategy within their customer service operation will drive the percentage of incoming customer inquiries handled by the VRU to 75 per cent or more versus the industry norm of 40 per cent to 50 per cent.

It is the goal of the telephone CSR to resolve all client inquiries as quickly as possible while reassuring the client that errors in the future are unlikely in order to retain the client relationship. To make this possible, most customer service environments are structured so the CSR is empowered to handle almost all non-monetary entries to the account system (such as making name and address changes or ordering a new plastic) and some monetary entries based upon pre-established policies (such as annual fee waiver based upon sales volume threshold).

Any client inquiry requiring additional investigation or research is documented and forwarded on to the research area for resolution, which can be done in a paper-based mode or an automated work case mode utilizing software designed to make tracking and resolving research cases simple.

Client inquiry – correspondence

The correspondence inquiry area within customer service also desires to resolve client inquiries as quickly and efficiently as possible. The only difference between this area and the telephone unit is that this area receives problems that need to be resolved via letter or documented branch visit as opposed to a telephone call.

In the correspondence unit, letter- and branch-generated issues are logged by date and nature of inquiry and then forwarded to the appropriate area for action and resolution. Most client letters involve issues that are more complicated than those received in the telephone inquiry area and generally require research and investigation to resolve.

Once investigated and resolved, the correspondence unit must communicate the outcome of the inquiry back to the cardholder by telephone call or letter.

Client inquiry – Internet

A relatively new aspect to customer service is the use of the Internet to enable cardholders to essentially service themselves. Many bankcard issuers make available large amounts of data to their cardholders via their website. Data can include several months' worth of previous bankcard statements, recent payment history, current and pending transactions and authorizations, and a number of other relevant informational items.

By making this information available to cardholders in a secure environment, clients can answer many routine questions themselves simply by accessing the financial institution's website, therefore offloading those calls and letters from the other client inquiry areas.

Research

The research area is the part of customer service that investigates cardholder inquiries that are not simple or routine in nature in order to resolve them to all parties' satisfaction. This area is usually separated from the client inquiry areas to assure that its time-intensive nature is not a direct impact upon the client contact portion of cardholder inquiries.

Client inquiry areas obtain the information necessary to investigate a cardholder dispute such as an unrecognized transaction or merchant dispute and similar problems. They inform the cardholder that the issue needs to be researched and that the financial institution will contact them upon completion of the necessary investigation. Then, they turn over the data gathered to the research area for follow up and resolution.

Research takes all necessary actions to investigate the problem and determine the resolution, and then it establishes the actions to be taken with the appropriate input areas such as monetary and non-monetary adjustments, cardholder inquiry, or credit. Then, they follow up to ensure the necessary actions are completed. Much of the investigation work conducted within the research unit involves the retrieval of sales drafts signed by the cardholder at the point of sale or electronically captured by the point-of-sale terminal or tracking down account adjustments initiated internally within the bankcard issuing organization. Great importance is placed upon the issuer's ability to store and retrieve relevant transaction data easily.

The research area is very important in resolving complicated client issues, so its ability to track all of the investigations it has in process to ensure timely resolution is critical to providing quality customer service. Much of this tracking can be accomplished in an automated fashion utilizing workflow software available in the commercial marketplace.

Chargebacks

Many cardholder inquiries result in the need for the issuer to initiate a chargeback to the acquiring financial institution due to a cardholder dispute, the merchant's failure to properly authorize the transaction, a processing error, or any number of other reasons.

Regardless of the reason, the issuer must obtain some important information from the cardholder during the client inquiry process (often this information needs to be in writing from the cardholder, including a copy of the sales receipt if available), then it must determine if a chargeback is warranted. It is this determination that is the responsibility of the chargeback unit within customer service.

If the chargeback unit decides that a chargeback is warranted, they post a provisional credit to the cardholder's account in the amount of the disputed sale, then forward the documentation provided by the client along with the provisional credit information they initiated to the chargeback processing unit in the back office for follow up and resolution.

Adjustments – non-monetary

Non-monetary adjustments are all of the changes to a cardholder account that can be made that do not involve money, including making name and address changes, ordering of additional cards, asking for payment due date changes, requesting to close an account, and numerous others.

Two schools of thought exist when it comes to handling non-monetary adjustments. One approach is to empower the client inquiry CSRs to make all non-monetary adjustments while the client is on the phone thereby providing the cardholder with quick, responsive customer service and eliminating any exchange of data between areas. This also requires that CSRs be allowed to have longer talk time on the phone with the client in order to process the non-monetary adjustment and mandates that the CSRs also utilize a security procedure to identify cardholders in order to guard against potential fraud.

A second approach to non-monetary adjustments is to have a separate unit within customer service just to post non-monetary adjustments received from the client inquiry areas after their validity has been established. This approach has the advantage of shortening the client inquiry phone call on the front end, but requires an exchange of data and information between client inquiry and the adjustments area, therefore exposing the process to additional potential for human error.

Regardless of which approach is utilized, the key in effective non-monetary adjustment management is to have a proper audit trail in place to ensure that only adjustments that are appropriate are undertaken.

Adjustments – monetary

Monetary adjustments are a critical area for any customer service operation as they are the ones that generate the most client attention. Waiving a fee or rebating a late fee or finance charge involve money, so they are sensitive issues from a client point of view and must be treated accordingly.

Most card issuers centralize the monetary adjustment area within the customer service group in order to properly control and monitor its activity. Since money is involved, this area has a direct effect upon the profitability of the portfolio in the shortest amount of time.

Client inquiry areas submit a recommended monetary adjustment to the monetary adjustment area. The recommendation is then verified and the appropriate entries made in the system to account for the adjustment and to credit the cardholder's account for the amount agreed upon. Strict controls and oversight procedures are required in this area to ensure that all adjustments are accounted for properly.

Quality control

As important as any operational function resident within the customer service unit is the quality control area. This group of individuals is tasked with measuring the effectiveness of the various processes within customer service to ensure that the strategy management has put in place is being followed effectively.

This measuring process involves a combination of quantitative and qualitative measures.

QUANTITATIVE

- Client inquiry
  - *Average speed of answer* – the time it takes a CSR to answer a ringing telephone. Usually issuers require a time of less than 20 seconds.
  - *Abandon rate* – the percentage of incoming telephone calls which go unanswered due to volume or staffing considerations. Usually issuers require 3 per cent or less.
  - *Average talk time* – the amount of time a CSR spends on the telephone with a client. Usually the goal is 3 minutes or less.
  - *Pending correspondence* – the number of client correspondence pieces still in the process of being resolved. Usually the goal is 75 per cent of all correspondence resolved within 24 hours, 85 per cent within 48 hours, and 95 per cent within 72 hours.
- Research
  - *Cardholder disputes pending* – the number of disputes currently being researched for resolution. Usually the goal is to resolve 75 per cent of all disputes within 14 days of receipt and 95 per cent within 21 days.
  - *Suspense account clearing time* – this measures the amount of time a transaction remains suspended from a cardholder's account while it is researched for resolution. The standards here usually correspond to the standards for cardholder disputes pending.
- Adjustments

  Both non-monetary and monetary adjustments should be monitored to ensure that they are entered in a timely fashion once the adjustment has been decided upon. The goal is normally 100 per cent within 24 hours.

QUALITATIVE

There are a number of non-quantifiable, but no less important, quality measurements employed in managing the customer service area including:

- Telephone proficiency

  This involves the monitoring of actual telephone client inquiry calls so that the accuracy of the information given by the CSR can be gauged as well as the CSR's tone and friendliness during the conversation. Both good and poor performance requires comment to the CSR from the monitoring employee in order to ensure continuous improvement.

- Sampling
  Taking a random sample of various processes within the customer service unit helps to ensure proper and accurate fulfillment of commitments made to cardholders. This would include checking monthly billing statements, account adjustments, plastic produces, and client correspondence initiated by the issuer.

Quality Control is critical in the delivery of quality customer service. Continuous monitoring of all functions, both quantitatively and qualitatively, is the only way to ensure that cardholders are receiving the best service the financial institution is capable of providing.

Cardholder retention

Another function is often performed within the customer service area, but it is not necessarily broken out into a separate unit, and that is cardholder retention. As competition increases and customers have more choices with respect to where they may obtain a bankcard, the ability to retain current cardholders becomes more difficult for issuers. As a result, many have put proactive cardholder retention strategies in place within their customer service areas.

Two basic schools of thought exist when it comes to organizing a cardholder retention unit within the customer service area. The first is to establish a separately staffed, specially trained unit that is empowered to try to retain cardholders who have indicated their intention to close their account with the financial institution. Incoming calls and letters indicating this intent to close are transferred to this special unit and the staff members are empowered to make concessions and counter offers to these cardholders to entice them to keep their account with the financial institution. Having a separate unit enables the financial institution to provide specific training and incentive compensation to staff members and provides for ease of tracking results. The separate unit approach has the disadvantage of requiring phone calls to be transferred to it that can result in an unhappy cardholder due to the inconvenience. It also makes retention the job of a few, as opposed to the job of all.

The second approach to cardholder retention within customer service is for all CSRs to be trained and empowered to save accounts that indicate their intention to close. This approach offers the advantage of not inconveniencing cardholders by requiring a call transfer and makes retention the responsibility of all people who have client interaction. It has the disadvantage of being harder to control and track than a separate unit. It also makes deploying incentive compensation schemes more difficult.

No right or wrong approach exists to cardholder retention in terms of structure. What is important is to have empowered CSRs who can offer meaningful countermeasures to cardholders who desire to close their account. Even then, the best retention units are lucky to achieve a success rate of 40 per cent of accounts retained: by the time a cardholder calls to close an account, they usually have already initiated the attainment of a new one with a competitor. The best approach to cardholder retention is aggressive existing account marketing designed to ensure that cardholders do not become disenchanted with their bankcard product.

SUMMARY

Because customer service may be the only organizational area with which bankcard clients interact, customer service *is* the financial institution to many customers. Accordingly, it is imperative that this area functions efficiently and effectively to ensure that cardholders continue to use their bankcard product in the future.

Organizing a customer service operation can be done in a number of different ways and will be driven by the bank's chosen customer service strategy, but the three key functions of timeliness, cardholder interaction, and closure must be addressed regardless of strategy or structure. Cardholders want issues they raise to be resolved quickly and without further effort on their part, so this must be the goal of the customer service unit, regardless of organizational structure.

Achieving timely problem resolution requires a combination of properly trained human resources and technology applied appropriately. Automating common, less complicated cardholder inquiries can free up the staff to deal with the more complicated items such as cardholder disputes and monetary adjustments.

Continuous monitoring of performance, both in terms of quantitative and qualitative measurements, is a requirement to ensure quality customer service.

A key responsibility of the customer service area is cardholder retention, which can be achieved in a number of ways, but all of which revolve around empowering representatives to make meaningful counteroffers to cardholders who have indicated their intent to close their account.

Ultimately, customer service is not likely to be the differentiator in why a customer chooses to take a new bankcard account with a particular issuer, but it can certainly be the reason a cardholder leaves a particular issuer if it is not done properly.

The combination of database management, with its corresponding emphasis on analysis and program testing, and customer service is what dictates customer management. Both must be wholly integrated within the bank card issuing organization if long-term customer relationships are to be developed and maintained.

CHAPTER 7

Operations Management

Business strategy means having a declared purpose and a plan to realize that purpose. It requires envisioning tomorrow's marketplace and the desired competitive positioning of the business within that marketplace. Card managers must ask the questions – what will the market for card issuing and consumer lending look like three years from now and what role do we want to play in that market? Do we want to be price leaders? What unique competitive advantage should we be striving to develop that will lead us there? The answers to these questions indicate the strategic choices that a business must make in order to compete.

At a basic level, the strategic plan must answer four key questions:

- What is the product or service on offer?
- Who will buy it?
- Why will they buy it?
- What is the optimum price?

But business strategy, no matter how ingeniously envisioned and how rigorously articulated, can only achieve its ends if the company has the know-how and practical means of implementing it. Business strategy may be clever thinking but it has no significance unless the company has charted for itself a clear and viable operational strategy to put it into effect.

In the minds of managers, operational strategy quite often plays second fiddle to business strategy – its sexier sister. But the truth is that the two are inseparable. Operational strategy provides the necessary answers to the equally important and fundamental questions about business viability that most strategy consultants overlook:

- What processes and resources are required to develop and deliver products and services?
- What are the options for delivering the products and services?
- How will the business retain its customers?
- How can processes be made inexpensive and efficient?

Operations management objectives

The successful management of payment card operations requires the pursuit of the following key managerial objectives:

- delivering business strategy
- cost optimization
- operational efficiency enhancement.

A good operations department will focus on continual savings in costs and enhancements in efficiency. The cost and efficiency of product delivery has a direct and significant impact on card program profitability and customer retention. This is especially true in mature and saturated marketplaces where it is very difficult to increase market share without lowering prices and nearly impossible to raise prices without losing market share. Genuine innovation can break this deadlock. But in the financial services industry, radical innovation is rare. The pressure to increase profitability falls on the cost side of the profitability equation. If revenues cannot be raised, costs must be pared down.

It is important to note that cost optimization does not necessarily mean cost reduction. Cost optimization, it is often said, is about cutting fat. Cost reduction, on the other hand, often results in cutting muscle, impairing the competitive strength of the business. Card issuers that offer simple no-frills cards depend on low-cost operations sometimes at the expense of customer service. Issuers that cater to the more affluent consumer segments incur higher operational costs as customers expect superior quality of service. Calls must be answered quickly and to the satisfaction of the customer. Operational costs, of course, also depend upon other factors that relate to the card issuer's policies and procedures. A more risk-averse issuer may choose to deliver cards to new customers via secure mail or courier service instead of ordinary mail. They may also invest substantially in fraud prevention technology and credit management to prevent losses.

Operational efficiency and cost optimization are intertwined. Generally, inefficient processes cost the company a lot more than may appear on the surface as shown in Figure 7.1.

- Customer spends 10 minutes on website but fails to get resolution.
- Customer decides not to use the website for future inquiries.
- Customer resolves query through call center.
- Total transaction cost to company = $15.25.

Bottlenecks can be identified and removed or quite often, part of a particular process may be reengineered or made redundant. Every process consists of a number of activities and it is only by examining such activities can we improve overall operational efficiency. This methodology is called activity-based management (ABM). Identifying activity costs for benchmarking and optimization is called activity-based costing (ABC). The chapter on profitability provides an activity-based approach to developing the card issuing profit and loss account.

Specific processes can be undertaken in-house or outsourced to specialist companies called third-party providers. These organizations invest substantially and continually in process infrastructure. By contracting out operations, card companies can enjoy greater efficiency and better quality of process delivery. They can also reap additional cost savings through scale economies if the outsourcing provider is able to obtain sufficient transaction volumes from multiple players in the market.

Operational excellence

There are seven operational 'virtues' in efficient card-issuing organizations which managers ignore at their peril. They are particularly relevant when the business is being set up, people

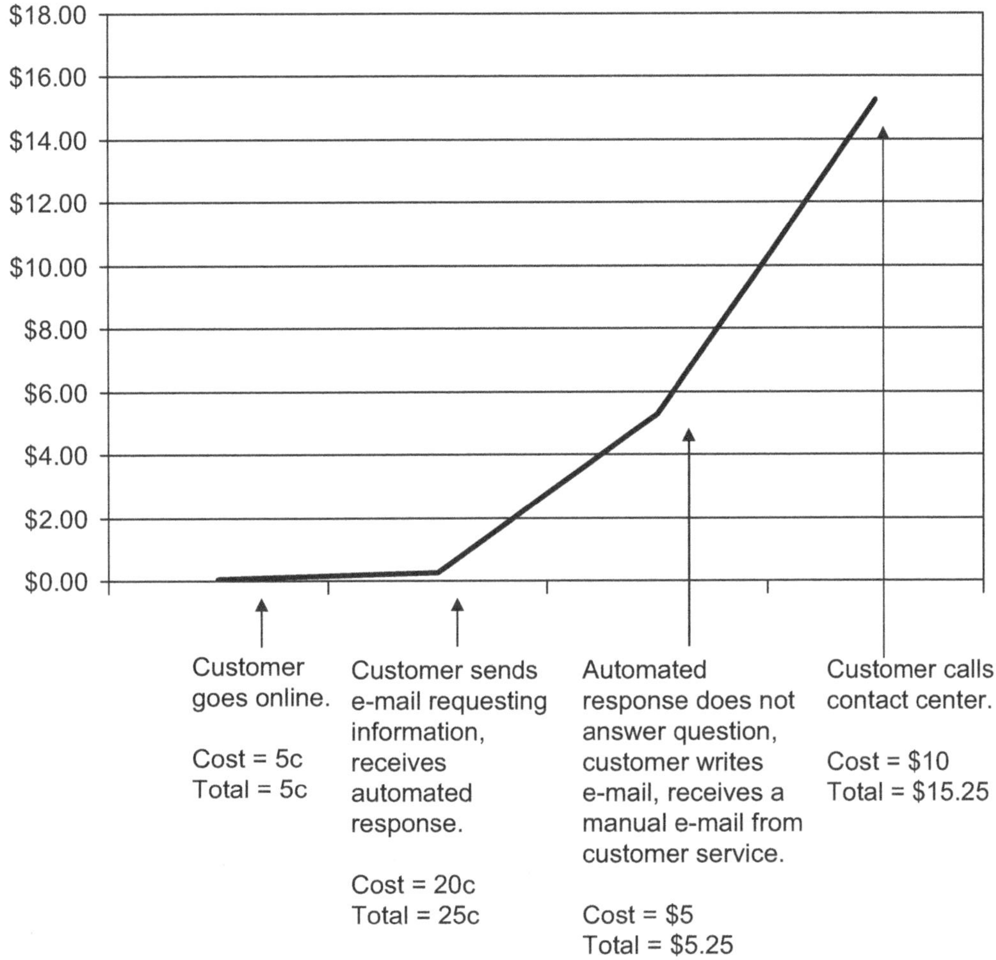

Figure 7.1 Example call costs

are being hired, and systems are being implemented. Banks planning to outsource their operations must look for these qualities in the third-party providers they are proposing to partner with.

SCALABILITY

A common problem of expanding businesses is the lack of production or delivery capacity. As transaction volumes grow, the infrastructure sometimes simply cannot cope with the additional volumes. The problem often lies in core systems or the underlying technological platform. The infrastructure may not be designed to handle high levels of transaction traffic. To avoid this problem, capacity estimates are made at the planning stage and revised periodically to avoid scalability surprises.

Scalability problems also often arise from the lack of appropriately trained staff. Human bottlenecks may be responsible for drops in efficiency. The obvious answer is more people. This usually means additional investments in systems for the new employees to work with.

Adding more call center staff means adding more desktop stations. This may solve the problem. But it can also be sometimes wasteful where alternative solutions can be found without additional hiring. The answer lies in freeing up capacity. To illustrate: a subprime card issuer was getting consistent negative feedback from customers who could not get through to the call center. Identifying this as a scalability issue the issuer was considering increasing call center capacity by 30 per cent – buying more equipment and hiring additional servicing staff. A quick analysis of customer calls revealed that a significant number of calls related to credit limit queries. Cardholders were actually calling up to check their available spending limit before making routine purchases like filling up their cars. By sending available credit limit information by text on a daily basis to customers who needed it (and were willing to pay for it) the issuer was able to resolve a capacity problem with a little bit of software engineering but without adding expensive capacity.

Scalability issues may be of temporary or cyclical nature: sudden transaction volume surges caused by incentive marketing campaigns, holiday shopping, or special events require temporary additional capacity. Instead of increasing in-house capacity, businesses often contract with third-party providers to provide peak volume back up.

Scalability is of paramount importance to third-party providers. Their business case is built on the promise of lower costs resulting from economies of scale.

FLEXIBILITY

The concept of operational flexibility is rather vague. In theory, it means that operational processes and systems should be able to incorporate new products, new attributes (a new feature or a new price point) of existing products, customer group parameters, and so on without much difficulty. Flexibility means quick time to market for new products, features, or services. Many issuers are still encumbered with legacy systems requiring considerable effort even for changing a simple product price point.

This flexibility is essential in today's card-issuing market where issuers have to quickly test and market a number of product variations, especially in markets where risk-based pricing is being used. The core card-issuing system should be capable of assigning specific price points to individual customer accounts in the master file. Usually, in traditional issuer systems a new product set has to be created and set up even for small parameter variations.

As new systems are added to the main systems infrastructure – say, a new application program designed to generate electronic statements over the Internet – the problems of making the old and new talk in the same language are often described as nightmarish by many system integrators. In a flexible operations environment it should be relatively easy to configure the existing systems to accept small changes or write a communication program that interfaces the old with the new. The gradual development and adoption of industry standard 'open' communication protocols is gradually making this easier.

A point of caution when selecting systems: vendors and third-party providers will always present their systems as fully flexible and easy to implement. The best thing to do is to directly obtain testimonials from their clients where the systems are already up and running.

Additionally, card systems and operations should be designed in such a way that incorporating a new product attribute in the main card system should not require many independent stand-alone changes in other peripheral systems. Issuer systems that have developed organically in a hub-and-spoke-like style, where a number of systems have been linked to the card host over a number of years, can take very long to set new product parameters.

After implementation, all systems have to be tested to ensure that all systems – core and peripheral – are in place to support and service the product.

SECURITY

The core appeal of every financial institution rests on trust. If trust is compromised, for whatever reason, the organization will face serious customer confidence and business continuity issues. A secure operational environment means that customer data and software applications that utilize this data must be protected against accidental or unauthorized access, use, modification, or disclosure.

Data security has specific resonance in the payment cards industry. Payment cards constitute sensitive information. Card details in the hands of fraudsters and hackers could result in serious damage and substantial losses to the issuer. The sustained growth in Internet transactions over the last decade or so has made card companies more vulnerable to fraud than ever before. Quite often one comes across stories of hackers operating over the Internet from far away countries breaking into databases that store information relating to millions of payment cards. Supposedly safeguarded by industrial strength firewalls and state-of-the-art encryption algorithms, these databases appear to be vulnerable to professional acts of high-tech crime. Hacking reports are unsettling for cardholders, even though they are protected against losses arising from fraudulent transactions. They are also extremely worrying for issuers who have to cancel the compromised cards and re-issue and mail new cards. When large card databases are compromised, the cost to reissue the cards can run into millions of dollars. But most important of all, such news is damaging to the integrity of the system and severely erodes customer confidence.

Card companies invest in fraud prevention measures to ensure transaction security and deploy advanced security systems to store and manage customer details, make sure that all transactions take place in a secure environment, and invest in systems and models that help them identify fraudulent activity before it happens.

Additionally, physical security is also important. It involves access restrictions to the facilities and regular checks even where advanced security software has been implemented. A security discipline must be in place that should be continually monitored and supervised closely.

INTEGRITY

In addition to providing security against unauthorized access to system applications and data, an operations department must always ensure controls are in place that ensure system integrity.

This means that systems and processes must continue to function even after an unexpected error, fault, or catastrophic disaster. If operations are halted due to such events, operations should recommence from backed-up data and procedures within an acceptable period of time. Unexpected disruptive events may be of a technical nature – such as hard drive crash, data storage loss, failure of circuitry, or software crash – or caused by external events – such as power losses, flooding, or fire. Business continuity is assured through backup systems, emergency power sources, regular data backups, and long-term off-site storage.

Third-party providers offering outsourcing services should be well prepared for any disruptive events that require contingency and immediate disaster recovery.

CONTROL

A key element in managing operational risk is the design and deployment of operational controls – checks and procedures – that identify errors and irregularities. These also serve as early-warning systems to prevent workflow breakdowns. Controls may be programmed into applications or consist of regular manual checks. Automated programmed controls can validate data against pre-designated rules, and automatically reject data that does not conform.

In a well-managed operational environment, all types of controls, their description, purpose, and ownership will be fully documented. Generally there are four types of control methods:

- Verification controls are designed to check the input data before input to minimize errors during transaction processing.
- Validation controls ensure accuracy of data.
- Preventive controls guard against unauthorized access to the system or data and form the core of the security infrastructure.
- Reconciliation procedures tally control totals obtained from different operational areas to double check data accuracy.

Controls are also categorized in other categories depending upon their location in the processing cycle – there are input, processing, output controls, and also data transmission and online controls.

COMPLIANCE

Working in conjunction with the legal/compliance department, compliance procedures are built into the operations infrastructure. A compliance checklist is agreed between operations and legal departments. Future compliance requirements must be anticipated so that resource requirements can be planned and earmarked for implementation purposes. In practice, especially with new products and services, there are usually gray areas where legal opinion must be obtained. While this may be the responsibility of the legal department, operations should be intimately involved in the process. A problem arises when new systems are being installed. These have to be configured to comply with the relevant regulatory environment. For companies with a global footprint who wish to deploy the same core systems in a number of markets, configuring systems for specific market compliance can be time consuming.

QUALITY

A number of frameworks and methodologies, such as Six Sigma or Total Quality Management (TQM), are available to card companies for monitoring the quality of their operations. Card companies, in this respect, are not any different from other business within the financial services industry or in other industry sectors. Any framework can be chosen.

What is important is that there is a discipline in place with quality control measures that have been designed based on customer and front-office staff feedback.

A common practice in this area is the use of detailed service level agreements (SLA) drawn up with third-party providers as well as with internal suppliers (for example, corporate IT department for communication network availability) to ensure the card business can deliver its promised service quality to its customers.

Top issuers invest substantially in training staff and management on customer management techniques. This includes training on technical matters, such as systems, processes, policies, and procedures so that customer queries can be quickly and efficiently resolved and also training in interpersonal and psychological skills such as attentive listening, empathy, and conflict resolution. Front-office employees, who are in regular customer contact, are trained to think in terms of overall customer experience and not just as problem fixers.

Operations organizational structure

Operational processes are carefully designed to maximize efficiency. Quite often when a business has evolved through acquisitions, there are functional overlaps as the organizational structure is impacted by considerations other than efficiency.

Operations departments organize themselves according to logical business functions so that not only they are more efficient but they benefit from common goals and have to observe common guidelines, control, and procedures. Information systems are also usually part of the overall operations area as well as are the customer services staff. However, in this chapter we will review core operations only which deal with the management of customer records, transactions, and billing (see Figure 7.2).

While core operations are similar across different financial institutions, organizational structures and staff volumes may be very different across entities. This is primarily due to two key factors. First, some of the activities may be outsourced to third parties which means that only a few staff may be allocated to the outsourced function to manage the vendor and functional quality. Second, the extent of automation within the issuer organization determines the number of operational staff. In less developed markets, a number of processes are handled manually owing to the high cost of specialized equipment and the relatively lower cost of labor. Large banks in developed markets are able to invest in equipment, especially imaging and workflow solutions, to automate and standardize their operational procedures.

Core operational functions

The operations department serves as the engine of the card-issuing business managing a continuous and large streams of data that have to be processed quickly and efficiently. Operations provides support to all other departments and to customers. In a sense, it can be regarded as the backbone of the issuer business. It must be able to handle surges in volumes without breaking down and the staff must be trained to handle exceptional situations.

While the staff usually have little or no direct contact with customers – the operational department is also commonly referred to as the back office (as opposed to front office – areas

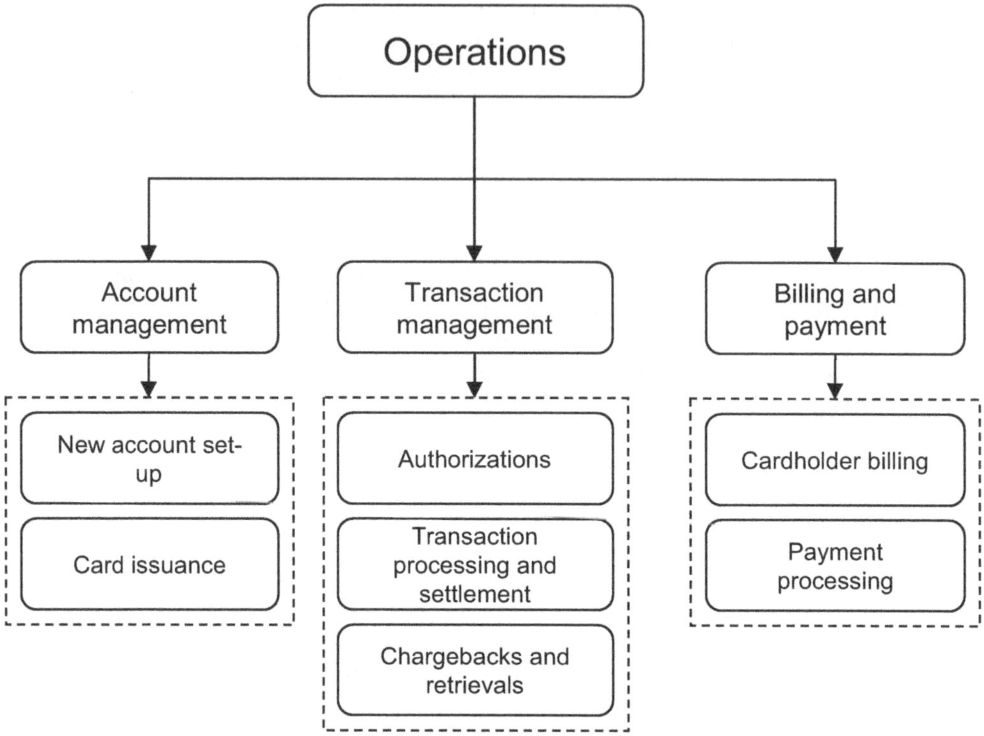

Figure 7.2 Core operations structure

that are customer facing). However, any mistakes or delays in the operations department directly impact cardholder relationships as it is responsible for transaction completion from transaction origination to cardholder billing. Putting this in a different way, it can be said that operational processes are invisible to the satisfied customer but visible to dissatisfied customers.

The operations department is also sometimes referred to as the production department. As in a factory, the focus is on error-free, cost-efficient, and fast-flowing throughput. When things go awry, cardholders' relationships can be adversely affected within a short period of time.

ACCOUNT SETUP

When an application for a new card account is approved, customer details have to be entered into the card issuer's primary and peripheral systems. Usually there is a customer masterfile that is the primary repository of key customer data. All other systems, such as billing systems and customer management systems, draw information from this file as and when required. The masterfile also ensures that any changes to customer records are made at one place only and only by authorized staff.

Account numbers for newly approved accounts are generated by the card approval system and are automatically fed to the masterfile. The masterfile contains customer personal and contact information, data about credit limits, product types to be issued, card reissue dates, and so on.

Any analysis undertaken for customer segmentation and analysis draws information from the masterfile. Some advanced financial institutions are beginning to deploy the concept of a universal masterfile which serves as the primary data source of customer records for all areas within the bank including retail, insurance, and brokerage.

CARD ISSUANCE

Once the new account has been set up on the masterfile, a message is sent to the card production area or a third-party provider, which is most often the case, to produce and deliver bankcards to customers. The same message is sent when a card comes for reissue or if it has been lost or stolen.

The card production area, or the third-party provider, utilizes the secure inventory of blank plastic to produce and personalize the card based on the information received. This process is more complex in the case of chip cards as the embedded microprocessors have to be personalized or programmed with cardholder personal information that cannot be tampered with. The process is discussed in a later chapter in this book. Here we will focus on the standard magnetic stripe cards.

Some advanced systems can approve applications online and generate account numbers very quickly. As a result, the cardholder can begin to make remote card-not-present purchase transactions minutes after approval of the new application.

In magnetic stripe cards, card personalization occurs on the front of the plastic as a result of the embossing process. Embossing means raising the plastic surface of the card to form words and numbers (cardholder name, account number, expiration, and sometimes start dates). This ensures that cards can be used in an offline environment with a 'zip-zap' (paper-based) mechanical reader. Some cards are not embossed but the information is printed on the front. These can be used electronically only. The magnetic stripe at the back is encoded with key account information (card and cardholder details and security information). Encoding involves electronically embedding the card and cardholder details on the magnetic stripe for use at electronic terminals or cash machines. It is very important that this information is transferred from applications approval area to card production without any errors. In addition, card production is a sensitive area and must be physically kept safe and secure at all times allowing entry to authorized personnel only, as theft of both blank stock and complete cards awaiting delivery can lead to fraudulent transactions if they end up in the hands of criminals. Card plastic inventory procedures are crucial and it is recommended that audit supervisors should make routine checks to ensure that the cards inventory is in order.

Card production is highly automated in most issuer environments these days. Special machines receive the information file, interpret it, emboss, and encode cards very quickly. This automated conveyer-belt system then uses machines that place cards in paper card carriers, insert them in to envelopes along with other materials to complete a new customer welcome pack and make it ready for mailing by applying the correct postage, or sorting the packages appropriately for delivery by courier or customer pick-up at bank branches..

For seamless use of cards at terminals all across the world, it is important that both plastic cards and card-reading devices such as point-of-sale terminals and cash machines follow the same standards in terms of the style, format, positioning, information storage, retrieval, and data field specifications. All card schemes and card companies have detailed operating regulations which must be complied with. They specify design and operational details to be followed which have been agreed to by all the major card companies to ensure there is interoperability across all markets.

AUTHORIZATION PROCESSING

Most card transactions are authorized which means that the card issuer directly or indirectly approves a cash withdrawal or purchase transaction request originated by the merchant. The authorization message format is also governed by the relevant operating regulations of the card schemes or the card companies involved. The issuer checks the authorization requests against the records it holds, such as credit limit or funds available, the amount of transaction, and various parameters that are designed to manage and control risk such as the frequency and total of cash withdrawals in a day.

In many markets, authorizations are expensive due to lack of economies of scale or simply due to inefficiencies in the telecommunications structure. Not all requests are authorized for approval and floor limits are often used. Based on the type of merchant, the issuer can allow transactions below a certain value to be approved without authorization. It is also possible that the electronic telecommunication links may be temporarily out of order. Card companies deploy special procedures known as stand-in-processing (STIP) that use some form of back-up systems, partial, or previous day's data to authorize transactions, where a link with the issuer cannot be established, so that customers can continue to use their cards without disruption. A message is then sent to the issuer so that they can update their records.

If no other form of authorization is available, the merchant may have to phone the issuer to obtain a voice authorization. This is kept to a minimum as voice authorization is the most expensive type of authorization. Even when all systems are functioning properly, the issuer's risk management systems may generate a referral asking the merchant to call and validate additional information about the cardholder.

Authorization processing is highly automated and the operations department usually does not employ any significant number of staff to supervise this area. Periodic regular review of authorization systems and management of risk control parameters is, however, continually required.

TRANSACTION PROCESSING

Authorized transactions are sent to the issuer by the acquirer or the card schemes for processing, clearing, and settlement. Most transactions these days are captured electronically although in some markets, paper drafts are initially used. Information on paper drafts is converted to electronic information by the use of scanning machines or data entry operators. The issuer will receive the transactions, process them, and finally post them to the relevant cardholder account. The whole process is automated with little or no manual intervention. The settlement message is also standardized by the operating regulations so that it can be produced and read by machines automatically.

Card payments in some countries are based on a single-message protocol for transaction completion. This means that the settlement message is sent along with the authorization message. Others operate on a dual-message system in which settlement messages are batched together, usually at the end of the day, and sent for processing.

CHARGEBACKS AND RETRIEVALS

Chargebacks refer to transactions that have been sent back to the acquiring bank by the issuing bank for several reasons. The operating regulations of card schemes catalogues these using reason codes which must be provided when a transaction is charged back. Usually cardholders contact their issuer to inform them that certain card transactions were not made by them or have not been appropriately charged (charged twice or with wrong amount). Card issuers also review transactions to ensure that all transactions received from the acquirers are complete and correctly categorized. If any errors are discovered, those transactions are charged back.

The acquirer then researches a chargeback received to obtain further information from merchants and from their own systems to resubmit the transactions. In the case of mail order/telephone order or MOTO and Internet transactions, under current rules, the acquirer will charge the transaction back to the merchant and the matter will be closed. In other cases, the acquirer will review the transaction and resubmit providing all the necessary documentation required to support the transaction parameters. The issuer will then review the received documentation with the transaction a second time and if there is still insufficient evidence, the transaction will be sent back again to the acquirer. This is called 'second presentment'. The whole process used to continue back and forth but now the card associations have placed a limit and the second presentment is final.

The acquirer must identify valid parameters for every transaction. For example, a paper transaction cannot be flagged as electronic in order to pay a lower interchange fee. This is why issuers check that all transactions are categorized properly in order to ensure that they are not receiving lower fees. Transaction parameters are provided and defined in the operating regulations of the card schemes and companies.

CARDHOLDER BILLING OR STATEMENT GENERATION

When a transaction has been accepted, cleared, and settled it is charged to the cardholder's account by the issuer. The level of detail provided along with the transaction message on a cardholder's statement depends upon the type of card used. Commercial cards provide more detailed information about the purchase transaction than do consumer cards. Card statements are printed and mailed periodically, usually monthly, to cardholders. Most issuers allow the cardholder to select the statement date but many have limited flexibility in that area with only one or two statement generation cycles per month. This process is fully automated with very little manual intervention and quite often outsourced.

Completed transactions are billed to the cardholders on a statement that is mailed to them and, in many instances, is available for online access and downloading. Timeliness and accuracy are the critical elements of this process. Different markets have different requirements for what is necessary to provide to cardholders via their monthly billing statement, but in general, each statement must contain the following data elements:

- cardholder data such as name, address, and account number;
- credit limit of the account, current balance outstanding, and remaining credit available;
- payment amounts, both to pay the account in full or the minimum payment required;
- payment due date;

- transaction data including the merchant name, date, and amount of the transaction;
- transaction reference number, an internally assigned tracking number that makes researching cardholder chargebacks and disputes easier;
- summary data showing payments, credits, new transactions, and any adjustments to the account since the last statement;
- interest rate being applied to the account and the amount of finance charge being added to the statement as a result;
- any fees being charged such as annual fee, late fee, overlimit fee, and so on.

Bankcard billing statements are usually structured in such a way to make the identification of each of the elements described above easy to find and understand. Often, specific boxes are created on the billing statement so that the cardholder knows where to look for items of immediate interest such as balance, payment amount, and due date.

Billing statements also must be produced and mailed in a timely fashion in order to allow the cardholder time to review the information provided and make a payment by the date due. In many markets, this timeliness is prescribed by regulatory agencies that often set a minimum amount of time the financial institution is required to provide to the cardholder to make a payment from when the statement is mailed to the cardholder. It is important that these timelines be incorporated into the statement production schedule.

After each step, audits and quality control processes must be conducted to ensure accuracy. The entire process generally takes between three and five days to complete depending upon the volume of statements being produced.

A number of issuers across the world offer electronic statements over the Internet. Cardholders can access their statements from anywhere in the world and download the data on to spreadsheet software or to their money management programs such as Quicken. However, this feature may not release the issuer from sending a paper statement to the cardholder which may require special approval under the law and regulatory structure of the issuer's specific market.

PAYMENT PROCESSING

The payment processing function is important to both the bankcard issuer and to cardholders. It involves the receiving, capture, and crediting of payments from cardholders to their bankcard account in a timely and accurate manner.

The payment process involves the following critical steps:

- *Payment receipt.* It is not as simple a function as it at first might appear. Cardholders make payments by mail, via ATMs, through direct debits, via electronic bill payment, and at financial institution branches. Procedures must be in place to ensure that, regardless of how the payment is made, it is accounted for in a timely manner.

  In paper environments, cardholders utilize the paper coupon to send a check for payment. They also utilize the remittance coupon to dispute transactions or for other correspondence. However, these items must be separated from the payment form and forwarded to the appropriate area for response.
- *Payment preparation.* The next step involves the batching of payments and remittance coupons for ease of future balancing and error recognition.

- *Payment capture*. Electronic payment transactions via retail banking transactions are received and processed automatically. Check payments are processed when information is entered into the bankcard processing system, either via manual data entry or via the reading of the Magnetic Ink Character Recognition (MICR) line of the remittance coupon if such technology is utilized. The critical data elements required are the cardholder account number, payment amount, and payment date.
- *Balancing*. Once captured, the amount entered into the system must be compared to the totals from the batches created during the payment preparation stage to ensure that everything is accurate.
- *Payment posting*. Once balanced, payments are then posted, or credited, to individual cardholder accounts. Accuracy and timeliness are once again critical elements of this back office function. Payments generally must be posted within 24 hours of their receipt, both for operational and regulatory considerations.

  From a regulatory standpoint, most markets have some type of statute requiring prompt posting of cardholder payments. From an operational point of view, failure to post payments promptly can cause cardholders to become delinquent, even though their payment was, in fact, received on time, which can cause great difficulty from a client relationship perspective and can result in account attrition. In addition, there are specific regulations in different markets that describe how payments are to be applied if there are multiple balances outstanding with the issuer.

In-house versus third-party processing

Globally, in many markets, bankcard issuers have a choice regarding how they organize operational functions. That choice involves one of three options including:

- Create and manage an in-house operation in which all of the required functions are performed within the financial institution.
- Contract with a third-party processing organization for all of the operational functions, including the core cardholder account and transaction processing system management.
- Utilize some combination of in-house and third-party processing to accomplish the necessary functions of the back office.

No one right answer exists when it comes to which way a bankcard issuer chooses to perform its back office functions. Each option offers advantages and disadvantages. Generally, the decision to outsource or keep functions in-house revolves around three key variables as follows:

- management
- flexibility
- cost.

Each of these variables is influenced by the in-house versus third-party decision as illustrated in Table 7.1.

There are no easy answers to which is the best option for a particular issuer. Third-party processors offer, potentially, greater flexibility in altering systems and processes at less cost

Table 7.1 In-house versus outsourced processing

	In-house	*Out-source*
Management	All personnel on staff. All systems managed internally. Direct reporting line to card division	Staff employed by third-party company. Systems managed by third-party company serving multiple clients.
Flexibility	Systems, processes must be modified via internal bureaucracy and procedures.	Systems parameter driven, easy to alter. Processes prescribed by issuer and executed by third-party.
Cost	All systems and process modifications 100 per cent funded by financial institution.	Systems and process modifications spread across multiple issuers

than an in-house operation requires, but at the possible expense of being able to influence which changes are made when the issuer is just one of many clients of the third-party processor.

The in-house versus third-party processor decision is one that merits serious deliberation within card-issuing organizations in competitive environments. It is a decision which also should be revisited from time to time as circumstances change, as what may be a good decision today may be a bad one tomorrow.

Management and controls

The final topic for consideration with respect to the operations management is the extent of management oversight required to ensure the timely and accurate delivery of the functions performed. Often, the operations department does not receive the attention it merits when it comes to consideration for investment, staffing, and similar decisions because it is normally viewed as a cost center with no revenue implications. However, as we have learned, there are significant revenue influences inherent in this area should the functions performed not be done in a timely and accurate manner.

Oversight of the operations department deserves significant management attention. In fact, much of the information required to manage a card portfolio is contained within the back office. Sales volume, payment trends, balances, and other critical management information are all created and tracked as part of the normal operational procedures.

Operational control is also crucial. As was discussed within each function, there is no room for error, and little client tolerance. As a result, investment in the proper staff and automated system controls to ensure quality service is a requirement for the success of any card-issuing organization.

CHAPTER

8 Fraud Prevention and Control

Cardholder fraud is the cause of much concern to the card industry. Every year the industry suffers substantial losses in the hands of fraudsters ranging from the occasional unscrupulous individual to organized criminal gangs that operate globally to steal and forge bankcards. The card industry, in this respect is a victim of its own success. The card industry business is so significant that for criminals, unauthorized access to even a fraction of the total industry business volumes translates into billions of dollars. While card companies have invested hundreds of millions of dollars in developing sophisticated technology to counter fraud, the industry is always in a state of constant conflict with the world of organized cardholder fraud criminals who concentrate their efforts in developing and devising novel ways to steal and manipulate bankcard information.

In addition to simply stealing cards, organized criminals gain unauthorized access to cardholder information and manipulate it to obtain bankcards fraudulently. They also use sophisticated technology to convincingly produce counterfeit bankcards in large quantities. These cards are used to make unauthorized purchases and draw cash resulting in huge losses to card-issuing companies.

Card companies have measures in place that detect fraudulent activity. They also devise risk parameters that reduce the possibility of fraud through verification and validation of cardholders and transactions. They also work closely with each other and with the various law enforcement organizations to keep a constant watch against organized criminals who perpetrate more sophisticated forms of card fraud.

Before we review the various tools and techniques for preventing and managing cardholder fraud, it may be useful to take a quick look at the primary functions of the fraud department within a card-issuing organization.

Organizational structure

Fraud departments in different banks and card companies have very different staff structures but at a generic level these primarily consist of two key functional areas as shown in Figure 8.1. The first relates to fraud prevention. This area is responsible for the management of the various databases and control procedures that are deployed as safeguards against potential fraudulent activity. The second area deals with fraud investigations. Once a criminal has bypassed the safety checks and fraud prevention controls the fraud investigation team take over the responsibility to fully research the matter and bring the criminals to justice.

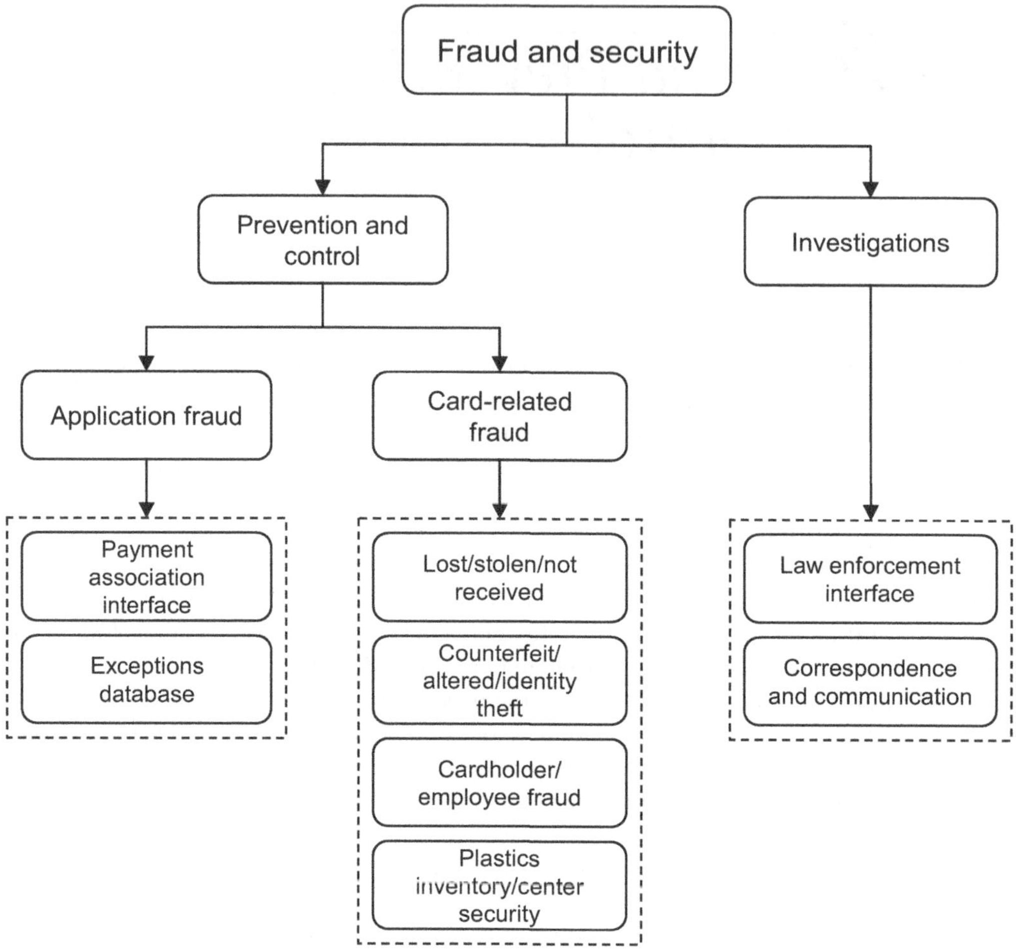

Figure 8.1 Fraud department structure

FRAUD PREVENTION TEAM

Staff in this team closely monitor transaction activity and applications received for new cards. Authorization messages and completed transactions are checked against preset parameters to safeguard against fraudulent transactions. They also look at overall spending volumes from a number of perspectives to identify emerging patterns leading to potential cardholder fraud. This type of activity is flagged for immediate action and review. It is essential to maintain comprehensive and easily available databases that keep updated records of recent fraudulent activity. In addition, there are software tools and analytical reports that are used to manage these databases. These databases and tools are the responsibility of the fraud prevention staff. Card associations such as Visa and MasterCard also keep centralized databases and maintain interfaces with fraud prevention systems with the bankcard issuer.

FRAUD INVESTIGATION TEAM

The fraud investigation team examine confirmed as well as suspected fraud activity. They contact cardholders, speak to merchants, and work with law enforcement agencies – providing evidence and testifying at court hearings to prosecute the criminals and bring them to justice. They also provide feedback for fraud prevention improvements so that procedures can be improved and additional technology investments are made in the right direction.

Risk management policies

It is crucial that all card issuers have a clear and well-defined fraud risk management policy that is well understood by all employees and not just risk management staff. This is because at the corporate level, financial institutions usually lay out the overall risk management guidelines that do not specifically cover card fraud in detail. The card business needs to ensure that its fraud risk management polices are comprehensive and aligned with the overall policies at the corporate level. In the first instance, these must deal with checks and controls for fraud prevention. These cover the types of authorization parameters to be set and by whom; data streams to be reviewed and monitored for flagging possible fraudulent activity.

Risk policies should also clearly define the procedures and controls in place to minimize exposure in each of the business functional areas such as new account application processing, card production and delivery, customer service, Internet purchases, and so on. In customer service, for example, risk controls make sure that the identity of the caller, when they contact the call center or the identity of the online user when they log on to change any personal information especially their mailing address, is suitably validated. In delivering bankcards, conservative risk policies mean that cards are sent via special courier or picked up by the customer at a branch. In both cases, the chances of new cards being stolen before they reach the intended recipient are minimized. Risk policies also deal with physical security procedures such as access to the vault where plastic cards may be stored and inventory control processes for personalizing new cards and destroying old ones.

Advances in technology are helping immensely in fighting fraud. The investment in new fraud prevention technology should reflect the risk management policies of the issuer. Chip cards with PIN are very effective at the transactional level. In some countries zero floor limits mean that every transaction is authorized thus increasing the chances of identifying fraudulent activity as early as possible. Sometimes the issuer asks for a cardholder referral requiring the merchant to contact the call center to verify certain cardholder details. Some issuers, however, simply decline or accept without offering any referral option. Internet transactions require advanced security protocols that validate the authenticity of the transaction using various security technologies. Mail/telephone order (MOTO) and Internet transactions utilize various other tools that help to mitigate fraud such as the address verification service (AVS) that enables retailers to match the cardholder's billing address with the requested delivery address; and the card verification value (CVV) or card security code (CSC) systems that requires providing an additional 3 or 4 security digits for a remote purchase. Fraud from remote or card-not-present transactions is generally on the rise and is a cause for concern. However, the incidents of hackers breaking in to card databases online to steal card details are extremely rare.

Clarity in an institution's risk policy assists the technology department to plan their future investments appropriately and to make sure that all new hardware and software additions comply with the prescribed security controls.

Types of fraud – prevention and detection

Criminals try to steal cards from consumers, apply for cards in their name, and intercept them before they arrive, and even steal legitimate customer identities to obtain bankcards fraudulently. They even attach fake devices to ATMs to 'skim' card number and PIN details to produce counterfeit cards. Payment cards with embedded microprocessors or chip cards that require the cardholder to enter a PIN instead of a signature prevent this type of skimming to a great extent. These cards are then used to withdraw cash or make unauthorized purchases at retailers or quite often via mail, telephone or over the Internet. Certain types of merchants, such as jewelers, unfortunately experience higher incidences of fraud than others such as supermarkets. Because it is not possible to verify cardholder identity in a remote or card-not-present transaction, card issuers under bankcard scheme rules, chargeback fraud losses arising from such transactions back to the merchants. However, new online technology initiatives that require PIN entry online, will guarantee no fraud losses for the merchants and are designed to encourage merchants to invest in online secure e-commerce.

APPLICATION FRAUD

Fraudsters supply false information to obtain new bankcards which they use to obtain cash and make purchases. Quite often part of the information may be stolen and relates to a person comprising of name, addresses, and related particulars. If the card is approved the criminals will attempt to intercept the card mailed by the issuer. A common tactic is to call the customer service helpline and try to change the card delivery address.

A more sophisticated line of attack involves identity theft and is usually found in more advanced markets. Criminals steal sensitive personal information from centralized databases such as those maintained by credit bureaus. They are able to manipulate that information and alter it to obtain social security documents, identity cards, and bankcards which they then abuse. Stolen identity information is used to acquire new cards or take over existing cards where the criminal calls the card issuer to cancel the card and have a new one sent to the fraudulent address.

Card companies keep track of fraudulent applications in databases which they share with each other and with third-party credit bureaus. These are checked against whenever new applications are made to detect any submissions that may be suspicious and require more scrutiny. Data and identity theft can be made more difficult by increasing the information points about a particular consumer. The chances that any 'red flags' may come up with a fraudulent card application are increased if more information points are required to be supplied and verified.

Card schemes are well positioned to maintain centralized databases that operate as repositories of all fraudulent applications received by card issuers across a market or region. Card issuers continually contribute information to keep these databases updated. Any indications of potential fraudulent activity triggers a warning alert to the relevant issuer.

This pooling of information for fraud prevention is indispensable and saves issuers hundreds of millions of dollars in potential fraud losses. In the US this service is called the Issuer's Clearinghouse Service. In the UK, a non-profit organization called CIFAS, formed by the major lenders and working in conjunction with the National Consumer Council and the police, is dedicated to the prevention of all financial crime relating to consumer lending including bankcards.

NEVER RECEIVED ISSUED (NRI) AND LOST/STOLEN CARDS

This is the oldest and most commonly encountered fraud. Cards are stolen from consumers or lost cards are picked up and used or sold to other criminals. Sometimes the criminals 'shoulder surf' a cardholder withdrawing cash at an ATM to read the PIN entered and then steal the card using various attention-diversion tactics. Criminals even attach special devices in ATMs that trap the card after the customer enters the PIN which is watched through a miniature camera or simply read by the criminal who is shoulder surfing. The stolen card and PIN are later used to withdraw cash.

Of course, as card issuers are able to block accounts, criminals try to make fraudulent transactions before the card is reported missing or as soon as the cardholder sees unauthorized line items in their card statement and reports them to the issuer. Issuers invest in cardholder awareness campaigns and in systems and procedures that make it easier for cardholders to report fraud. But issuers also attempt to detect this fraud even before it is picked up by the cardholders by using sophisticated technology solutions that monitor transaction activity and flag any irregular patterns. The issuer then contacts the cardholder to verify these transactions and if the cardholder does not recognize these, an immediate block is put on the card account.

Visa provides this type of sophisticated transaction monitoring for its members through its Visa Intelligent Scoring of Risk (VISOR), an advanced neural network system that monitors card transactions and assigns a risk score based on the spending behavior of the cardholder and the risk profile of the merchant. The issuer then can contact the cardholder to verify flagged transaction. MasterCard offers a similar risk prevention scheme to its users.

Mail interception is another common category in which cards are stolen even before they are received by the cardholder. This type of fraud is known as 'never received issued' (NRI) fraud. Properties with communal mailboxes such as apartment complexes or student halls are specifically at risk.

NRI fraud can be difficult to detect, especially for new cardholders, because predictive software usually compares current transaction activity with past patterns to identify irregular patterns. Past patterns obviously do not exist for new cardholders. But issuers use other techniques, the most common of which is card activation. Cardholders must call the issuer and identify themselves to activate the card. The call center agent will ask a set of basic questions to verify that the card is in the hands of its legitimate recipient and will activate the card. The telephone number and instructions are provided on a sticker placed on the new card. Many issuers deploy automated activation systems that detect the cardholder's home telephone number and activate the card or a VRU system may ask the caller to punch in basic information such as social security number or other previously supplied information such as mother's maiden name which is validated and confirmed by the system.

The PIN is also sent separately to reduce the risk of fraud.

COUNTERFEIT AND ALTERED CARDS

Most counterfeit cards are the result of card skimming in which the genuine data on the magnetic stripe of a card is illegally copied onto another. This usually takes place at retail outlets especially in bars, restaurants, and gas stations where dishonest employees skim the card data before handing the card back to the customer. The data is sold to other criminals who use the information to produce illegal copies or clones of the original card. Sometimes valid cards are stolen and altered or modified. The key advantage of chip cards is they are extremely difficult to copy compared to magnetic stripe cards. Some measures that card issuers use to prevent card counterfeiting are presented below:

- Security holograms are used – under ultraviolet light, a large 'MC' is visible on MasterCard-branded and a large dove on Visa-branded cards.
- Microprinting techniques are also used. What appears to the naked eye as a solid line, has very small words or letters when seen under a magnifying lens that are extremely difficult to recreate with normal printing.
- Tamper-evident signature panels that have 'Visa' or 'MasterCard' printed many times and are not plain white or damaged.
- Card security codes are available on the front or back of the card – which are unique three or four digit codes.
- Merchant education is also critical in which merchants are aware of key indications that a card being used is counterfeit.

CARDHOLDER/EMPLOYEE FRAUD

This category of fraud is initiated by dishonest cardholders or corrupt staff at card issuers. Cardholders dispute genuine transactions that they or members of their family made. Where family members are involved, cardholders sometimes refuse to acknowledge the fraud in order to protect them. They may report the cards lost or stolen before the transactions were made. In extreme cases, cardholders may collude with criminals to allow their cards to be abused and later claim such transactions to be fraudulent. This type of fraud cannot be prevented but through proper investigative procedures, it can be identified at an early stage to minimize losses and bring the fraudsters to justice.

The risk of fraud from unscrupulous employees is a risk inherent to any business. This mainly involves information theft by a staff member or by employees of entities who hold information on the issuer's customers such as credit bureaus, collection agencies, and third-party processing companies. Theft of unused cards is also a possibility. The stolen information is used by the thieves themselves or sold to organized card fraud criminals. It is important that there are supervisory checks and management controls that protect the issuer from such fraud or at least detect it at a very early stage. However, carefully laid out schemes by insiders are extremely difficult to unravel. Many financial institutions and third parties that control sensitive customer data for them have instituted special procedures to check staff backgrounds as there have been cases of staff infiltration by organized gangs. Some employers are very restrictive in the use of personal devices such as mobile phones that can potentially be misused in obtaining unauthorized data.

Internal control procedures include inventory controls of cards kept in stock, varying levels of access to information for different levels of staff, computer logs, regular reviews of fraud activity, and review of control procedures at the issuer's third-party outsourcing partners.

MERCHANT FRAUD

Merchants are also in a position to perpetrate fraud as they handle bankcards as a matter of routine. Corrupt merchants try to enter the same transaction twice or key in fictitious transactions using the card data of customers who have purchased products from them before. This type of fraud is much less prevalent but card-acquiring banks need to monitor transaction activity such as irregular authorizations, chargebacks, and daily merchant deposits on a regular basis and investigate where necessary. The investigation usually involves accessing past merchant transaction records and working with issuers to detect any suspicious transaction patterns or activities. Visa, MasterCard, American Express and others have detailed risk management policies and strict criteria in place against which new merchant applications are checked that review the business itself as well as the personal records of business proprietors before they are allowed to accept bankcards.

Fraud investigation

The fraud investigation unit researches suspicious or confirmed fraudulent activity. Any new card applications that have been flagged for possible fraud are investigated by the team. The applicant is contacted where further information may be required and to confirm that the new card application is genuine. Other parties such as the applicant's landlord, banks and insurance companies, employers, and other references provided on the application may be contacted as well. Where fraudulent cash withdrawals or purchases are suspected, the first line of defense is the transaction authorization. These days issuers are able to set up sophisticated parameters that allow for automated and quick decisions whether or not to authorize a transaction. A referral message may be sent back when more validation is required by the issuer to ensure the authenticity of the transaction. Where irregular activity is flagged by the computer, issuer staff will contact the cardholder to verify the transaction. Cardholders generally welcome this contact as it shows their issuer is being vigilant and proactive. However, referrals are expensive for the card issuer and may cause annoyance and embarrassment, and therefore should be selectively made.

Quite often legitimate transactions are flagged as fraudulent by the early-warning systems. The cardholder duly confirms that they did make those transactions. Such a transaction is known as a 'false positive'.

The first step to take if a transaction actually turns out to be fraudulent or where the cardholder has reported a lost or stolen card is to block the account immediately and place the account number on the shared fraud-watch databases and warning bulletins. The investigation team then begins to review the transactions related to that card account accessing old transaction documentation and other relevant information to ascertain the extent of the fraud and whether it is an early or late stage fraud.

Police and law enforcement agencies in most developed markets have units dedicated to financial fraud and especially bankcard fraud. The fraud investigation team prosecute criminals in conjunction with the police and prepare all the necessary evidence to document the case and bring the criminals to justice. Some cases can take a long time to complete but all forms of financial fraud are taken very seriously by the authorities and it is essential for the viability of the bankcard business that fraudsters are pursued and punished. Documentation is critical. Cardholder billing records, recorded statements that provide evidence, original documentation, authorization logs, evidence from other financial institutions and utility providers, and any other related evidence are necessary for preparing a robust case for prosecution. It is said that cardholder crime is a 'victimless crime' which somehow makes judges and juries less sympathetic compared to other crimes where the injury to the victim can be easily demonstrated. However, it should be kept in mind that these criminals usually utilize their ill-gotten gains from card fraud to pursue a host of other crimes and carry out organized rackets that are extremely dangerous to society as a whole.

CHAPTER 9 Collections

The key aim of the collections function with the bankcard issuing business is the management of risk and curtailment of losses relating to cardholder receivables. By definition collections is concerned with charge or credit cards. Debit cards make immediate payments and therefore there are no cardholder receivables. When cardholders do not pay the minimum amount by the due date the cardholder account is called 'past due' or 'delinquent'. The collections department sets about mitigating the risk resulting from cardholder delinquency. It should be noted here that the art of collection is not only focused on debt recovery. It requires diplomacy and customer empathy. Cardholders are usually helped and counseled back to being 'current' – to use their cards as before and pay their bills on time. In many situations, subtle persuasion is required to make cardholders settle their past due balances before other creditors.

Collections policy

Collections policy should be clearly formulated. It is important that every collection agent or 'collector' knows and understands the overall business philosophy towards collections. The strategy for collecting delinquent accounts must be consistent with the overall risk management goals and objectives.

Issuers realize cardholders are difficult and expensive to acquire. They must develop collection polices that aim to reduce the risk of non-payment while counseling the cardholder back to regular card usage and repayment. Cardholders having temporary repayment problems are sensitive to the treatment they get from collectors. Good collectors often turn around the situation without losing the cardholder and this can result in long and profitable relationships. An aggressive collections policy can yield the best results in terms of repayments of past due balances but can easily make the cardholder defect to other issuers. It is easy in this process to lose a potentially profitable cardholder who may be having temporary and resolvable financial difficulties by simply applying an inappropriate policy towards collecting debts. Such a policy is focused on the shorter-term profits.

Conversely, a more conservative collections policy will ensure cardholder retention but possibly at the expense of future profitability. In the end, an issuer may end up with an undesirable number of delinquent cardholders who may not become current, resulting in a riskier cardholder portfolio.

Issuers normally segment their delinquent accounts portfolio to decide the type of policy to apply to a specific segment. How aggressive the collections policy should be depends greatly on issuer judgment. Past experience with the cardholder, third-party information, and, of course, prevailing personal circumstances of the cardholder at the time of the delinquency combine to assist the issuer to decide whether or not the financial distress is temporary and determine the probability of bringing the cardholder back to current status.

Collection procedures

The cards industry normally deploys two types of procedures to collect past due accounts. The choice depends upon the issuer who must weigh the advantages and disadvantages of each procedure.

LIFE-STAGE-BASED COLLECTIONS

This procedure is based on the premise that early-stage collections (missed one to three payments) are very different from late-stage (missed four to six payments) collections. Each requires different training and experience. In the former category, cardholders require a softer approach with more help and advice to commence regular card usage and payment behavior again. The issuer must ensure at this stage that cardholder relationships are preserved while every effort should be made to collect the payments. Late-stage collectors are trained to be more firm and are experienced in handling client confrontations. Collection departments consequently work with two teams, each area of expertise applying special skills and procedures to manage the process effectively. Later-stage collections generally require more resources than early-stage efforts.

CONTINUOUS CONTACT COLLECTIONS

This approach is also commonly called 'cradle-to-grave' collections approach. A collector is assigned to an account when it becomes delinquent. The collector then continually deals with the account till it becomes current or is flagged for write-off. The obvious advantage of this approach is account specialization where one collector is made responsible for the account from start to finish. Greater responsibility brings greater effectiveness and makes it easier to monitor collector performance. While many issuers deploy this procedure, in general, life-stage collection requires fewer staff than continuous contact procedure.

Collections management

The management of an efficient collections function requires an understanding of four key areas. These are:

- an appropriate department organizational structure
- efficient undertaking of daily activities
- full use of supporting systems and applications
- risk management

The department organizational structure should allow for a judicious allocation of daily activities to staff members based on their skill and competency levels in order to avoid operational bottlenecks. Special customized training is required to develop and nurture customer management skills where call center agents regularly encounter difficult situations. Collections departments also rely heavily on outside specialist companies for certain key tasks.

Most issuers have also invested substantially in sophisticated systems and applications that raise collector productivity and help reduce cardholder risk.

Credit losses represent a significant part of total expenses in the card issuer's profit and loss account. Poor management of receivables, like in any business that involves lending, can spell disaster for the lender. Issuers with risky portfolios such as those that cater to the subprime market are cognizant of the risks involved and view collections as one of their core business functions.

Organizational structure

Collections department structures vary from one issuer to another. A typical structure is shown in Figure 9.1. However, there are two key areas within the department that undertake a bulk of all activities. These are:

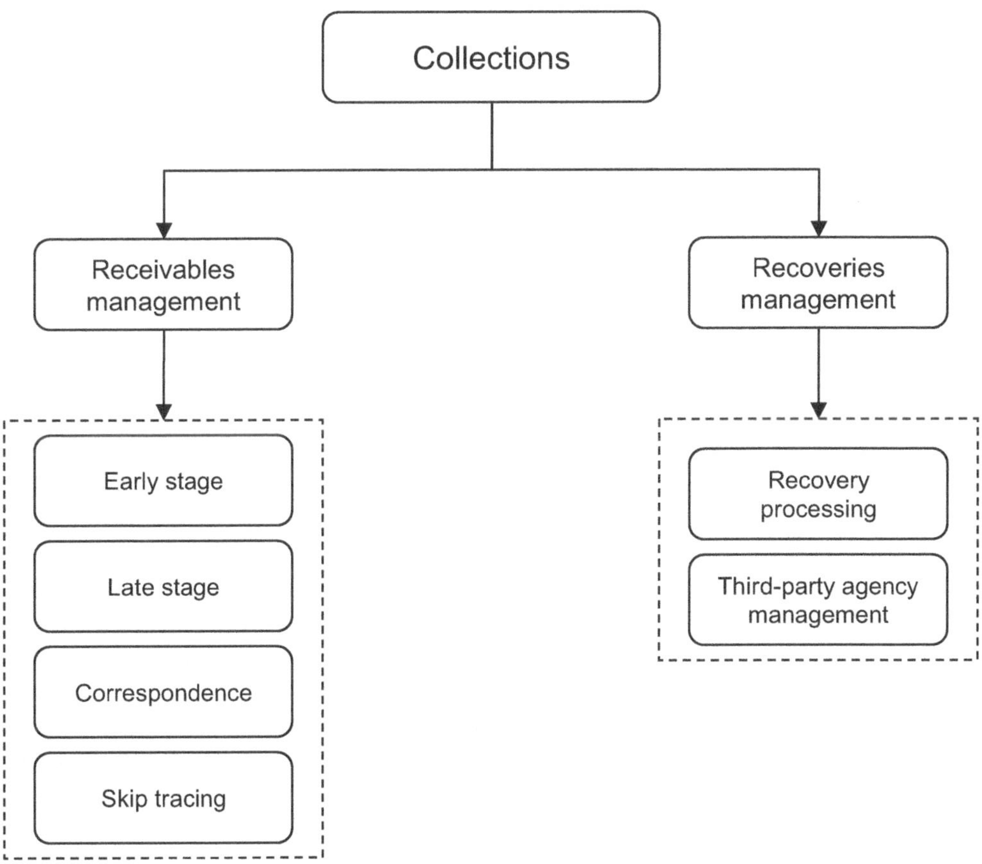

Figure 9.1 Collections department structure

RECEIVABLES MANAGEMENT

Identification, monitoring, and management of delinquent cardholder accounts is dealt with here. Seriously delinquent accounts, after all efforts to collect have been unfruitful, are charged or written off. This means that the issuer realizes that the amount is uncollectible or there is a very high probability of non-recovery from the account. The key responsibilities of staff in this area are:

- contacting and discussing/negotiating with delinquent cardholders;
- locating cardholders who are trying to avoid being contacted for non-payment of bills. This is also called 'skip tracing' in industry jargon;
- deciding on uncollectible accounts for charge-offs and provisions.

Contact is made with early- and late-stage cardholders in writing and over the phone which can, of course, be time consuming where cardholder details are no longer valid and their new whereabouts have to be researched and identified.

RECOVERIES MANAGEMENT

This area deals with accounts that have been charged off or provided for in the books of the issuer. Often, staff in this area work with third-party agencies and other creditors to recover the debts. Key functions cover:

- Recovery of all past due balances that cannot be collected are marked for charge-off or provisions as appropriate. The recoveries area deals with this type of accounts.
- The general policy in this area is aggressive collection, focused on recovering as much as possible of the loss incurred.
- This area also deals with third parties such as accountants and lawyers and works with specialist third-party agencies contracted by the issuer to help recover the losses.

COORDINATION WITH CUSTOMER SERVICES

The collections department is not the only issuer department in touch with the defaulting cardholder. In fact the cardholder more often speaks to the customer services department or other client facing groups within the organization which may also include branch staff in issuing banks. However, today, many issuers can flag accounts, so that any client facing staff who comes in contact with a late-stage delinquent cardholder, whether over the phone or in person at a branch, will redirect client communications to the collections department.

Nevertheless, it is critical that all customer facing groups are well coordinated. In this case, the collections department must work closely with the customer services department especially for early-stage collections to bring the cardholder back to current status. This usually happens when the delinquency is due to a transaction dispute. Quite often the cardholders will call the customer services department to request a credit limit increase. In such cases, the two departments must work together with the customer services department, transferring calls to the collections department as appropriate. These departments must work together and coordinate their strategies to share observations and lessons learnt on a regular basis.

COORDINATION WITH OTHER DEPARTMENTS

In addition to customer services, the collections department must work closely with the marketing and the credit underwriting departments to share management information and observations on the risk profiles of specific customer segments, product types, and marketing campaigns. This can prove invaluable for the two departments when designing new marketing and account acquisition campaigns.

Another indispensable component of overall collections management is the use of third-party organizations to assist the issuer in conducting both its collections and recovery activities. These agencies specialize in either current, or precharge-off collections, or recoveries, which are postcharge-off collections.

THIRD-PARTY AGENCIES

Collection agencies specialize in collections and general receivables management. As collections is their core business they usually invest significantly in state-of-the-art automated systems in order to deliver issuers better results than their in-house operations. They are generally paid for results, sometimes a percentage of amounts collected. For relationship management purposes, issuers normally keep precharge-off accounts in-house but outsource postcharge-off and also the most problematic accounts to third-party agencies. As agency compensation is performance driven, they are very effective in collection and recoveries. It is important to remember, however, that outside agencies, can also cause cardholder attrition by being over aggressive where a softer approach is required.

In the US, third-party debt collection agencies have been thriving. Increasingly financial institutions are outsourcing collection activities to them with good results. Now the large customer-service call-center firms have started venturing into this area. In 2004, Convergys, the world's biggest call-center operator bought Encore Receivable Management thus providing complete customer management solutions to financial institutions as well as other clients. While debt collectors may be based in the same country as the cardholders, small-value debts are often deemed too expensive to collect and are increasingly being outsourced to off-shore companies based in low-cost economies such as India. (*The Economist*: October 30, 2004).

STAFFING AND TRAINING

Collection staff must possess the rare quality of efficient empathy. While they must try to be firm and dedicated to recovering the debts due to the company, they must impress upon the customer that they truly understand their predicament and are interested in working together to resolve their financial problems. While some people are naturally good at customer empathy, there is no substitute for appropriate training to nurture the best collector. Experience is perhaps the most important element. Experienced collectors know the sort of issues being confronted by delinquent cardholders in genuine financial but redeemable distress. They can identify sooner than others which delinquencies have a reasonable chance of becoming current again and which ones are heading for charge-off.

Staff skills

CUSTOMER EMPATHY

As mentioned above, the primary quality of a good collector is customer empathy coupled with firmness. This indicates an attitude to problem resolution that is in the best interests of the customer, but makes it clear to the cardholders, at the same time, that empathy does not translate into any special waivers or sympathy-induced concessions. The primary task they have to remember is to bring the accounts back to current status or recover the past-due balances as far as possible.

PROBLEM RESOLUTION

Collectors have to review all the information provided to them in discussions with customers to develop pragmatic repayment plans. Issuer management must provide them with clear guidelines on negotiating pragmatic payment schedules with delinquent cardholders. The guidelines must stipulate the flexibility they can offer to delinquent cardholders and the limits within which they can operate.

EFFECTIVE COMMUNICATION

The art of persuasion is the central virtue of undertaking past-due collections. Good collectors are very clear in their written or oral communications what options the cardholder has and the choices that have to be made. These must be articulated clearly and confidently so that in all likelihood the cardholder will make an immediate or quick decision on how to proceed, saving valuable issuer time. One important factor is that most issuers forget that they are in a competitive situation while collecting. The effectiveness of collection lies in persuading the cardholder to attach a higher priority to paying back the debts over liabilities and obligations they may have to other lenders.

Training

Training is a critical element in the development and success of issuer collections. Because the collection process requires a blend of various skills, the collections manager should identify the strengths and the skills gap for each member of staff individually. As mentioned before, interpersonal skills that include customer empathy but with a strong pragmatic attitude towards problem resolution are necessary. But equally important are technical skills in terms of understanding of risk management techniques, using specialist computer applications, reviewing data from disparate sources, and reaching informed conclusions on how best to manage the delinquent customer. The degree of automation in systems and processes will determine the total staff requirements. An issuer wherein most processes are manual and documents have to be physically retrieved instead of being available in image format will obviously require more staff.

The first step is therefore to determine staff requirements. Issuers should hire staff who are naturally suited to this type of work and have considerable prior experience so that they can be productive from day one. More than any other area in bankcard issuing, collections benefits greatly from staff with experience. Good collectors are rewarded handsomely and their employers make every effort to retain them. The next step is to devise a complete training program against which skill gaps of individual collectors can be identified and measured. The program is based on specific training requirements of the issuer. Training can then be delivered in-house or through an external training house or both. Internal trainers can team up with external trainers to provide an all-round perspective of the collections area. In many issuers it is not unusual to find existing senior staff devoting some of their time to regular training of junior employees.

Managing collections productivity

To fully understand how a collector uses good business judgment by utilizing the tools and techniques available, we have to look at a list of the daily activities of a typical collector in a fairly automated issuing environment. A typical collector will:

- Review the account for current status and other relevant information including previous promises to pay and record of actual payments received.
- Obtain and review additional information from third-party sources including bank statements from other financial institutions and credit information.
- Contact the cardholder, either by telephone or in writing via one of a number of options.
- Update the details of the conversation with the cardholder in the cardholder case file maintained on the system.
- Where the cardholder is proving very difficult to contact, then undertake skip tracing which may include contacting friends, neighbors, and relatives.
- Negotiate pragmatic repayment plans based on the cardholder's financial position.
- Discuss the cardholder's situation with other financial institutions that may have a current relationship with them, subject to consumer data protection guidelines.
- Decide the limits to be placed on the account, or if the account should be blocked all together.
- Ensure these limits are implemented and monitored.
- Monitor the account and prepare recommendations for provisions and charge-offs.

Collection systems and applications

COLLECTION INFORMATION SYSTEMS

Issuer systems must be able to store and update information relevant to the delinquent cases in a systematic and searchable format. At a minimum this information should include:

- account details:
  - contact details and recent changes in addresses
  - employment and income details
  - past-due balance
  - balance details
  - payment history
  - number of days unpaid
  - reasons for non-payment (job loss, disability, legal problems, and so on);

- previous collections history of the cardholder;
- information on financial relationships with other banks and issuers and status of debts owed;
- information on past collection events with cardholder.

CUSTOMER CONTACT SYSTEMS

Contact systems enable collectors to minimize time and resources required to contact and converse with delinquent cardholders. Instead of manually dialing telephone numbers to contact cardholders, scribbling conversation details, retrieving documents and files, writing letters, and locating any necessary additional information or documentation manually, collectors at most bankcard issuers use sophisticated customer contact management systems that are also commonly called automated collections systems. These systems assist in queuing, contacting, and tracking of delinquent cardholder accounts.

The first major task in daily collection activity is to prioritize accounts based on certain criteria that may maximize customer contact and case resolution. Collection systems allow collectors to prioritize and queue accounts in a number of possible ways using the common case record variables: by location, risk measures (such as behavior scores), amount due, stage of delinquency, past payment history, and so on. By the touch of a button, the system will display all accounts listed according to the preset criteria along with all the necessary collections-related information for a particular case including collector notes from previous customer contacts. A collector can also append action items to the record such as next contact date and additional information expected so that the system can automatically alert an available collector to contact the customer on a future date.

A key feature of the contact management system is the 'power dialer'. The power dialer automatically dials up the cardholder contact numbers contained in the system. If contact is not made, it records the time of the attempt and contact result (disconnected, answer phone) for later review, and moves on to the next available telephone number or the next delinquent cardholder queued in the list. If the call is answered, it immediately transfers it to an available collector while at the same time, displaying the full account details on the collector's workstation.

After the completion of a call, a collector can select from a number of draft letters and written notices to send to the delinquent cardholder along with copies of billing statements if required. After negotiation with the cardholder the collector agrees on a date for payment which is input to the system. On that date, the system will automatically check against payments received to see if the cardholder has kept the promise to pay. If not, the system will move the account back in the collections list together with the reason.

Contact management systems are very similar in design to general call center customer service systems but have features designed exclusively for assisting debt collections. They enhance collection department efficiency by automating a number of cumbersome tasks which previously were undertaken manually.

RISK MANAGEMENT SYSTEMS

The collections department is also responsible for detecting and preventing bad debts before they happen. This is done by carefully reviewing cardholder usage and payment behavior. These early-warning systems are very effective in reducing credit risk and in detecting early signs of future delinquencies in regular cardholders. The most common form of an early-warning system is called behavioral scoring.

Behavioral scoring

Behavioral scores are often used to prioritize accounts for calls by collectors. Behavioral scores use predetermined algorithms that take into account card usage, frequency of transactions, average balance carried, regularity of past payments, and other criteria to develop numerical scores that can be compared across the portfolio. These are normally updated monthly. Collections departments utilize such scores along with other delinquent account variables, including delinquency stage, balance due, and past payments, to prioritize their calling plan.

A delinquent account with a low behavior score and a high balance that is approaching late-stage collection carries more risk than an account with high behavior score and low balance outstanding that is only in its early stage of collection. The primary object of a behavior score, when applied in conjunction with other cardholder variables, is to determine an immediate risk profile of the cardholder. Accounts can then be prioritized based on the risk profile and the collection system will determine when and how often the cardholder needs to be contacted

Predictive optimization

To identify patterns in the spending and payment behavior of cardholders, there are several techniques deployed by manufacturers of collections software. The algorithms contained in these applications attempt to identify such patterns by reviewing large quantities of data relating to individual accounts and to the portfolio as a whole. They are used to determine the probability of default of past due accounts. But more often they are used to enhance collection department efficiency by predicting and prompting optimal values for certain variables such as the best times to call during the day.

CHAPTER 10

Infrastructure and Delivery Channels

Advances in computer processing speed, storage capacity, and communications technology have combined to fundamentally change the way card issuers today develop products, process transactions, and service their customers. In the last two decades, the rapid development and deployment of advanced technology has revolutionized the payment systems marketplace. Technology has helped card companies develop more sophisticated, profitable, and customized products and services. The speed and accuracy with which payments are authorized over proprietary and public networks means retailers can safely sell and deliver their goods and services to anyone at anytime. The card industry has invested heavily in adding new systems to their overall technology infrastructure.

To cope with the substantial transaction volumes, the systems infrastructure in large card companies can be quite complex. Many large card issuers have a gaggle of disparate platforms, legacy and new, linked to each other in an arrangement that closely resembles a giant technology cobweb. Systems planners love to show 'aspirational' maps of how the cobweb can be rationalized to an ideal or 'point-of-arrival' infrastructure which would make things simpler for everyone. Almost always, this point-of-arrival vision is an unattainable state of operational nirvana that can only be wished for in the systems planning department. But as a card business manager, one need not get involved in the merits of rationalizing and untangling existing systems jumbles or attaining ideal future state scenarios.

Business managers, in order to understand the key impact of systems and technology must:

- have sufficient understanding of how the card systems are structured at a high level – front to back end – to appreciate the implications on product fulfillment and service design;
- understand the limitations of the various systems platforms that may adversely affect product features or characteristics;
- provide clear feedback to the technology team about additional features and functionality that may prove competitive and profitable in the marketplace so that they can evaluate development and implementation costs;
- be involved in future technology investment decision making and overall technology strategy to ensure the two areas are in alignment.

From a card business manager's perspective, the entire systems infrastructure can be divided into three key areas as shown in Figure 10.1:

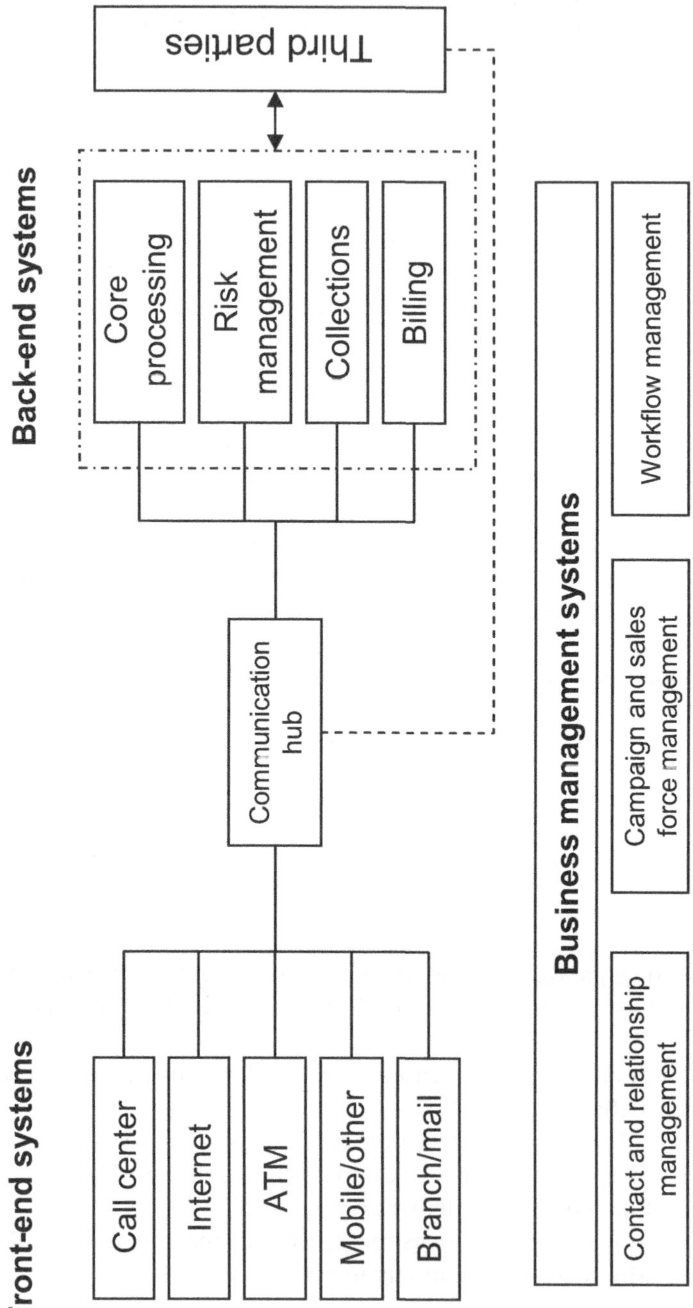

Figure 10.1 Systems infrastructure

- *Front-end systems.* These systems enable customers to communicate directly or indirectly with the company over a number of 'delivery channels' or 'customer touch-points'. These relate to new customer sign-up activities, transaction authorization and processing, statement generation, or customer help and service.
- *Back-end systems.* The core processing systems represent the 'guts and glory' of a card operation: these systems manage customer records and transaction histories, bill customers, monitor credit and fraud risks, and help collect delinquent account balances.
- *Business support systems.* These systems generally serve specialist tasks such as campaign or customer relationship management, which though essential for the success of the business, are generally not classified as part of the core infrastructure in a card-issuing environment.

Controlling and linking all these systems is the backbone communications network of the card organization. Some financial institutions have middleware components that operate as communication hubs enabling new components and platforms to be added and integrated with ease.

Many legacy systems have disparate platforms individually connected to each other instead of being linked through communication hubs. Communication channels are as important to the business as the systems they link. Communication faults frequently cause unwanted and costly business disruptions.

Front-end systems

Front-end systems support 'customer touch-points' – communication channels where customers come in direct contact with an automated interface (a machine, usually for self-service), talk to a live person, physically at a branch, or over the phone to an agent at a call center. In general, an automated interface is used to service the customer for simple activities such as ordering a statement and for routine procedures including cash withdrawals or balance checking. Call center agents, on the other hand, help the card company sell products where, in general, customers may require assistance, guidance, or specific knowledge-based advice, or resolve customer issues that they cannot resolve without speaking to someone.

CALL CENTER

In most mature markets, the call center is perhaps the most important part of the whole card-issuing organization. It plays a key role in marketing and selling, resolving customer problems, and providing an overall customer experience necessary for customer acquisition and retention.

Marketing and customer service managers rely heavily on call center efficiency and are actively involved in any new call center investment decisions. Call centers are critical especially where the card company does not have a branch network to rely on. Non-bankcard issuers, such as American Express, MBNA, and Capital One rely heavily on call centers to spearhead their customer contact function.

Modern call center systems now come with many advanced features that assist agents to better organize their work, speedily and satisfactorily resolve customer queries, and carry out marketing campaigns with effective results. Call centers execute card acquisition campaigns designed by the marketing department that include outbound calls using a specially formulated target customer list, and inbound customer calls received in response to advertising and direct mail solicitations.

Key features

Vendors offer a number of useful call center features but not all of these, such as advanced forms of computer telephony integration (CTI) or voice recognition, are necessarily 'must haves' and card issuers should carefully review the costs and benefits of implementing new call center features and functionality.

Call centers are now evolving to include data channels in addition to the traditional voice-based communication. These days vendors offering call centers with integrated Internet and emailing features refer to call centers as 'customer contact centers'. These contact centers integrate voice call management systems with e-mail and text messaging facilities.

The call center features presented below are not exhaustive but are presented for illustrative purposes only. These should be kept in mind when launching a new call center or enhancing existing facilities.

INTERACTIVE VOICE RESPONSE (IVR) FUNCTIONALITY:

- Menu driven – intuitive hierarchy of submenus that do not test customer patience.
- Ability to execute basic and frequently used functions (such as, access balance and pay bills).
- Fulfils the front-end function of identifying customer and retrieving data before handing over to a call center agent.
- Voice recognition – helpful feature, especially where key input is not possible or inconvenient such as for mobile phones or for sight impaired customers, but this feature continues to suffer from performance issues.

CALL MANAGEMENT:

- Call queuing – ability to prioritize inbound calls.
- Call waiting – call divert after lapse of specified time to overflow destination (VRU or voicemail).

AUTOMATED CALL DISTRIBUTOR (ACD):

- Recognizes and answers incoming calls.
- Programmable routing instructions – routing call to available agent, VRU or a recording machine.
- Provides management information relating to call handling and performance of center agents.

COMPUTER TELEPHONY INTEGRATION:

- Computer systems linked with ACD form what is called computer telephone integration (CTI).

- Enables quick and accurate call management. Enables screen pop-ups with customer data, relevant scripts, and instructions.
- 'Warm Hand-offs' – when calls are transferred from one agent or call center to another, customer data is also transferred along with the call so that the receiving agent does not have to retrieve the data again or ask the customer the same set of questions as the previous agent.

Outbound marketing

The use of predictive dialers has become quite common in outbound marketing and collections. The system dials out and screens out responses such as answering machines, operator intercepts, or busy signals to pass the call to an agent only when answered by a real person. Dialers also refer to a preset agent skills database, calculate agent workloads, then pass calls to the most suitable agent

Preview dialers are also used where the system pops up the target number details requiring the agent to decide whether to go ahead or abandon the contact attempt. For outbound marketing management, please refer to the chapter on marketing.

Communication infrastructure

Most call centers use tried and tested communication protocols such as IBM's SNA that has been the de facto standard in the financial services industry for many years. However, the open Internet protocol, TCP/IP, is now being deployed in a number of centers. As technology improves, the quality issues that previously prevented TCP/IP from being deployed widely in mission-critical environments, are now being ironed out.

Voice-over-IP (VoIP), the ability to use an Internet connection for reliable and clear voice calls, is making great strides even to the point where telephone companies are feeling the competitive pressure on their existing fixed-line businesses. VoIP is considerably cheaper than other communication options available.

Call centers offer great outsourcing potential. Many providers based in less expensive parts of the country or in offshore locations, such as India, with an educated and skilled English-speaking workforce, offer cost-effective and efficient solutions.

INTERNET

The Internet is becoming increasingly important for card issuers. It plays a vital role in marketing to technology-savvy customer segments both via relevant advertisement placements and targeted e-mails. Many issuers offer well-designed tools on their websites to help customers build the type of payment card they want by choosing the card features they want, and in some cases, selecting the best interest rate/annual fee combination that best suits their needs.

Account acquisition

New account acquisition over the Internet involves online credit decisioning which can be a complex undertaking from a systems perspective. This feature is offered by several issuers, though the degree of systems sophistication varies significantly. Online card applications are automatically approved or declined based on credit-scoring algorithms that involve instant checking of customer credit histories from outside credit bureaus and internal/external collection agencies.

If an online card request is not approved, the customer is sometimes referred to the call center or asked to leave a contact telephone number. This is because while the customer may not be eligible for the card they have applied for, they may still qualify for a different product or service.

Customer service

Online customer service is also undergoing gradual growth. Call center agents also manage customer e-mails and, in some cases, even provide online assistance over live Internet dialog/chat for all types of customer interaction including even debt collection and advice.

Online cardholder services include web-based access to routine customer information such as statement balance, credit line, available credit, last statement and new unbilled transactions (to appear in next statement). Past statements can also be accessed in various formats to view or download, the number of previous statements available depending on issuer policy and storage capacity available.

Online transaction management

This is a powerful tool if fully and successfully implemented. It can allow cardholders to click on items in the online statement to attach notes for their own reference, request the issuer for a copy or image of the transaction slip or other proof of transaction, and query the accuracy or legitimacy of a transaction. There is also a facility to search for transactions in past and present statements that match user input criteria.

Cardholder alerts

These are notifications based on cardholder-activated parameters and are sent by the issuer to the cardholder mailbox within the online customer service site, cardholder's normal e-mail, or even through to the cardholder's mobile phone. Alerts require cardholder attention where, for example, credit limit on their card has been exceeded. This facility can also be used for personal reminders such as for birthdays.

Other features

There are several Internet-related self-service features that can be deployed based on the capabilities and limitations of the implemented Internet support systems. These include:

- bill payment;
- ability to review past payments or make changes in address or contact information;
- transferring balances from other cards;
- online case capture (creating simple forms on company website to capture customer comments and queries and route them appropriately);
- auto-response e-mails to customer e-mails and intelligent routing of e-mails by subject/problem type to call center agents.

Case management

This involves creation and distribution of customer cases within the issuer support and service organization so that a problem is referred to the right group or agent immediately. This function also has the capability to escalate customer service issues to managers as and when necessary.

AUTOMATED TELLER MACHINES

Automated teller machines, from an organizational perspective, are generally not part of card-issuing or merchant-acquiring businesses but are part of the core retail banking network. On basic ATM units, customers can withdraw cash, and in some cases, deposit cash and checks which otherwise would have to be deposited over the counter at a branch. ATMs have come a long way from their original purpose of providing cash. They are now morphing into self-service terminals, information access points, and even multi-purpose vending machines.

A significant majority of retail banking transactions are general account access transactions dealing with issues such as balance inquiries, cash withdrawals and deposits, viewing recent transactions, and so on. It is important that these are automated self-service transactions so that banks can cut operational costs, and allow branch staff to spend more time developing customer relationships and selling products and services. ATMs offer the potential of migrating non-value-added routine transactions from expensive labor-intensive options to cheaper and more accurate automated routes.

ATMs play a very important role in customer management strategy as customers are familiar with how ATMs work. Properly persuaded, they can gradually use the machines for all routine transaction needs. In most markets, customers use ATMs a lot more for cash withdrawals than for deposits. Their reluctance to make deposits stems from the lack of deposit verification at the ATM. In the US, legislation referred to as Check21 is enabling check images to be deemed legally equivalent to paper checks. Customer-deposited checks will be scanned by the ATM and a verified deposit receipt issued immediately on the spot.

Information access points

Advanced ATMs these days boast color screens and provide considerable useful information ranging from weather forecasts to stock market quotes. The purpose is to gain more 'face time' with the customer albeit over an automated interface. The downside is that this may result in longer wait periods – annoying those waiting to withdraw cash only. Web-enabled ATMs with limited Internet access are also being selectively deployed.

Vending

Banks in Spain pioneered the use of ATMs for selling tickets for a number of activities and events. Customers can purchase tickets for entertainment, such as concerts and movies (some even allow customers to choose their preferred seating arrangements for theater bookings). They can also purchase tickets for local busses and trains, stamps and gift vouchers, and even place stock market orders.

Off-premises installations

The growth in ATM deployment today is largely driven by off-premises ATMs. These installations may be at airports, public places, and especially retail stores. Retail installations generally consist of basic cash dispensers without much added functionality. Security concerns must always be considered before choosing where to locate ATMs. Cash disbursement fees – fees payable by the card issuer to the ATM owner – are the main revenue generators for ATM owners and act as an incentive for increased ATM deployment. ATM surcharging also carries significant revenue potential.

Back-end systems

Back-end core systems are at the heart of a card-issuing business. They manage customer and product profiles, customer and transaction records, authorize and process monetary and non-monetary transactions, calculate charges and fees, and generate cardholder statements. Key core processing features include:

- application processing capabilities:
  - customizable tiered application processing criteria
  - formatted output for sending acceptance/regret letters
  - links to third parties for credit scores
  - internal updated assessment of credit scores and risk scores
  - alert files for flagging unacceptable credit histories;
- risk management capabilities:
  - track and prevent fraud
  - predict account performance using credit bureau and risk scores
  - alerts for unusual activity
  - flag and prioritize receivables for collections;
- chargeback processing for scheme transactions;
- transaction authorization:
  - automated decision making
  - accurate responses
  - manual referral diverts and processes;
- transaction processing and charging to accounts;
- calculation and management of finance charges with flexibility to use multiple interest rate calculation routines, for example, from transaction or charging date;
- application of payments to receivables;
- real-time changes to non-monetary items;
- overall and individual account roll-ups – for example, showing total insurance fees, total finance charges on statements;
- roll ups for multiple products by customer;
- generation of formatted data for card production – new cards/cards up for renewal;
- management of the customer information file (CIF);
- customizable reporting capabilities;
- creation of general ledger (GL) entries;
- create customer correspondence with account specific variables in text.

Many issuers have systems modules purchased from a number of software vendors. These software applications work alongside homegrown and bespoke systems. There are integrated suites available in the marketplace that cover the entire end-to-end issuing business. Integrated systems may also cover the merchant-acquiring business.

Business support systems

CONTACT AND RELATIONSHIP MANAGEMENT (CRM)

Contact management systems handle customer details and are now essential components of card-issuing systems infrastructure. They allow notes, memos, and other items to be attached to the customer record so that a complete customer electronic file is ready and available for any call center agent to retrieve and use. Computer telephone integration (CTI) applications will automatically retrieve the data as soon as customer input details are captured at the VRU or when the Automatic Number Identification (ANI) system identifies the caller.

Sophisticated CRM systems provide intelligence on customer preferences and needs by analyzing transaction and personal data. This data is used by the marketing department to develop card-acquisition strategies and campaigns and to design new products and services.

However, CRM systems can be exorbitantly priced and can be sometimes disappointing, their sophisticated algorithms rendered useless due to lack of accurate customer data for analysis.

CAMPAIGN AND SALES FORCE MANAGEMENT

In developed markets, marketing campaigns heavily rely on direct mail and outbound telemarketing. Of course advertisements, in print and on the Internet, and other marketing materials such as take-one brochures/application forms are also utilized in coordinated marketing campaigns. Campaign management software assists in campaign execution by providing analyses and statistical results on response rates from a number of perspectives. It can provide us with many useful insights into our marketing campaigns: the marketing channel that target customer segments best respond to, the customer subsegments which are most receptive to a specific offer, the geographical areas producing the best results, the sales groups which are outperforming others.

Sales force automation software serves a similar purpose but also provides tools for effectively managing sales leads and opportunities over a longer period of time. It is particularly useful where mobility is required as in commercial cards acquisition and also in merchant acquisition within bankcard acquiring. Sales agents visit merchants all over their assigned territories in an effort to sign them up. Advanced versions of popular sales force software packages allow all the necessary forms on agents' laptops to be available offline and enable necessary information verification through remote connections with central servers allowing quick decisions and the sale to be closed on the spot.

WORKFLOW MANAGEMENT

A business is critically dependent on its business processes. Card-issuing business processes are discussed in Chapter 12. It is important that its arteries do not get blocked by the inefficient flow of needless paper work. Workflow systems ensure the smooth flow of activity for all the card processes. Front-end workflow is usually integrated with contact center software. These systems can also handle back-end processes such as chargebacks and disputed items that originate from the front office and may need to be researched and resolved in other areas of the organization. Depending upon how the process is distributed within the organization, the workflow system may consist of one integrated application or a series of disparate systems connected to each other enabling a staff member to pass a completed step on to the next stage for escalation, decision, or further review. Workflow systems indicate the extent of automation in card organizations. In small labor-intensive card organizations, specific groups may pass on the results of their work to the next group manually or via ordinary corporate e-mail. In large card organizations, workflow systems create a sort of 'moving belt' from transaction origination to resolution with the ability to automatically handle exception items.

Card issuers have often experienced business disruptions where one or more of their workflow systems have broken down creating bottleneck situations. While workflow solutions are in the domain of the operations department, product managers attach a great deal of relevance to these as the inefficient working of any workflow system can destroy the value proposition of any product.

CHAPTER 11 *Profitability*

Although the terms profit and profitability are used interchangeably in the industry, there is an important difference that is vital to business decision making. Profit is essentially a short-term concept. It is the excess of revenues over costs in a specific period of operation, usually a year. Profitability, on the other hand, is an indicator of the continued viability of a business. It is the business's ability to generate future profits based on the demand for its offerings. In a wider sense this is measured in terms of shareholder value. Shareholder value is defined as the sum of projected cash flows discounted at an acceptable rate of return. Profitability is therefore a longer-term concept.

In this chapter we will review ways to measure and compare profitability. We will also discuss the variables that impact portfolio profitability including product pricing. Product prices in mature and saturated markets are always pushed downwards as can been seen by the virtual absence of annual card fees in recent years. Such competitive pressures squeeze issuer margins and have an adverse impact on profitability. Issuers have found that entering into price wars to acquire new customers can seriously damage longer-term profitability without any significant portfolio gains.

Key profitability indicators

Net profit for a card-issuing business is calculated by deducting operating expenses from total card related revenues. For credit cards, we usually start by taking net profit before taxes for calculating the various profitability indicators. The standard practice in many industries is to use EBITDA – earnings before interest, taxes, depreciation, and amortizations. But since interest – interest earned as well as interest paid – is an integral part of a credit card issuing business, we use net profits after interest and before taxes in our calculations. Profit alone does not represent how well the business has used its assets and resources and whether the investment in the business has earned an acceptable rate of return for its investors. To do so, we have to determine a set of profitability indicators or business ratios. The most common ratios are as follows.

PROFIT MARGIN

The profit margin is simply the net profit expressed as a percentage of total revenues. Commodity products are low-margin products and require an increase in sales volumes for overall profitability enhancement. Niche or more expensively priced products, on the other hand, command better margins but it is usually difficult to increase unit sales volumes.

RETURN ON ASSETS

As mentioned above, interest generated from lending on credit cards is a key source of revenue for issuers. Cardholder receivables, which generate this revenue, appear as assets on the books of the issuer and represent a substantial portion of total corporate assets. Return on assets (ROA) – defined as net profit as a percentage of assets – appropriately reflects the productivity and profitability of key business assets.

RETURN ON EQUITY

Another way to review and compare profits is by calculating return on equity (ROE) calculated as net profit expressed as a percentage of shareholder equity. Shareholder equity is equivalent to the net worth of the company which is the excess of corporate assets over all liabilities to third parties (short and long term) from the total assets that appear in the balance sheet. Refer to ROE data for various markets in Figure 1.1 earlier in the book.

Key profitability drivers

CREDIT CARD PROFITABILITY

The single most important driver of portfolio profitability in credit-based payment products is interest income, which from the customer's perspective is more commonly referred to as the finance charge. The finance charge is applied on an issuer's cardholder interest-bearing balances. The bigger the balance, the bigger the finance charge. Credit card issuing is a consumer lending business and as such its success lies in achieving a profitable and sustainable balance between risks and rewards. The economics of consumer lending are primarily a function of credit risk and interest income. All other factors are secondary. At a basic level, risk and reward are directly related – the more risk you take the greater your chances of generating additional revenues. The problem of course lies in the relative cost of risk taking. Higher levels of risk usually mean higher probability of default for the lender. This is reflected time and again in the boom and bust consumer lending cycles of many developed economies. Eager lenders extend credit to meet boom time demand for credit consumption. Consumers borrow beyond their means resulting in bankruptcies and reduced institutional profits. Increasingly in mature markets, issuers – under pressure to sustain their business growth levels – are lending to subprime customers: a high risk strategy that can easily destroy issuer profits and damage long-term business prospects. The Federal Deposit Insurance Corporation (FDIC) in the US says that lenders who lend to subprime segments account for only 2 per cent of its insured institutions but account for 50 per cent of problem loans – a staggering $19 billion. But if managed well, a subprime portfolio can generate high returns within acceptable levels of portfolio risk.

Many large issuers now follow risk-based pricing policies which are designed to ensure that this risk is appropriately factored in credit card pricing. But critics say that such policies border on exploitation and point to exorbitantly priced credit products that have been or are still being offered to the public. Recently a credit card issuer in the UK was marketed at an astronomical rate of over 60 per cent to high-risk revolvers.

The only remedy is preventive. A lender must always have a clear understanding of the ever-changing risk profile of its credit card portfolio and appreciate that card revenues need not depend solely on interest, the traditional key source of income. Card issuers must strive to maximize revenue streams from all possible sources while running, at the same time, an optimized and efficient operations department.

DEBIT CARD PROFITABILITY

Measuring debit card profit is very difficult. This is because the card is linked to a primary banking product, a checking or current account, making it difficult to meaningfully ascertain stand-alone product profitability: revenues and costs for linked products are shared and attempts to separate them are, at best, arbitrary, potentially inaccurate, and misleading. All non-lending card products – debit, charge, and emerging payment products – derive revenues solely from non-interest sources such as annual fees and interchange fees and obviously carry less profitability potential than credit cards in a credit-hungry market. For debit cards, it is best to review the overall current or checking account for profitability analysis.

Revenue drivers and product pricing

The individual revenue components of a card-issuing business, for the purposes of our review, can be classified into primary and secondary sources:

- primary (or traditional) sources of revenue
  - card fees
  - finance charges
  - interchange fees
- secondary sources
  - service fees
  - risk-related fees.

Revenue drivers differ for each type of card product. Consider, for example, the revenue drivers for three hypothetical issuers in Table 11.1.

It is clear that for Issuer A, traditional sources – card fees, finance charges, and interchange fees – bring in two-thirds of the total revenues. This is much less than Issuer B,

Table 11.1 Sources of revenue (per account)

Revenues	*Issuer A*	*Issuer B*	*Issuer C*
Card fees	$5.00	$25.00	$32.00
Finance charges	$35.00	$32.00	$1.00
Interchange fees	$29.00	$31.00	$35.00
Service fees	$14.00	$12.00	$23.00
Risk related fees	$23.00	$14.00	$6.00
Total issuer revenues	$106.00	$114.00	$97.00

whose structure is more traditional, deriving 77 per cent of its revenues from traditional sources. Issuer C, on the other hand, is a charge card provider with minimal interest income.

A key element in understanding payment card revenue dynamics is pricing. Over the years credit card pricing has become significantly more complex as issuers attempt to segment customers by their propensity to pay and their risk and behavior profiles. In the US, in the early 1990s it was not unusual to find issuers offering a standard product range to all customers with fixed and published annual fees and interest rates. This lack of cardholder differentiation was obviously beneficial to the subprime customers who managed to qualify for the card product and who, despite being riskier, paid the same rate of interest as the issuer's prime customers. With competition, things began to change: issuers devised risk-based pricing techniques that linked risk profiles with product price. This allowed more tailored products to be offered to a wider customer base instead of the one-size-fits-all approach.

Another trend, especially in the US and the UK, has been the gradual erosion of traditional annual fees. Issuers have instituted new non-traditional fees such as penalty fees for late payments to compensate for the loss of revenues.

We will discuss the key revenue and cost drivers of card-issuer profitability to understand the impact of each on overall profitability and to review the latest trends for each item.

CARD FEES

Issuers charge an annual fee to the primary cardholder and also fees for each additional cardholder. Currently, many payment cards come with no annual fees – a testament to the competitive pressures in the card marketplace. Card fees were considered a loyalty tool and a key source of revenue 10–15 years ago. But now in the face of competition, less than 15 per cent of cardholders in the US pay an annual fee. Recently, however, issuers have been busy developing new value-added products for which customers are willing to pay higher fees. Annual fees which accounted for just 28 per cent of total card revenues in 2000 rose to 35 per cent in 2003 and 39 per cent in 2004. Some issuers are cleverly charging monthly maintenance fees, which can potentially add up to more than the advertised annual card fees charged by their competitors.

In some markets, issuers still charge card fees on basic card products where, due to low transaction activity or low revolve rate, other fees or finance charges may not be sufficient to cover product costs and maintain profitability. But in mature and saturated markets, issuers can only charge card fees where they can communicate a clear value proposition to their customers. Card issuers should take into account three key considerations when developing their pricing strategies relating to cardholder fees.

Features and functionality

This refers to specific card value features such as co-branded airline or other rewards or discounting programs. Affinity products also command fees. In the US less than 3 per cent of customers who are not enrolled in a rewards program, such as a frequent flyer program, pay an annual fee.

Branding or market appeal

Where a card product is not unique in terms of features and functionality, branding becomes extremely important. Issuers with powerful brands can charge a premium price for that brand appeal only in some selected markets. Customers will also pay for a card product that gives them status or a feeling of belonging to an aspirational consumer class.

Credit access

Customers with an adverse credit history will pay for access to credit. Issuers charge higher fees to offset the credit risk. But other customers, with perfectly good credit histories may have pressing financial needs due to a life event – wedding, baby, loss of employment – and may be willing to pay for access to a quick and convenient source of credit.

FINANCE CHARGES

Finance charges refer to interest charged to cardholders by card issuers on credit card borrowings. Cardholders who choose to defer payment of their card balances are called 'revolvers' and the balance carried forward is called 'revolving balance'. Issuers ask for payment of a minimum amount to cover their credit risk and offer cardholders the opportunity to revolve the remaining balance for an agreed fixed or variable rate of interest.

In the US, a majority of credit card receivables revolve and almost half of those who pay interest make only the minimum payment. In many other markets, most cardholders pay their balances in full at the end of the month.

Successful marketing managers realize that interest income is directly linked to loan balances and not just the number of accounts. Marketing campaigns designed to enhance this source of income focus on increasing total interest-bearing balances. Many such offers are targeted at accounts that already revolve. As cash advances usually do not attract any free period, they are also targeted by issuer marketing programs.

Annual percentage rate

The agreed rate of interest on the borrowings is expressed as the annual percentage rate (APR) – a mathematical calculation which represents the true cost of borrowing and takes into account all charges billed by the issuer. APR uses the net present value of payments that take into account the timing of monies paid or received. Comparing APRs is more meaningful than just comparing rates of interest. It provides the consumer with a more reliable tool to compare the full cost of borrowing. An issuer may have a lower rate of interest than a competitor but a higher APR due to extra fees and charges to be paid during the year. As a sum of money has a greater present value if received or paid out in year 1 than in year 2 or thereafter, mathematically speaking therefore, APR is always greater than the annual interest rate.

Issuers offer lower interest rates on balance transfers and from time to time during selected promotional periods or for selected types of transactions. These days it is common to find 0 per cent offers on balance transfers for six months or more as card issuers compete for market share for outstanding consumer credit.

Transparency

To avoid unnecessary regulatory intervention, it is important to follow the relevant rules and regulations on how rates are advertised and communicated to customers. Quite often we hear of instances where card issuers are accused of deliberately misleading consumers by not disclosing the full extent of terms and conditions attached to an apparently generous offer. These conditions, if not understood properly, can result in the consumer being hit with higher finance charges due to the calculation policies and methods applied by the issuer. In the UK in 2003, the Office of Fair Trading (OFT) reviewed and challenged a '0 per cent forever' offer from a major card issuer as highly misleading. The 0 per cent rate was in fact only available on balance transfers and only if the consumer spent at least £50 per month on regular purchases which would attract the higher standard interest rate offered.

Regulators are working continually towards helping their governments enact rules and regulations on how the APR is communicated to consumers. These include indicating how the rate should appear on brochures and advertisements and, where a range of rates is available, what rate may be advertised. This is usually the 'typical' rate – the rate that a majority of customers are expected to pay when they borrow on the card instead of the minimum possible rate that may be available to only a few qualified card applicants.

Three essentials of pricing finance charges

When developing the pricing strategy for finance charges, product managers should keep in mind three related product characteristics:

- *Minimum payment and finance charge.* Credit card lending is open ended and the balance due to the issuer changes continually. Cardholders who wish to revolve must settle a minimum amount with the issuer. This is usually a fixed amount and a variable percentage of the balance. An issuer may require a minimum payment of $10 or 3 per cent of the balance whichever is higher. However, cardholders who revolve small balances may find this disadvantageous as the fixed minimum is charged irrespective of the amount revolved. The two most commonly used methods of calculating minimum payments are as follows:

  - x per cent of Principal + Interest + All fees owed
    or
  - x per cent of (Principal + Interest + All fees owed)

  The first method will create higher minimum payment amounts owed by cardholders, but have the advantage of collecting all interest and fees owed each month. The second method will create a lower minimum payment owed, but will increase the cardholder's balance outstanding over time, thus increasing the amount of interest the cardholder will pay.
- *Multiple APRs.* Issuers offer lower rates on promotional spending and balance transfers. This usually does not apply to cash advances which, in any case, attract higher rates of interest than purchase transactions. Due to multiple APRs, issuers should make it clear to cardholders the way in which part payments received against outstanding balances are applied to the account. Normally, a payment is first applied to reduce the outstanding balance that has the highest APR and so on.
- *Grace period.* Cardholders are allowed a free period within which they can pay their entire outstanding balances without attracting finance charges. Some issuers with low rates cut back significantly on the number of free days they offer. This not only reduces the issuer's cost of funds (discussed later in the chapter) but can earn more revenue in terms of penalty fees and interest charges on inadvertently late payments. However, it can damage the issuer's relationship with cardholders and may invite damaging protests from consumer associations.

Finance charge calculation

The finance charge calculation is not simply a matter of multiplying the outstanding balance with the applicable rate of interest. In fact, the method used to determine the outstanding balance can result in very different calculations for the finance charge. Every market has its own relevant regulations that prescribe how interest is to be calculated. In the US, Regulation Z of the Federal Reserve Bank details the methods that card issuers can use to determine the outstanding balance. The issuer must decide on the method and communicate it to its cardholders. But the issuer is not required to explain how each method works, leaving it up to the cardholders to do that for themselves. These methods are briefly described here using a very simple illustrative example.

- *Previous balance method.* This method takes the net outstanding balance (what is due from the cardholder on day 1 of the month) and applies the APR to calculate the finance charge. It does not take into account any activity – new purchases or payments – during the billing period. It results in the highest finance charge calculation compared to the other methods described here.
- *Average daily balance method.* The outstanding balance is determined every day after adding purchases to the previous balance and deducting payments received. Then the outstanding balance is calculated by taking the monthly average of daily balances. The APR is applied to this average to calculate the finance charge. This method is also called the 'straight average daily balance' or the 'true actuarial method'.

  A variation of this method involves determining the daily balance without adding new purchases. In other words the daily balance is the previous day's balance reduced by any payments received. The calculation starts from the net outstanding balance on day 1 of the month but then the average daily balance, for the purposes of calculating the finance charge, is determined without adding new purchases, but after deducting payments. This is obviously more advantageous for the cardholder as new purchases do not attract interest till the next billing period.

  Yet another variation is to apply this method over two billing cycles. The two-billing-cycle method is especially disadvantageous for those cardholders who previously paid their balance in full – when they revolve for the first time. The method effectively charges them finance charges for the previous cycle. This innovation, obviously, contributes positively to issuer revenues.
- *Adjusted balance method.* This method results in a lower finance charge calculation than the methods described above. From the net outstanding balance on day 1, any payments, regardless of when they are received, are deducted and the new outstanding balance multiplied with the APR to calculate the finance charge.

ILLUSTRATIVE CALCULATIONS

Data:

- Net outstanding balance on day 1 (starting point for all methods) = \$400
- New purchases = \$50 on day 18
- Payments = \$300 on day 15
- Monthly APR = 1.5 per cent

Calculations:

- Previous balance method = \$400 multiplied by 1.5 per cent APR = \$6.00
- Average daily balance method = [(\$400 x 15 days) + (\$100 x 3 days) + (\$150 x 12 days)] divided by 30 days = \$270 multiplied by 1.5 per cent APR = \$4.05
- Adjusted balance method = (\$400 – \$300) = \$100 multiplied by 1.5 per cent APR = \$1.50

INTERCHANGE FEES

Background and rationale

No card issuer can afford to ignore the importance of interchange fees in payment card profitability. The interchange fee is one of the mainstays of the payment card issuing business. It is paid by the acquiring bank to the issuing bank based on fee structures agreed among the members of a card organization such as Visa or MasterCard.

The rationale for interchange fees is complex, controversial, and deeply rooted in economic theory. The original economic framework, first developed by William Baxter, one-time law professor at Stanford University and an Assistant Attorney General of the United States, argued that a payment system should be viewed from an economic perspective that takes into account the demand and supply of payment services. The banks – issuers and acquirers – are the suppliers of payment services while the cardholders and the merchants are consumers of payment services.

The core argument in his theory is that the two banking entities *jointly supply* and the two consumers *jointly consume* payment transactional services. Joint supply means that one supplier cannot supply without the other and joint consumption means that one consumer cannot consume without the other. It follows that the demand for payment services by the consumers is joint and interdependent. This is intuitively correct: cardholders have no use for cards if there are no merchants who accept card payments and conversely merchants have no use of the card network if there are no card-carrying members of the payment network who are likely to use their cards at their outlets. If there is a large number of cardholders, most merchants would want to accept card payments. If there is a large number of merchants who offer the convenience of card payment, card members would find it beneficial to carry and use the card wherever they go. This is also referred to as the 'network' effect.

The joint supply argument indicates that the costs of supplying payment services are also joint. The issuer's costs and the acquirer's costs, together, add up to the total cost of supplying payment services. It therefore stands to reason that if there is an imbalance between the ratio in which costs are shared and the ratio of merchant and cardholder demand, it should be redressed and adjusted. In other words the total joint cost of supplying payment services should be shared between the issuers and acquirers in an equitable manner – for example, in the ratio in which their customers exhibit demand for payment services. For practical purposes, revenues are taken as representative of demand patterns. Baxter viewed the interchange fee as primarily an adjustment fee to redress this imbalance. He stressed that without this adjustment, the issuers (who happen to foot a majority of the total costs but receive the smaller share of total revenues) due to market realities will find the payment card business unviable and will consequently exit the marketplace. For the payment system to be viable, there must be a monetary adjustment that redresses the cost-revenue imbalance between the issuers and acquirers. This is the primary purpose of the interchange fee that is the cornerstone of all open-loop payment systems.

Importance of interchange fees

This economic theory has been challenged by many economists, practitioners, and regulators around the world. Alternative arguments put forward assert that interchange fees are anti-competitive and arbitrarily computed. Thanks to their arguments and an almost constant pressure from the large merchant community, there has been tremendous downward pressure on interchange fees. Retailers, especially in the US, regard interchange fees as a major and non-negotiable component of the service commission they pay to the banking community for processing card transactions.

In other parts of the world also, interchange fees are coming under pressure from the regulatory watchdogs. The Reserve Bank of Australia recently reviewed the fee structure in Australia and opined in favor of the fees being substantially reduced.

Unfortunately economists postulating against interchange fees do so without a clear understanding of market realities and the unique character of a four-party payment system where a certain degree of cooperation is required among competitors. It is frequently argued that interchange fees necessitate the acquirer to charge a fee (the merchant service commission fee) to merchants, who in turn penalize cash-paying customers as all customers pay the higher price. This is because goods are sold at the same price whether the customer pays by cash or by card. In championing the merchant's cause, these economists overlook the fact that a merchant establishment offers many services and benefits to its customers and does not charge differential prices. Should customers who use elevators pay a higher price for an item than those who prefer to use the stairs? This argument, and similar ones used against bankcard interchange, are divorced from economic theory and reflect little or no appreciation of the complex market realities of global payment systems. Bankcard issuers in turn often complain that this lack of understanding only provides the closed-loop card companies, such as American Express and Discover, with an unfair advantage simply because of the way they are structured from an organizational perspective.

Interchange fee structures

Interchange fee structures vary with the type of transaction. Local and international transactions attract different rates. Rates also vary by the technology involved. Paper, electronic magnetic stripe, and electronic chip transactions work on different rates. Additionally card products have different interchange rate structures: debit, credit, and commercial card products have their own rate schedules. This complexity in terms of variances in rate by geography, technology, and product are due to market forces and the different cost and revenue structures involved.

International card associations play a key role in setting international interchange rates and also assist local member associations in devising their own domestic rate structures (see Figure 11.1).

SERVICE FEES

In addition to the three primary sources of revenue described above, there are also transaction based fees that issuers need to incorporate in their pricing schedules.

Cash advance fees

Fees can be charged on cash advances made on credit cards. Consumers normally use their cash or ATM cards to withdraw cash without being charged fees by the issuer. However, ATM

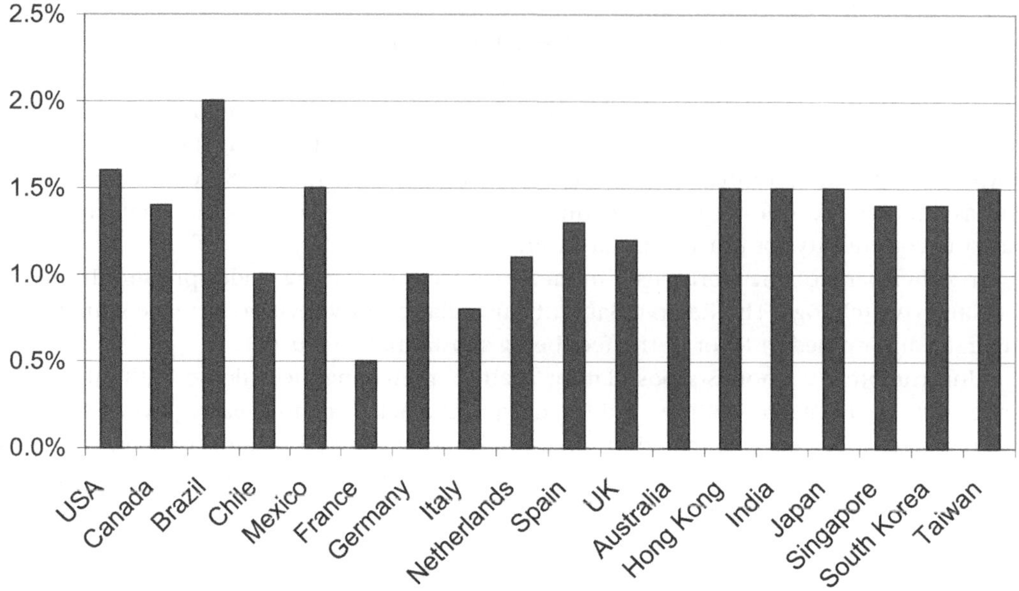

Source: Morgan Stanley Report 2003
(*Note*: Australian Interchange has since been reduced to under 0.60%)

Figure 11.1 Global interchange as per cent of merchant sales

owners sometimes also charge for the use of their machines. Other cash-equivalent transactions may also attract fees such as purchase of casino chips. This is based on the premise that cash transactions inherently carry greater fraud risk for the issuer. In general, issuers commence charging interest on cash advances from the day of cash withdrawal without any free period.

Foreign transaction fees

Banks charge fees for converting foreign transactions into local currency. The card associations charge currency conversion fees for doing the necessary exchange conversion and issuers further charge their own additional fees.

Currency-related fees are different from a disclosure perspective to other fees which are governed by credit terms disclosure rules and regulations such as the Truth in Lending Act in the US and regulations developed by the Federal Reserve Bank. The cardholder does not normally see these charges as they are built into the exchange rate. Even with these fees the cardholder gets a highly competitive rate against alternative currency mechanisms available.

Balance transfer fees

This is a relatively new type of fee that covers administrative and service costs related to balance transfers but is designed to reduce 'rate surfers' – cardholders who move card balances continually to take advantage of introductory interest rates.

Other fees

Issuers charge fees on a number of cardholder requested transactions such as stop-payment requests, statement copies, replacement cards, and so on in order to cover operational and handling expenses relating to these transactions. In some markets, issuers also charge a phone payment fee assessed on customers who pay their card bill over the phone.

RISK-RELATED FEES

There are also risk-related fees which are charged for activities or events that increase the default risk for issuers. These events do not necessarily mean that a debt has become bad or doubtful but indicate the issuer exposure to possible credit losses in the future.

Late payment fees

Issuers charge late payment fees if the payment is received after the due date for whatever reason and may even raise interest rates for future card transactions. While issuers claim that these fees cover risk elements, it is clear that as the card market has become more competitive, issuers have increasingly looked towards risk-related fees to compensate loss of revenues from traditional sources. In the US, late fee revenues for credit cards have increased very significantly in only a few years.

Overlimit fees

This fee is charged if the cardholder exceeds their credit limit and can be as high as the late payment fee.

Costs

In a highly competitive market, issuers are continually under pressure to reduce costs and improve portfolio profitability. But as discussed in the chapter on operations, a card issuer, like any other business, should focus on cost optimization and not simply on cost reduction. Cost optimization is concerned with reducing or containing costs as much as possible but not beyond a level where the business's ability to generate profits is in danger of being impaired. In other words in an attempt to run a lean and mean operation, cutting fat should not result in cutting muscle.

Business managers with product P & L responsibility need to understand the difference between direct and indirect costs. This classification is important for making informed decisions but not for any regulatory or statutory reporting requirements. It is also based on general industry convention which ensures consistency of comparisons across issuers for benchmarking purposes where possible.

The cost categorization is also helpful in understanding the operational profiles resulting from different marketing and operational decisions. Consider the cost schedules of three different issuers as shown in Table 11.2.

- Issuer A operations are relatively more manual and rely primarily on in-house transaction processing with some activities outsourced.
- Issuer B is relatively more automated but retains its technology and operations in-house

Table 11.2 Issuer cost schedule (per account)

	Issuer A	*Issuer B*	*Issuer C*
Direct costs			
Salaries, wages, and benefits	$12.34	$11.73	$4.33
Data processing	$5.89	$11.04	$4.93
Outside processing	$4.55	$1.29	$12.10
Other operational	$13.20	$9.49	$7.20
Sub-total direct costs	$35.98	$33.55	$28.56
Indirect costs			
Credit losses	$11.40	$8.04	$6.43
Fraud losses	$2.40	$1.97	$1.81
Membership fees	$1.76	$1.56	$1.75
Cost of funds	$52.33	$49.88	$34.71
Sub-total indirect costs	$67.89	$61.45	$44.70
TOTAL ISSUER COSTS	$103.87	$95.00	$73.26

having invested significantly in systems and technology. It also demonstrates better results in controlling credit and fraud losses.

- Issuer C has outsourced its operations to third-party processors and has also performed well in controlling risk. Issuer C has a charge card program which explains its relatively low cost of funds. (Charge card issuers fund the purchase during the free period only and do not extend credit beyond that period.)

It should be noted that these costs are 'fully loaded' – in other words they include both fixed and variable costs. For making financial projections for different activity volumes, one must treat the two cost types separately otherwise incorrect calculations will be made.

DIRECT COSTS

This category includes all cost items directly linked to activities or processes that support a card issuing program.

Salaries, wages, and benefits (SWAB)

All costs for salaries, wages, and related benefits, all bonus payments, overtime and shift payments – for both full-time and part-time employees – are included here.

The total number of staff is calculated in terms of full-time equivalent (FTE) employees. For example, an issuer with 20 full-time and 10 part-time employees, who work only half the time every day, employs 20 + (10 x 0.5) = 25 FTE. Direct SWAB costs per FTE is a good indicator of relative labor costs. The FTE calculation is also used to compare productivity through productivity ratios such as 'applications reviewed per FTE' or 'chargebacks processed per FTE'.

At a basic level the extent to which a particular issuer has more labor-intensive or manual operations, as opposed to automated, can be ascertained by a simple comparison of FTE productivity ratios. Issuers with highly automated operations show relatively favorable FTE productivity ratios. In markets where labor is inexpensive, direct SWAB costs may be low, but FTE productivity ratios may be relatively unfavorable. It is also important to note here that issuers who have outsourced their operations will also register favorable productivity ratios as the FTE number will be reduced. Where full general ledger data is not available for assembling total costs, an estimated benefits percentage can be worked out and applied to the total basic salaries and wages amount to calculate total SWAB costs.

Data processing

All system and technology costs – hardware, software, network, and so on – for day-to-day management and maintenance of operations plus apportioned software development costs for the period under review are included in this category. Some costing methodologies also include SWAB costs for data processing staff in this category.

Outside processing

This includes all payments made to third-party providers for transaction processing and other fees paid to outside suppliers. In markets such as the US where there is a general trend to outsource operations, this is an important cost category. Other than authorization and transaction processing charges, this cost also includes fees paid to outside collection agencies for recovering overdue receivables. Any charges paid to local or international payment schemes for transaction processing are also included in this category.

Other operational

All costs not included in the categories above are included here. These cost items are incurred for the general operation and management of a card-issuing business. These include:

- rent and occupancy costs
- telephone and general telecommunications
- furniture and fixtures
- postage
- travel and entertainment
- stationery and supplies
- expenses from other units – branch/corporate banking costs (allocations).

While these cost descriptions are self-explanatory, it is worthwhile to discuss the cost subcategory 'expenses from other units' within a bank in the context of payment cards. Bank branches perform a number of activities for payment cards especially marketing and customer service. In general, from a product perspective, most credit and charge card activities are performed by the card center. Customer servicing enquiries received at the branch are referred to the card center. However, for debit cards, branch costs assume much greater significance because debit cards are part of the checking or current account. Checking or current account costs are recorded in the retail banking business unit and not in the card center. For costing purposes, costs have to be identified from the retail banking business ledger and included in debit card costs. Similarly for corporate card products, a number of cost items are included in the books of the bank's corporate banking arm and suitable allocations need to be made to arrive at the full or complete payment card costs.

INDIRECT COSTS

Indirect costs do not directly relate to activities or operational business processes and include the following.

Credit losses

Most credit card loans are unsecured. This means that, unlike in other financial services such as mortgage lending, the lender (the issuing bank in this case) does not hold collateral assets that they can dispose of to recover their debt. Irrecoverable loans are charged off, and provisions are made against those considered doubtful. A provision keeps the debt on the books but charges it (or a part of it) against issuing income for that period. If a written-off debt is recovered, the amount is accounted for as other income or used to reduce the credit loss for that period. If a debt which has been provided for in the books is recovered through the debt collection efforts of the company or outside agencies, the balances for receivables and for provisions are accordingly adjusted. The cost category here therefore represents total losses and provisions net of any recoveries. Credit losses are usually expressed as a percentage of the cardholder receivables.

For debit cards and commercial cards products, credit losses are relatively small. This is because cardholders do not normally borrow on these products. Debit card payment is immediate and most commercial cardholders pay on the due date like other accounts payable transactions.

Fraud losses

Fraud losses, under most circumstances, are borne by the issuer. This category includes losses resulting from all types of fraud, such as counterfeit, lost and stolen, card not received, and so on. Fraud losses are usually expressed as percentage of card sales volumes.

Fraud losses are equally relevant to all types of card products. However, certain transaction types, such as offline, mail order, or Internet transactions, attract higher fraud losses.

Cost of funds

Cost of funds is usually the single largest cost item in the books of a credit card issuer. When a purchase is made, the acquiring bank pays the merchant immediately or in a few days depending upon the market and the technology involved. The issuing bank then pays the acquiring bank and charges the item to the cardholder's account. The issuing institution has to finance the purchase from the time it pays the acquirer to when it actually receives payment from the cardholder. This financing cost is called cost of funds.

The cost is directly linked to two key categories: the free or grace period in terms of number of days and the cost-of-funds rate. In some developed markets, the free period for credit cards averages from 40 to 60 days for ordinary credit cards. The cost-of-funds rate varies from issuer to issuer depending upon the borrowing capacity and credit profile of the card issuer. Large banks are able to borrow more cheaply in the open market than their smaller rivals. Banks with large retail deposits that do not attract high rates of interest also have inexpensive access to funds with which to finance the card receivables.

For debit cards, this cost is very low because the issuer deducts the purchase from the cardholder's account and the payment is immediate. In some markets where transactions work on a delayed debit cycle, funds have to be financed, though for a shorter period of time.

This funding cost is highly significant for commercial cards which offer generous free periods due to competitive pressures but generally do not revolve. In other words there is a financing cost involved without much financing income to be generated.

Credit card securitization helps in reducing cost of funds. Many issuers, like mortgage lenders, securitize part of their receivables which means these loans are used to issue asset backed securities to investors who then effectively own the risks and rewards in relation to those assets. Securitization is discussed at length in a chapter at the end of this book.

Product profitability

Product managers should be familiar with the 'marginal costing' techniques for decision making.

In full costing, we use fully loaded costs. That means all direct and indirect costs are included. Any long-term investments, for example in systems and technology, are apportioned, depreciated, or amortized over their useful lives and included in the profit and loss account in the usual manner in accordance with generally accepted accounting principles.

But for business decision making, we are interested in marginal costs and revenues only – the additional costs and revenues that will result from the proposed undertaking or project. To draw up the projected future cash flows expected for a new product or service, we simply use the additional revenues and additional costs that are directly due to introducing the new product. In other words, when preparing the business plan for a new product, product costs should not include corporate overhead or any other allocation. Additionally, the business plan should only focus on future revenues and costs: any past costs – also called 'sunk' costs – should be excluded from projected cash flows for determining the net present value of the business investment under review.

CHAPTER 12 *Business Process Analysis*

In previous chapters we reviewed how a card-issuing business is structured into various departments and groups: departments such as marketing, operations, and risk management represent the workplace organization and staff hierarchies. In an earlier chapter we discussed the various business processes related to the operations department. We also looked at costs incurred in running a card-issuing business and how various cost items, such as salaries, data processing, credit losses, and so on are classified into direct and indirect cost categories. But this type of costing does not tell us anything about how the business is being managed: which parts of the business are running efficiently and profitably; which are slow and expensive?

To analyze the card-issuing business and look deeper into its constituent parts, we need to undertake business process analysis for the issuing business as a whole. The card-issuing business consists of a number of business processes or functional activities that are undertaken to run and manage the business. Some processes such as fraud investigation may be completely managed within one organizational department. Others such as new account acquisition may traverse more than one department (marketing, risk management, operations). To fully understand how a process works, how much it costs, and how efficient it is, we must map a process end to end across all departments.

In this chapter, we will review end-to-end card-issuing business processes in detail for credit and charge cards and how they vary for debit and commercial cards.

It is important for card managers to construct a complete view of the card-issuing business and also of its constituent parts. To enhance efficiency one must be able to identify processes that have room for improvement or where it makes sense to outsource a specific process altogether.

To determine the operational cost for each process, direct costs (such as salaries and wages described in Chapter 11) obtained from the cost ledger are allocated to the various business processes to which they relate based on acceptable and reasonable criteria such as FTE numbers, square footage, computer processing time utilized, storage capacity required and so on. This allocation process helps us to understand how the costs are incurred and what parts of the process value chain are costing too much without adding much value. By definition, only direct costs are allocated to business processes. The allocations should be made with reasonable but not exact precision. This is important because quite often management accountants spend considerable time, effort, and money in making precise allocations (finding exact square footage details for allocating occupancy costs of heat and electricity to all business processes) without a proportional increase in costing relevance.

So if we analyze the activities of a card-issuing business and classify them into business processes, we can develop a list that covers the entire business value chain. The processes are listed below:

- marketing
- credit evaluation and account acquisition
- card production
- authorization processing
- transaction processing
- statement generation or cardholder billing
- payment processing
- credit risk management
- fraud risk management
- customer service
- general management and non-core operations.

The cost schedule in the previous chapter can be presented in an alternative format, as shown in Table 12.1, that shows costs of the card-issuing business processes instead of ledger cost items.

Note that the direct cost sub-total in Table 12.1 is the same as the (sub) total cost of business processes in Table 11.2.

Table 12.1 Issuer cost schedule (per account); alternative format

	Issuer A	*Issuer B*	*Issuer C*
Direct business processes costs			
Marketing	$2.12	$2.36	$3.20
Credit evaluation and account acquisition	$1.00	$1.73	$2.34
Card production	$3.10	$3.44	$0.95
Authorization processing	$5.20	$6.73	$2.30
Transaction processing	$4.30	$3.66	$2.30
Statement generation	$3.34	$1.32	$1.45
Payment processing	$6.60	$7.21	$3.30
Credit risk management	$3.45	$2.48	$4.40
Fraud risk management	$2.40	$1.50	$4.23
Customer service	$1.12	$1.48	$2.10
General management and non-core ops	$3.35	$1.64	$1.99
Sub-total costs of business processes	$35.98	$33.55	$28.56
Indirect costs			
Credit losses	$11.40	$8.04	$6.43
Fraud losses	$2.40	$1.97	$1.81
Membership fees	$1.76	$1.56	$1.75
Cost of funds	$52.33	$49.88	$34.71
Sub-total indirect costs	$67.89	$61.45	$44.70
TOTAL ISSUER COSTS	$103.87	$95.00	$73.26

Card issuer business processes

What does each card-issuing business process consist of? In this section we will review these at a high level.

MARKETING

Marketing includes all activities involved in developing or modifying offers to acquire new cardholders or persuade existing cardholders to spend more on their payment cards. These cover market research, customer profiling and segmentation for preparing target customer lists, product development and testing, product enhancements, promotions, and advertising across all channels (summarized in Figure 12.1).

Credit and charge cards

Marketing activities include:

- commissioning and acquiring external market research;
- purchasing/acquiring external customer lists;
- segmenting and profiling customers from internal customer database;
- developing and implementing new products and services;
- developing and implementing enhancements or modifications to existing products and services;
- design, development, and execution of marketing campaigns;
- design and development of solicitation materials across all channels;
- testing new offer and recording feedback.

Debit cards

Debit cards require minimal marketing if offered as part of the checking or current account product of the bank. If debit cards are offered as separate products with rewards linked to spending, marketing activities include most of those listed above. However, even if debit cards are offered as products in their own right, they are only offered in conjunction with the checking accounts offered by the banks. From this perspective debit card marketing is essentially marketing for the checking account.

Commercial cards

Commercial card marketing is directed at businesses and large companies. This results in longer solicitation cycles requiring more time, effort, and expense to complete a sale. For large corporations, the sales effort is targeted at the CFO or the COO level or to the head of the procurement division. The ownership of the marketing effort usually rests with the

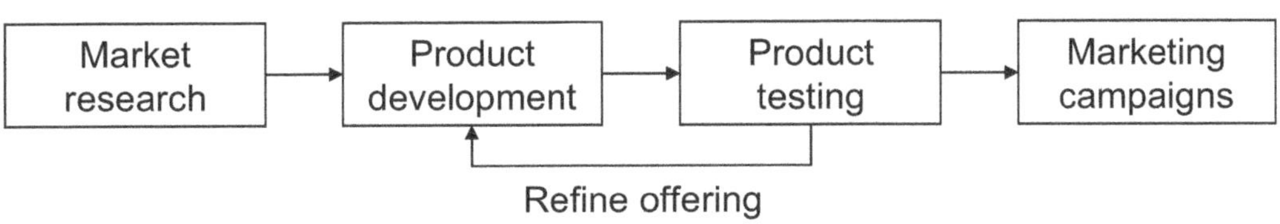

Figure 12.1 Marketing; process flow

corporate banking division. But for business card products designed for smaller businesses, the business owner or manager is the key decision maker and card marketing techniques for business cards are not too dissimilar to those for consumer cards.

CREDIT EVALUATION AND ACCOUNT ACQUISITION

This business process includes activities related to new accounts such as credit reviews using credit-scoring techniques for evaluating new customers and modifying credit limits for existing customers. Account acquisition includes the setting up of new accounts on the customer information file and other related databases. The process flow is shown in Figure 12.2.

Credit and charge cards

Activities include:

- obtaining credit reports from credit agencies;
- reviewing and processing inquiries for balance transfer applications;
- setting up balance transfers on system;
- reviewing and processing modifications in credit limits for existing customers based on customer requests or automatic prompts based on programmed criteria;
- setting up credit limit changes on system;
- ensuring necessary compliance procedures;
- reviewing and processing applications for new accounts;
- communicating decision to customers;
- setting up new account on customer information file;
- storing credit evaluation details;
- generating and mailing PIN information (if applicable).

Debit cards

Debit cards do not involve detailed credit checks or the setting up of separate and standalone customer accounts on the system. Debit cards work as access devices to a customer's checking account just like checks. Information verification is completed when an account is opened and any credit reviews are undertaken at that level particularly when a credit facility such as an overdraft is requested. The relevant activities for debit cards within

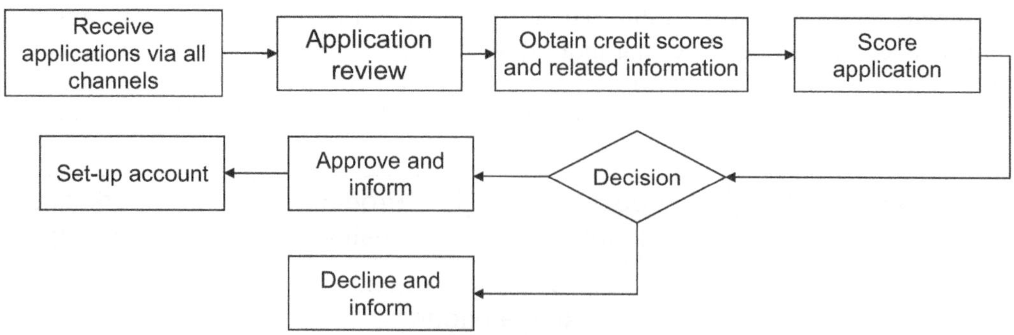

Figure 12.2 Credit evaluation and account acquisition; process flow

this business process are the setup and linkage of card details to the checking account and PIN generation and delivery.

Commercial cards

Commercial card activities in this area are generally similar to the ones detailed above for credit and charge cards with a few key differences. Credit evaluation is usually undertaken at the business or corporate level. The credit standing of the business is reviewed as a whole based on available information, recent financial statements, and tax returns. Banks and non-bankcard companies offer a portfolio of products and services to their business clients. Credit evaluation is undertaken for the entire offering not just cards. In most cases individual employees are not credit checked. However, work steps relating to account setup on the master file, notifications, and PIN generation and delivery are undertaken at the employee level.

CARD PRODUCTION

Plastic card production consists of developing, preparing, personalizing, and delivering cards and related materials to new customers and reissuing cards to existing cardholders (see Figure 12.3). The activities of PIN generation and delivery are included in the account setup function above.

Activities for all types of card are similar, as follows:

- procuring new magnetic stripe or chip embedded cards in bulk;
- maintaining and controlling card stock;
- developing new card information file;
- preparing cards – embossing, encoding, and personalizing;
- developing information file for reissue of cards;
- preparing card envelopes/packets ready for delivery;

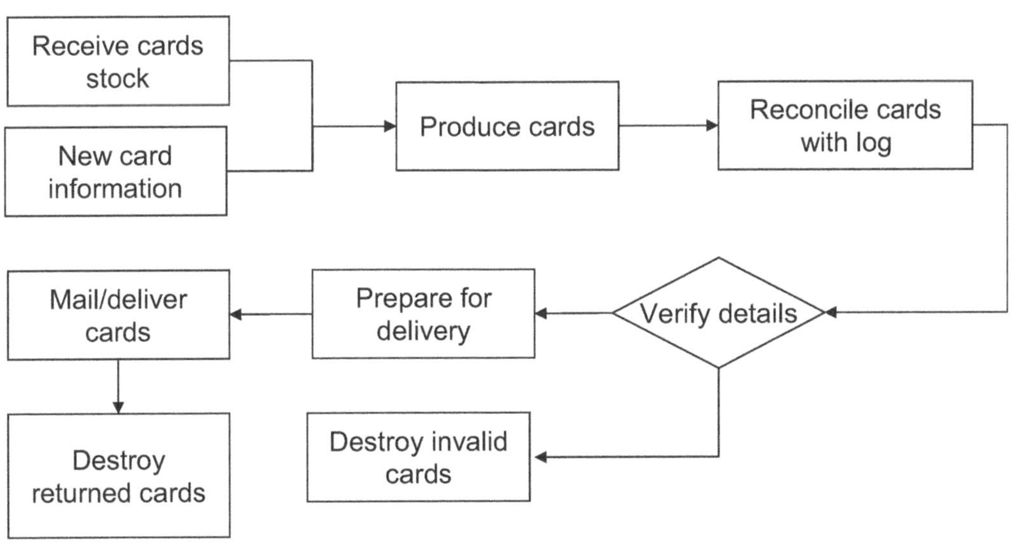

Figure 12.3 Card production; process flow

- delivering cards to customers by:
  - mail
  - secure delivery
  - special courier
  - customer pick-up at branch or other physical location;
- researching reasons for undelivered cards.

AUTHORIZATION PROCESSING

Transaction authorization consists of receiving and processing transaction authorization messages from acquirers and merchants across all channels; then communicating approval or denial back to the requester based on available funds or credit limit and/or credit and fraud risk parameters (see Figure 12.4).

Authorization activities for credit and charge cards include:

- setting up and managing of floor limits for authorization requests;
- receiving and processing automated and manual transaction authorization requests;
- approving or denying requests;
- communicating authorization decision to requester;
- handling manual authorization requests relating to referral inquiries;
- managing and maintaining authorization files and system parameters.

Debit cards and commercial card activities within the transaction authorization process are similar to those for credit and charge cards. In many markets, it may be necessary to authorize all debit card and commercial card transactions based on local payment system rules.

The reduction in telecommunication costs over the past several years, due to increased competition – especially in markets where previously state-owned telecommunication companies operated in monopolistic environments – has made it possible to reduce floor limits and approve a greater percentage of transactions than previously viable. Chip cards

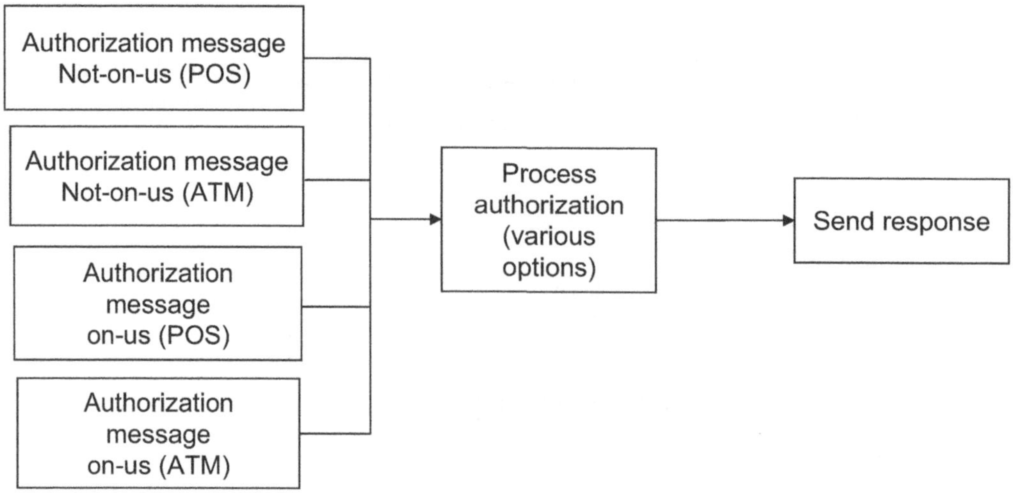

Figure 12.4 Authorization; process flow

do not require high levels of online authorization as they can verify cardholder identity against security parameters personalized on to the card.

TRANSACTION PROCESSING

This covers activities related to the receipt and processing of incoming transactions (both POS and cash) including charging of transactions to individual accounts and processing of cardholder chargebacks (see Figure 12.5).

Transaction processing activities for credit and charge cards include:

- receiving and processing incoming transactions in real time or in batches, and classifying incoming data into on-us transactions and interchange transactions (data received from other acquirers for settlement purposes);
- reviewing transaction logs and exception file logs;
- researching exception file logs;
- preparing data for settlement of interchange transactions;
- charging of transactions to individual cardholder accounts;
- receiving and processing requests for copy (transaction vouchers) from cardholders and from risk management in connection with fraud and credit research;
- handling exception items and disputes including root cause investigation;
- reviewing, preparing, and processing chargeback transactions;
- preparing and posting ledger entries for settled and charged-back transactions and losses resulting from chargebacks.

Debit cards and commercial card activities within the transaction processing area are similar to those for credit and charge cards.

A key advantage of corporate and business cards is the additional transaction-related information that is captured at the POS and passed on to the issuer. The issuer processes it and presents it back to the cardholders in individual and consolidated billing statements.

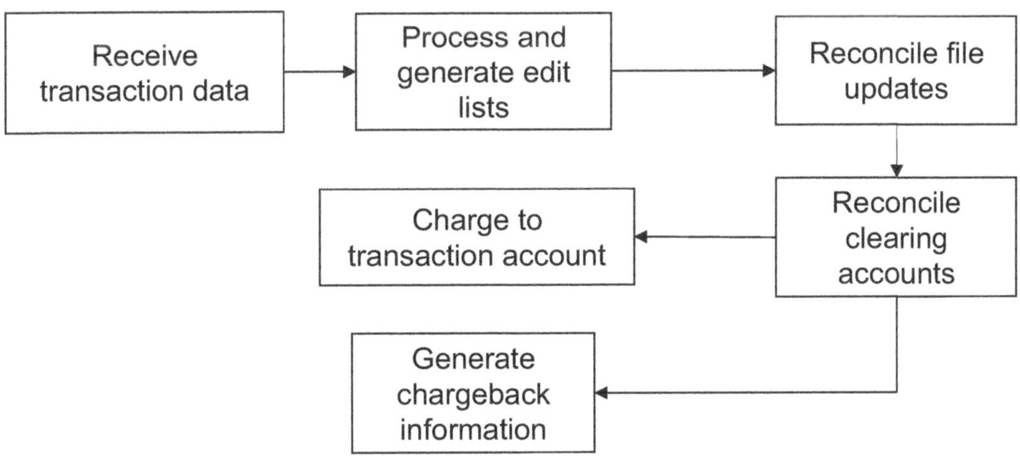

Figure 12.5 Transaction processing; process flow

However, in many markets, no additional information is captured and transaction processing activities are the same for all card products.

STATEMENT GENERATION

Statement generation or cardholder billing relates to the preparation and delivery of cardholder statements by mail or over electronic means such as e-mail, the web, or SMS text messaging (see Figure 12.6).

Credit and charge cards

Activities include:

- developing statement format and design – for paper and online statements;
- extracting monetary and non-monetary transaction information;
- formatting and generating cardholder statements;
- storing statements for availability across available channels;
- delivering statements: preparing, sorting, and mailing envelopes for paper statements; e-mail notification to cardholders of online availability of latest statement; special handling for selected statements where applicable;
- researching returned statement mail and undelivered e-mails;
- correcting delivery information and where applicable re-mailing paper statement and re-emailing.

Debit cards

Separate statements are not prepared and mailed for debit cards. Debit cards purchases and cash withdrawals appear on the regular bank statement in the same manner as check payments or deposits.

Commercial cards

In commercial card products, statement generation for corporate T&E and purchasing cards differs markedly from regular consumer cards. Line managers throughout the purchasing organization and the central procurement department staff need to review, monitor, and analyze purchasing activity on a continuous basis. Issuers provide regular detailed statements from a number of perspectives such as purchasing activity by department, cost center, merchant sector, and by specific merchants – with line item details and tax information, if

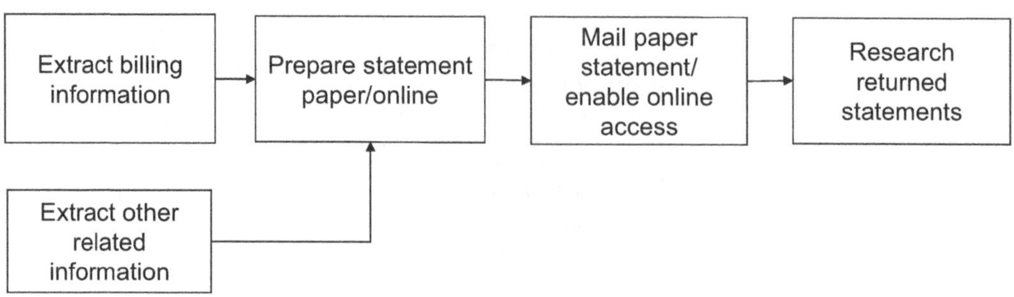

Figure 12.6 Statement generation; process flow

available. Issuers also offer customizable reporting and tools to access raw transaction data, over a secure closed network or over the Internet, which can be manipulated and utilized for consolidated reporting purposes by the purchasing organization. For the business card product, issuers in general supply regular consumer card type statements but some provide some flexible and customizable reporting features as described above.

PAYMENT PROCESSING

Payment processing broadly covers activities linked to cardholder remittances (via branches or physical collection points, checks, electronic bill payment, automated transfers) and crediting of payments received to cardholder accounts (see Figure 12.7).

Credit and charge cards

Activities include:

- receiving and processing payments received – cash, checks, payment slips, electronic transaction files for online bill payments files from third-party billers or website with payment option and so on;
- balancing control totals and investigating incomplete information on remittances or checks received without cardholder information;
- processing direct debit mandates where payments are automatically debited to checking account on specific dates every month;
- receiving and processing electronic payments through online bill payment providers;
- handling exception items – returned checks, balancing and posting errors and so on;
- crediting online bill payment provider/collection agent/lockbox bank's account on receipt of funds;
- crediting cardholder accounts;
- storage of payment records as applicable.

Debit cards

Payment processing is irrelevant for debit cards as funds are immediately deducted from the customer's checking account.

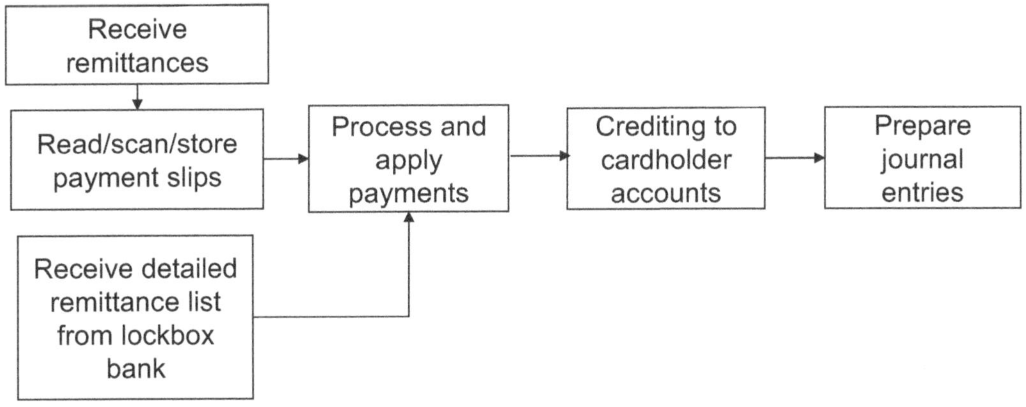

Figure 12.7 Payment processing; process flow

Commercial cards

Commercial card payments are usually made with direct debits to the business checking account especially for business and purchasing cards. For corporate T&E cards, the payment processing function may involve payment by cash, check, or online bill payment.

CREDIT RISK MANAGEMENT

The process of credit risk management involves reviewing, monitoring, and collecting outstanding balances. This includes behavior profiling for predictive purposes, management of delinquent, overlimit, and written-off accounts, and recovery procedures (see Figure 12.8).

Credit and charge cards

Activities include:

- preparing and utilizing behavioral scoring models for predicting credit defaults;
- preparing ageing reports for cardholder balances;
- preparing and sending payment reminders and notices;
- initiating recovery procedures through recovery call plans usually in conjunction with collection agencies – pre and post provision/write-off;
- reviewing and taking action on delinquent cases;
- reporting to credit bureaus where applicable;
- card retrieval procedures – blocking account and capturing cards at customer contact points;
- reviewing overlimit cases – obtaining updated credit reports, extending credit limits or blocking accounts;
- unblocking accounts where payment is received or alternative settlement arrangements have been made;
- making accounting provisions or effecting write-offs.

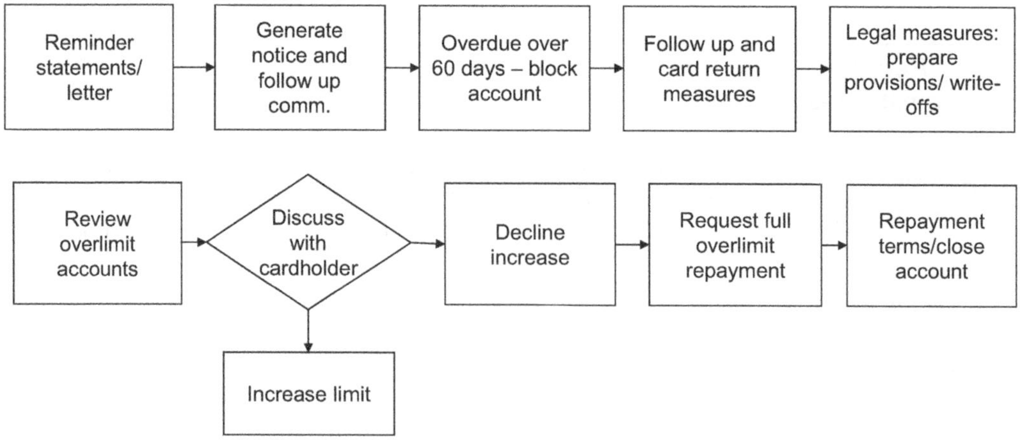

Figure 12.8 Credit risk management; process flow

Debit cards

Credit risk management and collections risk activities relating to debit cards are part of the overall retail bank credit risk management. Debit cards do not have a standalone collections function and any debit balances on customer accounts (receivables) are linked to overdrafts or overdrawn checking accounts.

Commercial cards

For business card products, net receivables at the end of a statement period are usually transferred to the business checking account and any risk management or collection activities form part of the overall relationship management between the bank and the business organization. For corporate T&E and purchasing cards credit risk management falls within the ambit of the corporate banking division where the bank's overall exposure is reviewed.

FRAUD RISK MANAGEMENT

Risk management activities for the prevention and investigation of cardholder fraud including identifying and monitoring suspect activity, receiving lost/stolen reports, investigating missing and counterfeit card usage and so on, are included in this business process (see Figure 12.9).

Activities for all cards are broadly similar, as follows:

- developing, modifying, and enhancing fraud management systems and procedures as applicable (internal, bureau operated, local payment networks, or international scheme);
- identifying, reviewing, and researching fraudulent applications for new cards;
- identifying, reviewing, and researching reported fraudulent transaction and reports of usage of lost, stolen, or counterfeit cards;
- where applicable reporting fraudulent activity for scheme-operated risk bulletins to other issuers and for hot card files;
- undertaking manual fraud prevention procedures such as flagging of suspect transactions, initiating customer contact, and undertaking related research;
- blocking card accounts, creating new accounts and transferring customer details, balance, and transaction information;
- preparing legal casework and providing assistance in criminal investigations.

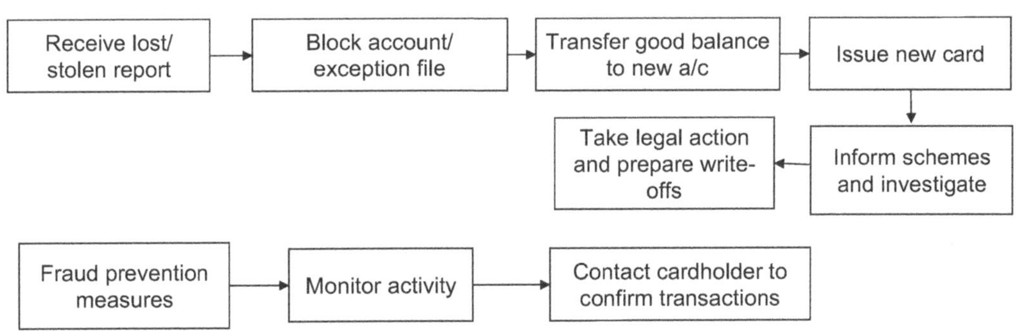

Figure 12.9 Fraud risk management; process flow

CUSTOMER SERVICE

Customer service activities involve responding to and resolving customer queries and requests across all channels (see Figure 12.10).

Activities for credit and charge cards include:

- developing and modifying customer service strategy including related quality control measures;
- receiving, reviewing, and incorporating new customer information on primary customer databases as reported by customers or received from other sources;
- receiving, reviewing, researching, and resolving queries and requests from customers;
- effecting account transfers;
- managing account terminations;
- cardholder behavior profiling and activity tracking to stimulate card usage;
- initiating service-related customer contact across all channels for notifications, general communications, or overall relationship improvement endeavors.

Customer service activities for debit cards are part of the overall retail banking relationship.

For commercial card products, service activities are similar to those for consumer cards. For large organizations, the card issuer, however, may allocate special service teams and dedicated account representatives exclusively to relationship management with the client organization.

GENERAL MANAGEMENT AND NON-CORE OPERATIONS

This area consists of a number of activities for the general management and supervision of the card-issuing business. At a high level these include:

- general management;
- liaising on payment system or international scheme related programs;
- strategic planning and development;
- management information reporting;
- financial management and accounting.

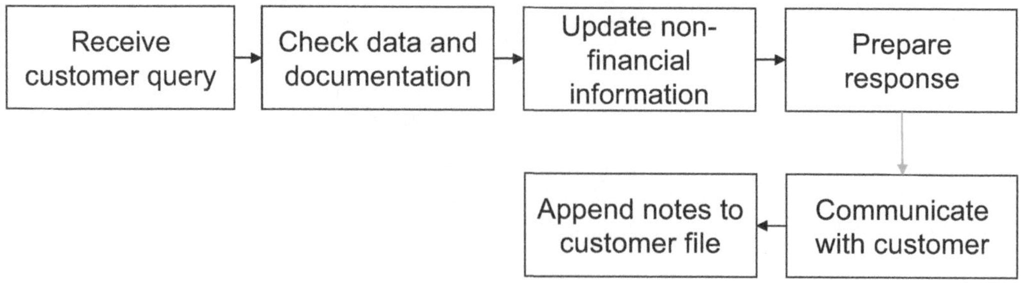

Figure 12.10 Customer service; process flow

Benchmarking

Benchmarking is a process of comparative analysis and evaluation of a business's performance against internal or external competitors. For it to be effective, benchmarking analysis is usually undertaken regularly over a period of time to fully understand the strategic and operational underpinnings of variations in competitor performance.

Once business processes have been analyzed, costed, and where possible, re-engineered, the card issuer should monitor process efficiency and costs over a period of time. The reasons for any efficiency gains or losses should be investigated and identified. Similarly the rise and fall in process unit costs should be explored to yield valuable information about the management and control of operational costs.

INTERNAL BENCHMARKING

Issuers regularly compare marketing campaign performance by comparing take-up and usage performance. Direct mail response ratios, applications reviewed, and applications approved are some of the performance indicators used. These indicators or ratios can be purely performance based (efficiency ratios) or may use cost data as well (cost efficiency ratios).

Internal benchmarking is also very useful where there are competing internal units in a geographically dispersed organization and also for tracking progress over time. A key convenience in internal benchmarking is the ready availability of internal data that does not face any confidentiality issues.

EXTERNAL BENCHMARKING

External benchmarking is a highly useful exercise because it allows issuers to make comparisons with competitors within the card industry and, where possible, with other organizations across industries.

The key problem with external benchmarking is the availability of information, as many market players are hesitant to contribute data for fear of breach of confidentiality. Specialist organizations undertake such comparisons utilizing strict confidentiality codes and present their results in a manner that shows the participant's results against the pool average only if the participant pool is large enough that no single data contribution can dominate the average. Visa and MasterCard undertake cost studies with their member banks and publish benchmarks. However, these reports are circulated selectively and are not available to the general public.

CHAPTER

13 *Future of Payment Cards*

In the dot-com years so many payment products were developed that credit card companies began to seriously worry about their future. They feared that, in an increasingly networked world, smaller and nimbler competitors, harnessing the openness of the Internet, would bypass the established, expensive, proprietary, and closed payment networks of the card companies.

These new payment products introduced novel ways to pay for purchases over the Internet – touting speed, convenience, additional functionality, and enhanced transaction security. A majority of the new products were designed for the Internet. Focus-group wisdom and countless consumer surveys indicated that people were afraid to use their credit cards over the Internet for fear of online fraud. These new fully secure methods of payment, it was claimed, would liberate legions of previously cautious buyers to shop like mad over the Internet. To match the cool image of the Internet, these products came with colorful names like Beenz, Flooz, and CyberCash. As it turned out, credit card companies need not have worried. Today many of these products populate the virtual graveyards of cyberspace while payment cards continue to be the preferred means of payment over the Internet in most countries and are likely to remain so in the near future.

Payment cards are also the dominant non-cash method of payment in the real world. Every year, billions of dollars of purchases are made with payment cards at shops, by mail order, or over the telephone. It is highly unlikely that people's preference for plastic will change in the coming years. In lesser-developed markets, where most payments are still made by cash, payment cards are undergoing remarkable growth and transaction volumes continue to rise.

Reasons for success

The reasons for the phenomenal success achieved by the payment card industry in such a short time can be attributed to the following.

CONVENIENCE

The success of payment cards is rooted in customer psychology. Familiar customer experiences are extremely difficult to displace or substitute. Familiarity does not necessarily breed contempt: it breeds preference and a perception of relative convenience. Paying for purchases is routine stuff – and everyone hates to learn new things for routine stuff. None of the new Internet payment products offered the familiar customer experience of paying with cards but demanded, instead, that consumers invest time and energy in following multi-step instructions to download and install odd pieces of software which often required more work and helpdesk calls than expected.

There has to be a very strong reason to use a new payment instrument designed for a specific channel. Why use a new payment method, when payment cards can easily do the job? If a transaction takes place remotely – by mail or over the phone or the Internet – all a buyer needs to do is send the card details to the merchant to process payment. It does not matter what mode of communication exists between the two parties – the only requirement being that card details be sent safely and securely. The Internet, telephone dial-up, broadband, mobile phones, interactive digital TV, and wi-fi are all card friendly.

GLOBAL BRAND

Consumers and merchants globally do not speak of bankcards; they talk in terms of Visa, MasterCard, or American Express. Global brand recognition places the bankcard product on the same level as Coke and Nike in terms of consumer awareness and confidence. Similarly, for bankcards, the global interchange system inspires confidence in both consumers and merchants that the product will work as anticipated and that all parties will receive the benefits they desire.

WORLDWIDE ACCEPTANCE

The near ubiquitous acceptance at all types of retailers – even at unattended places such as car parks – and the ability to obtain cash from automated teller machines at any time are of critical importance to the customer.

Retailing is not a local phenomenon anymore. When paying a merchant in a different country the buyer cannot just write a check and mail it. Banks are still not efficiently geared for personal cross-border payments and foreign payments can be expensive and quite frequently, time-consuming. With payment cards, it is as easy to make a cross-border payment as a local one. The exchange rate conversion is built into the billing system: the buyer and seller pay and receive in their local currencies. Additionally, there is the added convenience of obtaining local currency from cash machines, bank branches, and currency exchange bureaus for travelers.

Plenty of payment products claimed to offer some or all of these winning features but consumers were not impressed. Other than clever names and funky websites, there were no additional features on offer, no extra conveniences to benefit from, and hardly any innovations to make life easier. And not just that, some products even required consumers to pay with their payment cards first in order to 'fund' these payment instruments.

But one payment system, PayPal, has skillfully exploited a key weakness in the existing payment card systems. It caters to sellers on the popular online auction marketplace eBay. These sellers are generally too small or too risky to meet the card-acceptance criteria set by the card companies and rely on checks to get paid. Quite early on, PayPal recognized the opportunity to serve the needs of eBay sellers. More on PayPal later.

FLEXIBLE LOW-COST INFRASTRUCTURE

The technology involved in operating a bankcard issuing business is powerful and flexible, and consequently provides financial institutions with a great deal of latitude in managing the infrastructure required to issue cards. It also enables issuers to locate facilities in low-cost areas while servicing clients thousands of miles away.

The ability to manage the cost associated with servicing cardholders anywhere in the world provides issuers with the capabilities required to expand globally without having to make significant capital investments in new facilities and systems.

Perspectives on the future

GROWTH IN PAYMENT CARDS

Card numbers and purchase volumes continue to grow for all the major global and regional payment systems. In the more mature markets of the world, where card penetration is near saturation point, innovative marketing techniques and technology developments are helping to increase transaction volumes and reduce inefficiencies. Brand and product loyalty are becoming increasingly important factors. In some markets, such as the US, debit cards are driving market growth. While in others, such as Turkey, it is expected that future growth will come from good old-fashioned credit card products.

Debit cards replace the expensive and inefficient method of paying with paper checks. In European traditionally check-heavy economies, such as the UK and France, debit cards have already made substantial inroads with millions of cards in use.

PAYMENT CARDS ON THE INTERNET

Internet access is becoming cheaper, faster, and more reliable. In many households, thanks to broadband, the Internet is always available. You can quickly and easily search for an item, compare prices and features, order, and safely pay for it using your payment card from the comfort of your living room. From buying groceries, to books and clothes, to purchasing tickets for a movie in your local area, the Internet is gradually becoming an indispensable and reliable shopping tool. Online retailers are continually improving the reliability of their order fulfillment and delivery systems. Websites such as Google, Yahoo, and others are assisting information-based buying by locating relevant information on features and prices about millions of products from all across the world. If you are thinking of buying a digital camera, you are much more likely to go online, read up, find one that suits you, and seek the best price available.

The online buying process is simple. The buyer enters their card and relevant personal details on an online form and in a few seconds the order is completed and goods can be shipped. Of course you have to wait before you lay your hands on the camera but the wait is well worth the money you may have saved. The process is simple with no extra software to be downloaded or payment registration process to go through or a long password to remember. You pay for your purchases in a retail store with your payment card. Why not use the card online and have all your payments appear on one statement?

However, there are certain markets where customers prefer other forms of payment. Germans prefer to pay through a direct bank transfer, a mechanism called 'accept giro', but they are an exception and it is likely that at some point their payment preferences may change in favor of payment cards. The general trend in the US and Europe is that online card usage dominates all forms of payment and is on the rise. It is safe to say that payment cards will continue to dominate the Internet for many years to come.

One area where online sales are booming is the travel and entertainment sector. Customers book flights, hotels, and cars online for vacations and even business trips as they realize they can get better deals over the Internet. Many airlines offer discounts for online purchases as they save travel agent commissions and call center costs on online transactions. Indeed a few, like easyJet in Great Britain offer online ticketing only.

THREAT FROM ONLINE FRAUD

But the good news about this significant and growing trend in online sales comes with a significant and growing problem. Online card fraud is increasing at an alarming rate and in the US alone, by far the largest market in the world, online fraud now accounts for nearly half of all cardholder fraud. Grim news indeed for the retailers. Under current payment scheme rules, all fraud on card-not-present transactions which include mail order, telephone order (collectively called MOTO), and Internet orders, can be charged back to the retailer. Retailers have always considered this unfair and yet another example of banks forcing them to accept non-negotiable conditions that work in their favor. Banks say that these card-not-present transactions are risky as customer verification, such as PIN, signature or picture identification, and other counterfeit checking measures (that can only be applied when the card is used at a POS terminal) cannot be satisfactorily undertaken. Without verifying identity of the cardholder and the authenticity of the card, the transaction is highly risky. Actual fraud data supports this view.

There are initiatives in place that mitigate this risk, such as the address verification service (AVS), in which all goods ordered remotely are dispatched to the cardholder's registered address, but still a majority of total fraud takes place on card-not-present transactions (Internet and MOTO).

Large retailers can negotiate better terms with their acquirers. For business relationship purposes the acquirer will sometimes bear the chargeback loss and not pass it to the retailer. But since ultimately the responsibility for absorbing the loss is the retailer's, this situation does not encourage retailers to invest in online commerce infrastructure. Insurance companies have been quick to spot this and offer chargeback insurance on card-not-present transactions to retailers, but premiums are relatively high and do not always make financial sense to wary retailers.

To remedy the problem, card associations have developed initiatives to enhance online security and reduce fraud. Visa, MasterCard, and American Express developed the secure electronic transactions (SET) protocol that relies on public key infrastructure (PKI) technology. It was engineered elegantly but proved too cumbersome for retailers and cardholders alike. Digital certificates from a trusted authority (TA) have to be downloaded and uploaded and updated making the whole process confusing and complicated. The technology never gained wide acceptance except for a few small markets. Tiny smartcard readers in computers designed to turn personal computers into personal POS terminals were another option explored by card companies, but like SET it did not gather enough support from stakeholders involved. Computer manufacturers did not see the need to produce and supply smartcard readers, being already under extreme market pressure to cut unit prices.

The payment schemes offer simpler online security solutions. It is hoped that these will be implemented by both card companies and retailers. The schemes are actively encouraging all participants to implement these measures. Visa's 'verified by Visa' and MasterCard's 'SecureCode' both require a PIN from cardholders wishing to make an online purchase. It is argued that remembering and entering the PIN is not a new customer experience and therefore will be more acceptable to customers than downloading special software containing digital certificates. The only hurdle being that they will have to register first – a simple one-time process that is relatively painless. To encourage retailers they are using a 'liability shift' approach roughly similar to the one deployed in the chip card initiative. Retailers who implement these initiatives will not be liable for fraudulent transactions anymore, thus making a considerable improvement in their bottom lines.

Cardholders are generally protected against fraud. By scheme rules, their liability is limited to a small amount. Many issuers even offer complete protection although many consumers appear to be ignorant of this simple benefit.

DIGITAL WALLETS

The focus in recent years has been to make things easier for cardholders on the Internet. Special software solutions such as digital wallets make online buying easier while other customizable applications help issuers offer better customer service online. Digital wallets have been developed to automate the card details entry process. Instead of entering card details with every online purchase, a laborious, repetitive, and often annoying process, consumers can store their payment card details that the wallet software can automatically enter on to the online order form.

Payment segments

The payment cards industry offers a number of opportunities in the existing as well as in new and unexploited market segments. We will review these opportunities in three categories:

EXISTING PAYMENT SEGMENT OPPORTUNITIES

Further globalization

Continued expansion of the bankcard product into new markets around the globe is already well under way. Emerging markets and developing countries are areas of future growth for bankcard issuers. Cultural aversion to credit in other markets around the globe is slowly fading, and consequently increasing the attractiveness of these markets for issuers.

Expanded product utility

Even in the most mature bankcard markets today such as the US, UK, and Canada, cash and checks are still dominant, so there is a lot of room for bankcard usage to grow.

To capture this growth, issuers need to exploit the opportunity to add further utility to the bankcard product, most likely by capitalizing on the information accumulated via card use by consumers.

New partnerships

Bankcard issuers have many opportunities to create new, more valuable product offerings by expanding the current partnership model beyond co-branding and affinity relationships. Unique partnerships with government, technology suppliers, and service companies hold the promise of expanding the base of potential bankcard clients.

EMERGING PAYMENT SEGMENT OPPORTUNITIES

While cards dominate retail sales there are other types of payments that continue to prove elusive. Card companies have been trying hard to make headway in these emerging payment areas without much success. New entrants, not just start-ups, but established large organizations, especially mobile telephone operators, have their eyes firmly set on getting a slice of the payments pie and are likely to provide tough competition to card issuers. In this section we review four key emerging payment transaction segments.

Small value or micro-payments

While there is no standard industry definition, transactions below $10 are generally called micro- or small value payments. A significant majority of transactions in any country's economy are of small value made with cash and coins. Payment cards are rarely used to make micro-payments. These payments are expensive to process for both the card company and the merchant. The cost of processing a micro-payment transaction can be nearly the same as the value of the transaction itself. The micro-payment business is not a viable business for the payment cards industry.

More importantly perhaps, cash and coins are preferred by customers for small value payments because they are convenient. Everyone carries cash and coins – a quick and easy way to pay for a newspaper or a cup of coffee. Paying with a card takes a lot longer. Smartcard-based electronic cash solutions for micro-payments, also known as electronic purses, have been piloted in many markets over the last few years but have failed to achieve mainstream acceptance.

An electronic purse is a smartcard-based reloadable stored-value card that holds electronic cash just like your pocket holds real cash and coins. You can take out or put in electronic cash, store other information, and check your balance whenever you need. At the point-of-sale terminal, the value units are transferred to the retailer's terminal who then owns the value attached to the electronic units. If the purse is lost the value is also lost.

Mondex, an electronic purse developed by NatWest Bank in the early 1990s in the UK and later sold to MasterCard was the first large-scale attempt at capturing low-value physical transactions that cannot be cost-effectively captured on payment cards. Mondex was based as a smartcard plus smartcard-reader solution. It was piloted in stores in smaller towns in Europe and America without much success. Later MasterCard absorbed the expensive technology in its suite of smartcard based solutions.

The primary causes for failure for Mondex and other similar schemes are linked to its inability to offer the same level of convenience that payment cards offer for mid-value transactions or the speed that cash offers for small-value payments. Mondex retailer terminals were clunky and took a long time to process a transaction. In the New York City pilot, both Mondex and Visa cash were offered to customers. The advertisements claimed that these new cards would shorten lines at grocery stores by cutting payment time. But as consumers quickly realized, paying with these smartcards took much longer than paying with cash and coins forcing retailers to encourage shoppers to use cash. Some retailers simply put the card terminals away during busy periods. The inconveniences did not end there. The cards had to be reloaded at ATMs or special reloading machines. A small device was needed to read the card balance. All this added up to a consumer experience riddled with small, inconvenient, and time-consuming tasks. Pilot launches, therefore, were doomed from the start. Misleading marketing joined hands with incomplete technology to deal a prenatal blow to payment cards in their quest for capturing small-value payments.

A dozen or so schemes have been on offer in Europe competing for low-value payments but only a few have gained wider acceptance such as the Chipknip scheme in the Netherlands and Danmont in Denmark. Geldekart in Germany is being supported by prominent players but perhaps the most successful so far in Europe has been the Proton card with presence in Belgium. Estimates made by research organizations suggest that as much 60 per cent of adults in Belgium use the Proton card. But, as in the case of Chipknip, the relatively wide acceptance has also been due to the payment method being the only one available at specific POS – such as parking meters.

So far the approach to capture small-value payments has been based on stored-value cards using smartcard technology but mobile phone operators are investing in phone-based payment solutions that are already being used for downloading software, games, and phone ring tones. Wider acceptance is still far away and will depend on consumer preferences for payments at physical points of sale such as at newspaper kiosks or coffee shops.

Micro-payments over the Internet

People generally pay for small-value transactions with cash but making such payments over the Internet is a problem. The only payment product that has achieved significant acceptance in this area is PayPal, an online account payment system now part of eBay, the online auction marketplace. But similar competing schemes such as Citibank's c2it have not succeeded and been discontinued.

No article or book on electronic payment systems is complete without the mention of PayPal's phenomenal success in the midst of a gaggle of well-funded failures that offered better technology. It is not its simple business model, user-friendliness, or innovative use of new technology that made PayPal the preferred payment mechanism for millions but rather the way it positioned itself by identifying an opportunity riding on the explosive growth of eBay online auctions – eBay is one of the few dot com ventures that have lived up to the hype that surrounded it right from the start. The reasons for PayPal's success are inexorably linked with those of eBay.

The Internet is particularly well-suited for creating virtual marketplaces that bring fragmented buyers and sellers together. Small businesses or individuals who want to set up shop can easily do so at eBay and instantly make their wares accessible to millions of buyers. In the real world this would be like opening a store in a 24-hour gigantic shopping mall with a capacity to house millions of people from all over the world under one roof. Anyone can buy or sell through an auction system that gets the seller the best possible price. Most sellers on eBay are not established traders and are therefore not in a position to accept card payments that rely primarily on personal checks and bank transfers. PayPal offers them the benefits of accepting credit cards too. By charging sellers a transaction processing fee in the same range as the merchant fees on card payments, PayPal provides a funds guarantee to these sellers, allowing them to dispatch their goods as soon as the auction is completed.

The core component of the PayPal system is an online payment account maintained by the buyer that can be used to make payments to PayPal-registered sellers. The account is funded by the buyer via payment cards or bank transfers. It is more economical for PayPal that the account is funded from the consumer's bank account as it costs very little to process the transaction. PayPal acts as a merchant in a card-funded transaction and pays the merchant service commission to its acquiring bank.

The seller, similarly, maintains an online account with PayPal. All transaction messages and communications take place via e-mail. The seller is sent an e-mail that funds are waiting to be accepted. The funds are transferred to the seller's bank account. PayPal charges fees to businesses and provides other value-added services, but has kept the service free for individuals for sending or receiving money. This, some say, is a key reason for its massive customer success but then many free Internet payment schemes have failed to achieve customer acceptance in the past even though they were free.

Person-to-person payments

A payment between individuals may or may not be a commercial transaction but just one friend paying another, say for their share of a dinner bill. The occasional seller getting rid of some items from the back of his truck, at a garage sale, or over the Internet need to receive ready cash. Sometimes checks can be accepted if the buyer is known to the seller. Payment cards have no penetration in this area and past attempts to introduce super-smart card solutions were ahead of their time and faced technical, consumer, and regulatory issues. Online account payment products such as PayPal can be used to make person-to-person payments but this market segment is largely untapped at this stage.

Cross-border person-to-person payments are another story. Millions of migrant workers send money home. They earn their wages in the host country but because they do not have regular bank accounts, they are paid by checks which can be cashed for a fee at check-cashing establishments. They send part of their wages home using money transfer services, such as Western Union, paying yet another hefty fee. They can end up paying nearly ten to twenty percent in fees just to send money abroad. Online payment accounts such as PayPal are free for non-commercial users and should provide a viable alternative for these transactions. But there are three main problems to acceptance. To send and receive money, both parties must have an e-mail account, have access and familiarity with the Internet – still relatively unusual in many countries outside the developed world – and both parties should have bank accounts to fund, send, and receive money. Expensive international money transfer services, which do not require Internet and bank accounts will continue to be preferred by migrant workers for these reasons. These may be expensive but provide a practical, quick, and hassle-free solution.

But banks and other organizations developing person-to-person payment products should not give up. Transaction volumes may shift as consumers become more sophisticated in terms of technology usage and more settled in their host countries to overcome these hurdles and understand the alternatives on offer.

Card companies have also come up with cross-border offerings that utilize their existing international payment networks and access to foreign exchange markets. These services offer card-to-card money transfers.

For all international money account-to-account transfers, legal and regulatory provisions have to be complied with. These deal with money-laundering prevention measures and must follow general operating rules and regulations for efficiency and consistency. Within the European Union, clear rules and directives have been laid out for electronic money transfers between two bank accounts. Price tariffs must be clearly explained to customers and double charging, as has been the practice of many banks in the past, is strictly disallowed.

Ultimately this type of payment will become part of normal Internet banking services as bank technology improves. In the EU, the expensive nightmare of sending funds abroad is already being resolved. Not many years ago sending money between two European states could sometimes take two to three weeks. Enterprising banks tried to develop fast international payments services over private networks by leveraging their correspondent banking relationships. But these proved restrictive and achieved limited success. Banks will have to be careful that money transfer services are priced correctly so that they do not cannibalize payment card transactions. They also need to monitor transfer activity to ensure person-to-person payments are not being used for commercial purposes. The main reason why retailers accept card payments and pay for the service is that they get a payment guarantee from the acquirer that they will get their money for card transactions. If they are able to receive funds from local and even international buyers instantly through a simple anyone-to-anyone bank transfer, there will be no need to accept payment cards at all unless there is a risk of losing the sale.

Online account payments, therefore, offer a significant opportunity to retail banks all over the world as Internet banking slowly becomes mainstream in the developed world. While they threaten to substitute online debit card transactions to some extent, they hold the promise of capturing the person-to-person payment transactions that have eluded banks and other financial services companies for so long.

Business-to-business (B2B) payments

Currently when making large-value business transactions, purchase orders, invoices, and a bundle of other documents are exchanged, and payments are finally settled by check or electronic transfer of funds. In some countries paper checks are still widely used.

Card companies have developed commercial card products to target this sector. Commercial cards include business, corporate, and procurement (or purchasing) cards. The growth in commercial card volumes has been slow but issuers remain optimistic as the potential market is significant and relatively untapped. Commercial card penetration is relatively low except for the T&E sector which is well served.

Advances in corporate treasury systems technology are making it easier for payments to be made via the normal commercial banking channels resulting in slow take-up of card-based payments in this area. Sellers, unless prompted by large buyers, do not want to pay the merchant service fees, and buyers are not motivated to modify or replace their existing accounts payable solutions. Due to these difficulties, procurement cards face tough challenges in the marketplace.

Opportunities – new card-based products

SMARTCARD-BASED PAYMENT PRODUCTS

It is possible that advances in microprocessor technology will result in payment cards that look nothing like the small rectangular pieces of plastic we have today. Already some issuers are experimenting with new colors, shapes, and sizes – one issuer has developed a small key-chain attachment that is in fact a credit card and can be used at a POS terminal. One day even extreme possibilities may become reality, such as a small microprocessor embedded underneath the skin for initiating a secure and reliable payment transaction message.

The common factor in all these possibilities is the microprocessor, an extremely thin computer chip, small enough to be embedded in objects of various shapes and sizes.

Microprocessor-embedded cards, usually called integrated circuit cards (ICC) or simply 'chip' cards are already standard in some markets having replaced the original cards with the familiar magnetic strip at the back. Chip makers are working continually to develop smaller and smaller microprocessor solutions.

The old magnetic stripe on the back of the payment card stores all the necessary transaction origination information which is read when the card is swiped at a payment terminal. But it has limited memory – around 220 bytes on three tracks – and can easily be copied or forged. A chip on the other hand can store and process information many times greater than the magnetic stripe. It converts the card into a tiny computer that can, in addition to the payment information, store a great deal of non-payment details such as loyalty points, gift certificates, or security parameters containing electronic approvals that can be used to allow or deny access to shared assets such as a computer network or secured office premises.

The very basic chip cards that store simple electronic information are not especially secure and can process very little data. They can store prepaid credits which are consumed as the card is used to make payments. The card is inexpensive and cannot be reloaded. Once used it is disposed of. Common examples are cards for telephone calls, pay television, teleshopping, and so on. The more advanced 'smart' card operates with two memories: a non-volatile or read-only memory containing un-erasable data; and a volatile memory where data can be stored and deleted as necessary. The smartcard carries the necessary operating system and applications software.

The chip itself is made from silicon and to avoid breakage it is restricted to only a few millimeters in size. Once the card has been fabricated by a manufacturer in compliance with international standards, the card issuer 'personalizes' the card. Details about the cardholder's identity, account numbers, PIN, security policy limits, and so on are stored and locked on the card. The card is then ready for use.

The security features of the card make it very difficult to copy it, thus helping to reduce counterfeit fraud that plagues the world of magnetic stripe cards. It can also communicate and verify the authenticity of the terminal or other devices. France's card fraud losses plummeted after the country migrated to chip-based technology.

Chip cards help in verifying the:

- identity of the cardholder
- authenticity of the transaction
- authenticity of transaction data.

The internationally accepted standard for smart payment cards is the EMV standard (stands for the original Europay MasterCard Visa) which is being implemented in selected markets all over the world. This standard ensures uniform and consistent interoperability between the card and the POS terminal. Under the EMV process, the PIN at the point of sale replaces the cardholder signature for cardholder verification purposes. Cardholders enter their PIN by tapping on small numeric keypads attached to the terminal.

Markets with a clear commitment to EMV migration are introducing a liability shift, which means if the POS terminal is not EMV compliant, the merchant will have to bear the losses from fraudulent transactions. While Europe is committed to EMV with deadlines for the liability shift already in place, the US has not formally signed up. This is because the US is the world's largest market by far and the effort involved to upgrade terminals is indeed gargantuan. The US market, with its low-cost telecommunications infrastructure, has always relied on online authorizations for fraud prevention and projects a less viable business case for chip-enabling the entire marketplace.

GIFT CARDS

Gift cards are stored-value cards that can be used just like gift certificates. A grandmother can send a gift card to her grandchildren for them to buy books and music of their choice. For retailers they replace cash which is expensive to handle. Gift-card schemes are cheaper to manage and the cards are more difficult to forge than paper gift certificates. Most gift-card schemes are closed-loop schemes which means a particular gift card can only be used at the retailer that has loaded value on the card.

The US is by far the largest market in gift cards with most major retailers managing their own proprietary schemes. The gift-card market in Europe is relatively less developed. There are possible opportunities in the future for banks to market multi-retailer cards but the economic benefit to banks is not very clear at this stage. Multi-retailer cards can be used by shopping malls and complexes where all retailers located in that area can manage one shared scheme that can be used at all shops in a mall, saving considerable costs and resources. Individual retailers can develop and promote their own branded versions but the overall business infrastructure can be shared.

RELOADABLE RETAILER CARDS

A more advanced stored-value product is the reloadable retailer card. In the US, the Starbucks reloadable card has been hugely successful. But such products are essentially retailer initiated and controlled, the key benefits being customer loyalty and savings in cash handling. Financial institutions do not see any major financial benefit in offering such schemes to retailers. Multi-retailer reloadable cards offer an opportunity to third-party processors especially those already providing outsourced gift-card schemes to retailers. Although reloadable cards can operate with the magnetic stripe alone, increasingly these are chip based. A key issue with such cards is the reloading cost. As far as possible, retailers should look towards inexpensive but secure and automated reloading solutions for unattended terminals or remote solutions such as VRU or the Internet.

Stored-value products are linked to transport systems and also find use at car parks, on street metered parking, and also at automated vending machines.

CONTACTLESS CARDS

These cards use radio frequency identification (RFID) technology and do not require physical contact with a terminal for payment. Such contactless cards have great potential on toll roads and fast-food service outlets where payment has to be made quickly. Contactless cards do not necessarily need value to be stored on them and can be linked to payment cards such as credit or debit cards. The card communicates with the receiving device and transfers the necessary details so that the user's credit card can be debited with the appropriate amount.

Perhaps the greatest immediate opportunity for RFID technology lies not in payments but in supply chain management. Goods are tagged with tiny radio transmitters that can be tracked all the way from the manufacturer's factory to the retailer's premises. It enables the buyers to monitor their inventory requirements and accurately forecast times when inventories will be replenished. It also helps retailers in tracking, on a real-time basis, what products are doing well and in which stores. However, there have been protests by customers against plans by some retailers to continue tracking items that have been sold to collect customer data. To date, any such plans have been shelved.

BANKING ON CARDS

Companies and organizations in Western European countries pay their employees by automated credit. In the US, however, according to some estimates, nearly half of all payroll payments are still made by check, but checks are expensive for the banks to process.

Stored value 'payroll cards' offer the possibility of replacing these expensive check payments. Employees are able to load their payroll cards by inserting them in machines at the workplace in a manner not too dissimilar to time cards. Wages are transferred to the payroll card and employees can withdraw cash at participating ATMs. These cards make sense for employers as they reduce the cost of preparing checks and all the paperwork that goes with it. For millions of American households that do not have bank accounts this is a far better option than check cashing which can be quite expensive. The cards are safe as they do not actually carry any value in electronic form but access funds on deposit.

Other countries also see significant promise in payroll cards. South African stored-value cards offer a suitable opportunity to gradually extend retail banking facilities to a large, previously ignored, un-banked population. Payroll cards can offer competitive interest rates on positive card balances.

In practice there are significant obstacles to overcome before un-banked consumers will begin to accept and adopt the payroll card as a little bank in the wallet. Cash is still the main measure of value. It is something tangible and readily accessible. Value on a card is invisible and less tangible. Moving from cash to card requires a radical shift in consumer perceptions – always a difficult challenge for those pushing new products and services. It is quite likely that consumers will go straight to a cash machine and withdraw the entire amount viewing the card as just an additional step forced upon them by their employer. Another issue, which by no means has been fully resolved, is that of security. Such programs need to be carefully designed to ensure no value credits are fraudulently loaded or withdrawn on these cards.

Currently government organizations are planning to or are already in the process of setting up schemes to distribute social security benefits through stored-value cards. A few employers are also designing proprietary schemes to distribute workplace incentives to employees.

The possibilities are unlimited but it will take considerable time before such schemes become widespread. The advantage for such products is that organizations distributing benefits or incentives can mandate card take-up. Voluntary consumer acceptance is always more difficult to achieve. Multi-purpose benefit or incentive cards can also be used for security or identification purposes.

CHAPTER

14 Alternative Payment Products

There is every indication that payment cards will continue to hold their privileged position in the payment systems industry in years to come. Challengers have come and gone. Now there is an understandable feeling of complacency in the industry. However, serious funding is being directed by major corporations towards the development of new payment systems or enhancing existing ones that can seriously compete with payment cards in new if not in existing payments business.

The most potent threat perhaps comes from mobile phone operators. The mobile phone has taken the world by storm. Everyone has a mobile phone and those who don't, aspire to acquire one in the near future. The mobile phone is now as ubiquitous as a payment card or bank account.

Mobile phone operators want to grab a slice of the payments market by capitalizing on their consumer billing infrastructure. Payments can be directly charged to the mobile phone bill, bypassing credit and debit cards in the process. In this section we will discuss the threat faced by card companies from mobile and other alternative payment products.

Mobile payments

Every year the latest phone models, additional services, and all types of peripheral gadgetry, games, and ringtones appear on the scene to be snapped up by eager consumers. In less developed countries, where ordinary landline telephone connections are difficult to obtain and often highly unreliable, growth in both numbers of subscribers and billed business has been phenomenal. Already there are reliable technology platforms available for managing and processing payments. Industry observers forecast that the mobile handset may soon become the primary communication device for millions as reliable and fast video exchange and Internet capabilities become mainstream.

To capitalize on this growth, there has been no dearth, in recent years, of mobile payment schemes but like digital cash, consumer demand for mobile payments has remained abysmally low. But it would be hasty to draw a conclusion from poor customer adoption rates. Customers have not rejected altogether the idea of paying with their mobile phones forever. Currently, for regular card-and-cardholder present transactions, they see little use in switching from cash and cards to mobile phone payments simply because the phone is capable of making certain types of payments. The age-old problem in payment services is changing consumer behavior, which is notoriously difficult. Moving from a familiar experience to an unfamiliar one requires a very strong incentive and clear value proposition. PayPal found its 'best-fit' market in online auctions. To gain acceptance, a mobile payment scheme must clearly address a marketplace need where perhaps existing payment methods are unworkable or less convenient. Marketing a mobile payment scheme that simply offers an alternative to cash, cards, and checks for all types of transactions is courting disaster.

But a need for making small-value payments for 'digital' or electronically downloadable goods via mobile phones is growing, where you browse, pay, and download over the phone. This market owes its existence to the phenomenal success of the mobile phone industry itself. There is significant demand for digital products among the younger subscriber base for downloading ringtones and games and playing digital games remotely with friends. Advances in mobile communications technology are already improving the download speed. New wider and clearer screen handsets are offering Internet-on-the-go. Ten years from now, high bandwidth Internet access over a mobile phone may be commonplace. The future is certainly encouraging and mobile phones may well provide a payment solution for mobile Internet payments of all transaction values.

MOBILE MICRO-PAYMENTS

At present the opportunity is in small-value mobile transactions or micro-payments for digital items. These micro-payments are billed to the consumer's regular mobile phone bill.

But there are also several real-world applications for handling micro-payments with a mobile phone in the medium term. Robust technology already exists to allow consumers to pay for products and services with their mobile phones at unattended terminals such as parking meters and vending machines, but this is one of the areas where mobile transactions will find it difficult to displace cash or cards, due to entrenched consumer behavior.

MACRO-PAYMENTS

While transactions over $10 can also be charged to the phone bill, mobile phone operators provide the option of charging the purchase to the customer's payment card. Since it is cumbersome to enter card numbers each time a purchase is made over a mobile phone – say for movie tickets – a mobile wallet can do the job. The mobile wallet software holds payment card details either on the phone or in a more secure location, such as on a server at the mobile operator. Mobile phone users can select the card they want to use from the wallet and the system will send the card details contained in the wallet to authorize and validate the transaction. The authorization message is routed to a mobile Internet gateway and on to the normal payment card networks. In this sense, mobile payments will not displace payment card transactions, much to the relief of the card companies.

MOBILE PAYMENTS TECHNOLOGY

At the basic level, text messages can suffice to complete a payment transaction. Early experience with wireless access protocol (WAP), a data exchange protocol for mobile communication has been disappointing but that is mainly due to low bandwidth causing inordinate waits while browsing content online. Whatever technology is used it is essential that the key requirements for a remote payment transaction are complied with: buyer and seller authentication, transaction authorization, and non-repudiation. Security is obviously very essential. A simple PIN – like the one used for ATMs – will be necessary for buyer authentication. It is also likely that mobile phone operators will require registration via the Internet or over voice before mobile phone users can start using the payment service. But for very low-value transactions these steps may be waived. The mobile operator will assume the risk. At this stage the key challenge is the bandwidth. For transaction at the point of sale, infra-red technology is already available in the form of Bluetooth and other protocols. The consumer will point and click to pay at a vending machine or at a POS terminal. In such cases the main hurdles to widespread acceptance are terminal modifications to accept mobile payments.

TIMING OF BILLING

Like billing for regular phone charges, mobile payments can be billed to customers in two ways: prepaid and postpaid billing. Prepaid phone calling cards are available at high street shops, kiosks, and filling stations for purchase. The retailer earns a commission from the mobile phone operator. The consumer uses the calling card till the purchased units run out. Under this option no bills or statements are sent to the user, though transaction details can be confirmed if required. This is commonly known as pay-as-you-go or prepaid service. These prepaid cards can be used to make payments on a mobile payments scheme just as they are used for voice and data.

The other option is postpaid billing where the consumer settles their bill for calls or purchases made in the past period. This option carries more risk for the mobile operator but is obviously advantageous for customer relationship purposes. In a payment scheme, the mobile phone user will be able to review all payments charged to the phone just like regular calling or data charges.

Digital cash

The heady days of dot-com hype offered us a plethora of colorfully named and brilliantly engineered payment schemes designed for the Internet. The Internet was quickly creating a whole new digital universe parallel to our real one. We needed a parallel digital currency to go with it. Entrepreneurs and venture capital firms began pumping billions into online shopping businesses, and digital cash payment schemes popped up in every corner of the world.

Digital cash technologies boasted industry-strength impregnable encryption algorithms specially engineered to complete financial transactions securely and efficiently. But these payment schemes were ahead of their time and the digital micro-payment market had not sufficiently developed for these to succeed.

That said, digital cash may well find consumer demand in the future as lessons about customer preferences are learned from past mistakes and more attention is paid to market realities and less to the finer points of exciting technologies.

The traditional definition of digital cash describes it as identical to real cash. This 'virtual' form of real money should be untraceable, of immediate value to the bearer or holder, and accepted as legal tender wherever real money is used. Digital cash is electronic currency – accepted in the virtual world as readily as real cash and coins are accepted in the physical world. To describe this in a more fanciful way: it is the migration from 'atoms to bits' for cash and coins.

A 'purist' framework sets out ten properties of digital currency and it may be useful to review these to understand the nature of an ideal digital cash product:

- *Security*. Good money cannot be counterfeited. The integrity of the digital cash algorithms must be beyond reproach. No one, except the issuing authority, should be able to create, copy, or delete digital cash units.
- *Anonymity*. Like real cash, digital cash units must be untraceable. This means that they should not leave a trail behind that could be traced. The identity of the payer and the payee must remain completely confidential.
- *Portability*. The units must not be dependent upon one particular channel (such as the Internet). The digital cash units must be fully transportable.
- *Durability*. Digital cash units must remain valid legal tender until replaced.
- *Two-way flow*. Value must be transferable between any two parties at any time. Unlike payment card transactions where transacting party roles are clearly defined between buyers and sellers (only sellers receive funds), digital cash transactions can flow either way.
- *Offline capability*. Digital cash must be legal tender in the real world as well. This means it could be exchanged for, or used just like, cash and coins.
- *Divisibility*. As in cash and coins, digital cash units must be divisible into smaller units to handle low-value transactions.
- *Wide acceptance*. Any digital currency must have acceptable value in all the markets in which it operates.
- *Simplicity*. Though it may seem obvious, this requirement is very important. Most highly secure and multi-channel schemes have been too difficult and counterintuitive to gain consumer acceptance.
- *Unit of value*. There must be clear value attached to the digital units. In international markets, a currency, in order to be convertible must be traded on the foreign exchanges. So a true global digital currency is not only backed by the government of the country where it is legal tender but must be exchangeable against other currencies.

Cash and coins possess all the above properties. Unlike payment cards, cash requires no identification or authentication. Digital cash schemes need to comply with some if not all of the requirements stated above if they are to serve as true substitutes for cash and coins.

Electronic bill payment and presentment (EBPP)

BILL PAYMENT

Straddled by the inefficient economies of processing millions of paper checks, retail banks are forever under pressure to devise new ways to switch check payments to electronic payments. In most markets non-business checks are processed free of charge. Check processing is not in itself revenue generating but forms the core of the banking business. The bank account with its key functionality to receive and make payments is usually a loss leader. It is provided free of charge or at reduced rates with the assumption that account holders will acquire other more profitable products from the bank whenever the need arises.

This position, based on the relationship between the bank and the customer, has changed appreciably over the years. Direct mail marketing campaigns, outbound marketing and Internet offers provide the customer with considerable choice. These days, more than ever before, consumers are likely to buy financial products from a number of providers. They can pick and choose the best offer available. As a result the potency of loss-leading products is weakening and the pressures to reduce costs on such products, and lower the break-even point, are growing. Banks are finding that long-time loyal customers are not so loyal anymore. While they may retain their bank accounts with one bank for decades, they shop around for cards, mortgages, investment accounts, financial advice, and also – bill payment.

Electronic bill payment and presentment offers an attractive opportunity for banks to reduce their check-processing costs for loss-leading products. But it also provides a viable substitute to payment cards. Retail banks – using the 'bank assisted' model – are competing with card issuers in the market for payment transactions. Retailers, working with third-party EBPP providers, such as CheckFree Corporation, are also actively competing for retail payment transactions using the 'biller direct' model. These two models are described in more detail below.

BANK ASSISTED – PAYING VIA BANK WEBSITE

The consumer receives a bill from their phone company in the mail and logs on to their bank's website. The payer registers for the bill payment service. In the next step, the company to whom the payment is to be made – referred to as the biller – must be set up as a payee. This involves selecting the biller from a list and providing customer details such as billing reference or the customer account number as appropriate, and selecting the right address of the biller in case of multiple payment locations. Payments can be made to any registered biller. If the payee is not registered, some providers will generate and mail a paper check, allowing this service to be used for any-to-any payments. Many banks offer this service over multiple channels (call center, Internet, ATM, and so on).

BILLER DIRECT – PAYING DIRECTLY TO BILLERS

Billers offer bill payment services directly. Customers can access the website of the retailer, provide their bank account details and pay directly. For obvious reasons, retailers prefer this model as they are able to gain 'face time' with customers, during which they can market their other products and services.

However, consumers prefer, if they have multiple bills to deal with, to pay through one familiar process where all billers are set up in one place, that is, via the bank website. For online customers, the process of bill payment is now fairly commonplace in North America. Customers can review past payments and check when the payment was processed. As there are administrative delays between payment origination and completion (when the money is actually received by the biller), customers have to be careful, and they run the risk of missing payment deadlines.

BILL PRESENTMENT OR E-BILLS

Presenting a bill or statement online is cost effective for the biller. It saves the cost of printing and mailing bills. An e-bill is convenient for the consumer as it can be received or accessed over the Internet – useful for frequent travelers. The e-bill provides all the detailed information that is shown on a paper bill. The bill can be downloaded in various formats and for those who prefer a paper version, the e-bill can always be printed. Whilst not mainstream at this stage, e-bills are gaining popularity especially as Internet access is becoming more widespread. In the future most bills will be presented online and payable by simply clicking on a pay-now button.

What PayPal is to online account payment, CheckFree, a US-based company, is to electronic bill payment and presentment. CheckFree processes much of the EBPP traffic in the US and has a sizeable biller file.

In the US, electronic bill payment via the bank website has experienced relatively gradual adoption. Consumers prefer to pay directly by visiting biller websites but payment via bank website is now on the rise. One reason for this is that, unlike Canadian banks, banks in the US charge for bill payment (except for some notable exceptions). In Canada, consumers feel a lot more comfortable paying bills though their bank websites.

Europeans, on the other hand, do not use electronic bill payment. Direct debits are set up to pay for regular bill payments. Utility companies, credit card issuers, and others automatically charge their current/checking account on a specified date shown on the bill. Many offer discounts for payment by direct debit.

Electronic checks

Though overall transaction volumes are declining, paper checks continue to dominate many large markets such as the US, UK and France. Converting paper checks to electronic transactions promises to make check payments more efficient and cheaper for financial institutions. To a great extent, automated clearing houses (ACH) have played a key role in this profitable transition from paper to a paperless environment.

Designed for the Internet, digital (or electronic) checks – digitally signed using PKI (public key infrastructure) technology – failed to achieve widespread acceptance. The idea was to compose an encrypted secure electronic message, the digital check, that can be sent by the payer to the payee in an e-mail. The payee forwards the digital check to their bank. The bank, using the payer's public key, confirms the authenticity of the check and processes it using the details provided in the message. The concept is simple and based on the logical appeal of PKI technology. But as with all other digital payment instruments using PKI, the setup and use are complicated with users having to continually update their digital certificates to avoid compromising system integrity. As digital checks have not achieved any success, the focus in financial institutions is now more on check truncation – the conversion of paper checks to electronic messages.

CHECK TRUNCATION

Paper checks go through a long and complex chain of manual or semi-automated business processes. Each process takes time and increases the risk of error that eats away at the bottom line. The banking industry, at least in the check-intensive markets, is developing initiatives to truncate this inefficient paper process as early as possible in the business process flow. Bank operations already involve a mix of electronic and paper interchange. Strategic investments in infrastructure are now shifting the traffic more and more to electronic means but it will be many years, perhaps decades, before the entire bank transaction traffic is safely rendered paperless.

Let's briefly review the paper check processing cycle to understand how truncation can accelerate the payment process. Take the example of the UK where, until a few years ago, paper checks required presentment at the branch of the payer bank at which the check-writing customer's account was maintained resulting in a long and laborious movement of paper. To illustrate:

- The buyer writes a check and gives it to the seller.
- The seller deposits the check at their bank's nearest branch who 'prepares' the check.
- This involves encoding the amount of the check in magnetic form at the bottom of the check and sending it for clearing to the centralized clearing house, the Check and Credit Clearing Company (C&CCC) which works under the auspices of the Association of Payment Clearing Services (APACS) in the UK. Here all banks exchange checks written on them and their accounts are accordingly debited or credited.
- The checks are sent to a centralized area at the payer bank. Checks used to be physically sent to the branch where the customer's account is held, but that step in the process has now been "truncated" and checks no longer need to be sent to the original branch.
- The banks review the checks for balance and authenticity and decide whether or not to honor the check. They do not review every single check but take a decision using agreed relative risk parameters based on their risk management policy.
- The banks agree among themselves the actual value of the total checks exchanged the day before and settle this through their accounts at the Bank of England via the CHAPS system, a real-time settlement system.
- The paying bank must communicate to the payee bank information on checks it has decided to dishonor. This takes more time and many banks receiving checks do not credit customer accounts until they are sure that the check has been honored, further delaying the process. Processing checks between English and Scottish banks may take even longer.

This whole process is gradually being automated, which promises to make it significantly more efficient. Truncating paper checks into electronic information as early as possible in this process will greatly help. This truncation can take place as early as at the point of sale (purchases) or at the ATM in countries where ATMs accept check deposits. The best option would be to truncate the check at this first step in the chain and treat the captured electronic data as a debit card transaction. This way immediate authorization will be available and the merchant, with guarantee of payment, will be able to release the goods. Reading checks at ATMs would help too. Many consumers in the US are still hesitant to deposit their checks in these machines because they cannot obtain a validated receipt.

A more expensive option is to read and scan the checks at the point of sale or deposit. The captured image can be exchanged between banks instead of the physical paper. If this proves too expensive, only the check data can be exchanged for clearing and settlement along with selected images required by the paying bank. This requires investment in check-scanning equipment and can be significantly more expensive than just capturing the check data. Alternatively, the merchant can scan the paper check and retain the image in its accessible archives.

In the US, the Check Truncation Act, or Check 21 as it is more commonly called, will allow financial institutions to use documents created from check images as equivalent to physical checks.

Electronic checks, truncated and authorized at the point of receipt, offer a viable payment mechanism for the twenty-first century. With new technology, government backing and support of the entire banking community, electronic checks are poised to compete effectively against payment cards, especially debit cards. But they also offer a formidable challenge to banks, who must understand and embrace the new technology advantageously.

CHAPTER 15 Securitization

Ask most people what they know about the bankcard business and they'll say 'I know I use one, and that is pretty much the extent of my knowledge about how these little pieces of plastic operate.' This is to be expected. After all, you don't need to know how a watch works in order to tell the time. You don't need to know the mechanics of the internal combustion engine to drive a car. And you don't need to be an expert in agriculture to enjoy the taste of fresh fruits and vegetables. Is it any different when it comes to a bankcard?

While it is certainly true that one does not need to comprehend the intricacies of the Visa and MasterCard global interchange systems or the details of the credit scoring process to obtain and use a bankcard, people might be surprised to learn just how much bankcards play a role in other aspects of their daily lives. Consider the impact upon prices of just about any retail goods or services you can think of if the seller could not accept plastic in exchange for payment. It is a proven fact that consumers spend more, on average, when utilizing a bankcard for payment than when they pay by cash. This increases the sales volume of the seller, thus helping to lower prices for everyone. And what about the sale of more costly items such as refrigerators, washing machines, televisions, stereos, and similar durable goods? If credit in the form of bankcards was not so readily available, these items would be more difficult to sell. This, in turn, would lead to less manufacturing of such items and, therefore, fewer jobs and a lower economic output in countries where such products are produced.

It is quite apparent that as the convenience and flexibility of bankcards as a payment mechanism grows throughout the world and their share of total personal consumer expenditures (PCE) increases, their impact upon the lives of everyone also grows. Try to pay for an item purchased via the Internet with something other than a bankcard; it is almost impossible to do. Try checking into a hotel or hiring a rental car without a bankcard to ease the process; it is inconvenient at best, and completely inconceivable in some instances.

Payment cards are an essential component of our everyday lives and it is hard to imagine life without them. But one area relating to payment cards that has a significant impact on the lives of consumers the world over is probably the least understood. Its global repercussions go unnoticed. This little understood fact involves the impact that bankcards have upon the world's capital markets. Every business day, billions of dollars worth of securities which are backed by credit card receivables are bought and sold throughout the world. The legal sellers of these instruments are trusts created by the large credit card issuers in markets in Europe, Asia and North America and beyond. The buyers are corporations and wealthy individuals who seek diversification within their investment portfolios through the purchase of a security which yields a better return than traditional government-backed bonds or similar instruments, but which has a broad and deep global trading market, thus ensuring liquidity.

How does this impact the average consumer? After all, very few individual consumers actually own one of these credit card asset-backed securities. The impact comes from several sources. First, credit card issuers are able to grant more credit, and on more favorable terms, if they can count upon the global capital markets for liquidity. Second, many of the buyers of these securities are corporations which sell shares to the public, thus enabling ordinary investors with share holdings in their personal investment portfolios, pension plans, and stock trading clubs to indirectly invest in the bankcard business. Finally, the corporate buyers of these securities are able to improve the yield of their investment portfolios while maintaining the liquidity crucial to long-term stability of their operations, thus helping to ensure continued growth in jobs and income for their employees.

This process of creating securities which are traded in capital markets throughout the world is called 'securitization'. It is a critical aspect of the bankcard business. Without it, the cost of capital in the bankcard industry would rise, thus creating reluctance on the part of card issuers to grant credit as broadly as is done today. This reluctance to lend would lead to lower credit availability and slower economic growth in most markets as consumers would have less money to spend on goods and services; consumer spending represents two-thirds of most western economies' gross domestic product (GDP). A significant impact indeed!

Bankcard securitizations are part of the broader asset-backed securities market, a global market of some US $7 trillion (*ABS Yearbook 2004*, Banc One Capital Markets, Inc.: January, 2004)! Over two-thirds of this market is comprised of securitized first and second mortgage loans (Philadelphia Federal Reserve Bank). The remainder includes other retail lending products such as home equity lines of credit, automobile loans, and credit cards. Recently, small business loans have also begun to be securitized.

Credit card securities constituted about US $421.3 billion of the $7 trillion in ABS available – a shade above 6 per cent of the total market (Standard & Poor's *US Credit Card Quality Index*, 'Performance data results continue positive trends': July 29, 2004). The vast majority of these bankcard securitizations were issued in the US – over 70 per cent (The Bank Market Association *ESF Securitization Data Report*: Winter, 2004). In the first six months of 2004, $45 billion in new securitizations had been issued in the US.

What is a securitization exactly? Why do so many bankcard issuers utilize it in the operation of their business? How does it work? The nature of bankcard securitizations is such that its impact is felt throughout the financial markets of the world as well as within the economies of a number of individual countries. It impacts the daily lives of literally billions of individuals globally on an almost daily basis, yet few people outside of industry specialists truly understand how it works and the many ways in which it influences capital and retail markets throughout the world. It is important that bankcard professionals, bankers, merchants, investors, financial advisors, and countless others have at least a basic understanding of this amazing capital redistribution mechanism so that they can better perform their daily activities.

Securitization – a primer

In order to fully appreciate the impact bankcard securitizations have upon consumers and individual country's economies, it might be useful to first understand the process and how it works.

In simple terms, securitization is a form of financing. In case of credit cards, it provides a source of funds for the daily funding of customers' transactions which is a significant portion of the costs associated with operating a credit card issuing business. This financing, or funding, is accomplished via the pooling and sale of bankcard assets into an independently managed trust which, in turn, sells securities to public and private investors backed by the future revenues, or cash flows, to be generated from the assets pooled in the trust. These securities pay a rate of return to the investors who purchase them, which can be either fixed or floating, for a specified duration which can range anywhere from three to ten years.

Credit card securitizations are one form of what is more broadly termed 'asset-backed securitizations' (ABS). As the name implies, any form of asset can be securitized. Within the financial services arena, the most prevalent form of ABS is mortgage loans, followed by second mortgage loans, home equity lines of credit, automobiles, credit cards and, most recently, small business loans (*Source*: www.vinodkothari.com; Standard & Poor's article 'US ABS credit ratings show solid performance', Dr. Joseph Hu: 2003). Perhaps the most famous securitization of non-financial assets involved the sale of securities backed by the future royalty payment streams of David Bowie music and videos. Yes, you too can have a financial stake in the continued success of one of rock and roll's most venerable performers. What the David Bowie example demonstrates is the incredible flexibility the ABS process enjoys. Almost any asset which generates ongoing revenue can be securitized and sold to investors if it is structured and marketed properly. It is this structuring process which ultimately determines the success of a securitization.

Securitizations have been used for years in the mortgage lending business and serve as the primary source of funding for mortgage lenders throughout the world. Most originators of mortgage loans grant credit following strict guidelines with respect to loan amount, loan-to-property value ratio and similar parameters. This is done to facilitate securitization after the loan has been approved. As credit cards are a relatively new asset class within the securitization markets, with the first securitization taking place in 1987 in the US, there are fewer generally accepted compliance rules applicable to credit cards. Instead, credit card securitizations use a different structure to gain market acceptance.

CREDIT CARD SECURITIZATION STRUCTURE

While there are an almost infinite number of nuances to the creation of credit card securitizations, all ABS backed by credit card receivables have certain core elements in common. The first is the creation of an independently managed trust into which the credit card assets to be securitized are sold. The creation of the trust is the first step in the securitization process. It is necessary to reassure the prospective buyers that the investments will be managed and supervised in a satisfactory manner.

Trusts

There are two basic forms of trust structures prevalent in the industry:

- *Standalone trusts*. In a standalone trust a single pool of credit card assets is used as collateral for a single security to be sold to investors. Utilizing this approach, a credit card issuer creates a trust and sells securities to investors backed by the credit card assets housed within that trust. If, later on, this same issuer wishes to securitize a new pool of

credit card assets, then a new trust must be created and a new security issued against this new pool of bankcard accounts.
- *Master trusts*. Master trusts differ from standalone trusts in that a master trust acts as a reservoir for bankcard accounts and the corresponding assets they represent. This structure allows issuers to add accounts to the trust periodically and to issue multiple securities against the assets housed in the trust over time. For large, growing card issuers the master trust structure provides greater flexibility and lower costs than standalone trusts.

Regardless of the trust structure it must be managed by an independent 'trustee'. The bank's role in the process is to originate the credit card accounts to be sold to the trust and to service them on an ongoing basis over the life of the trust. The trustee's role is to ensure that the credit card accounts serving as collateral for the securities the trust will issue and sell to investors (a role also overseen by the trustee) are maintained properly and that all revenues due to the trust from the bank are received in a timely fashion.

The trustee's role as independent overseer of the collateral contained within the trust and as seller of the securities backed by that collateral is crucial to the global liquidity of credit card securitizations. Investors need to be reassured that someone other than the bank which originated and sold the credit card accounts to the trust is keeping an eye on the performance of the cards over the life of the securities issued.

CREDIT ENHANCEMENT

The next step is the credit enhancement of the trust so that when the rating agencies evaluate the trust's ability to pay the rate of return promised to investors on the securities issued by the trustee, it will receive an investment grade rating of Aaa (AAA+ is the highest rating attainable), or equivalent (in most instances). The role of the investment rating agencies in the securitization process is more fully explored later on. For now, let's look at some of the ways bankcard issuers credit- enhance their securitization trusts to obtain the all important Aaa rating. The following areas are critical in the evaluation of a trust:

Spread account

The spread account, sometimes referred to as 'excess spread', measures the difference between the revenue coming into the trust from the credit card accounts securitized and the return paid to investors, losses, and servicing costs associated with the trust accounts. The originator of the trust (the bank issuing the credit card accounts) receives the excess spread. Many securitization trusts contain an agreement whereby the cash generated by the spread account must remain in the trust as a cushion to ensure payment of the return to investors if the ratio of the excess spread to assets held in the trust falls below a pre-set threshold. This is sometimes referred to as 'trapping cash' in the trust. For example, excess spread is returned to the originator unless it falls below 6 per cent of the assets in the trust, at which point the cash remains in the trust in order to pay investors their return each month.

Cash collateral account (CCA)

A cash collateral account is exactly what the name implies. In this instance, the trust's originator places an additional amount of cash in the trust to be accessed in the event that the revenues generated by the trust are insufficient to meet the expenses of the trust, most particularly the payment of the return to investors.

Collateral invested account (CIA)

This is a form of subordination (see below) in which the poorest performing accounts contained within the trust, usually referred to as the class C accounts, are broken out and a different class of securities is created and sold to investors at a better rate of return than the rest of the securities the trust issues. This process enables the risk of the C class of securities to be expressed and priced to investors separately while improving the quality of the primary portion of the securitization trust.

Subordination agreement

A subordination agreement is the breaking up of the securities issued by the trust into two distinct classes, each with its own price to investors, whereby the A class securities are backed by the best performing credit card accounts held within the trust and the B class are backed by the less-than-best performing credit card accounts contained within the trust. The B class securities will offer a better rate of return to investors, but are also highlighted as riskier than the A class.

Letter of credit

Similar to the common process within the commercial lending operations of banks, some securitization trusts sometimes utilize a promise to pay a certain amount of money into the trust from another bank or financial institution if certain thresholds in trust performance are triggered, such as higher losses, greater than anticipated attrition, and similar triggers.

Third-party guarantee

A third-party guarantee is a contractual agreement between the trust and a third-party entity, usually a bank or other financial institution such as an investment bank or insurance company, to step in and provide the funds necessary to ensure investors receive their return should the trust fail to generate sufficient revenues on its own.

Insurance

This type of enhancement is not commonly utilized, but functions much as any form of insurance does. Trust originators pay a premium to an insurance company which, in turn, agrees to put sufficient cash into the trust to ensure that investors receive their promised return should the trust itself fail to generate the cash necessary to do so.

All of these forms of credit enhancement to a credit card securitization trust are designed to obtain an investment grade rating from the various rating agencies which evaluate each trust and the securities issued against them in order to assist investors with determining the risk associated with each security.

RATING AGENCIES

A key player in the credit card securitization process is the group of rating agencies who monitor and observe the marketplace. These organizations evaluate each credit card trust created and rate the risk to investors of receiving the stated return on the securities issued by the trust. This rating and evaluation process is a major factor in determining the price trust originators will have to pay to investors in order to sell the securities their trust will issue, thus providing them with the funding they seek. The higher the agencies rate a given trust the lower the interest rate the trust will have to pay out to investors to entice them to purchase their securities.

There are three primary rating agencies evaluating credit card securitization trusts around the globe:

- Moody's Investor Services
- Standard & Poor's
- Fitch IBCA.

RATING TRUSTS

Issuers seeking the best price on their securities must obtain a rating from at least two of the above three agencies to have credibility in the marketplace. But how do these rating agencies determine their ratings? What do they look for in evaluating the bank that originates a trust and services the credit card accounts? There are many factors which are evaluated through a combination of statistical analysis and management interviews conducted with the trust's originator, but they generally fall into three categories.

Product and pricing considerations

PRODUCT TYPE

As securities backed by credit card trusts are issued for specified periods of time, rating agencies concern themselves with the nature and structure of the card products contained within the trust. Factors such as co-branding partners, loyalty schemes in effect, plastic color (for example, Gold, Platinum), and similar structural components are reviewed and analyzed to determine their potential to impact the trust's ability to pay the return to investors as promised. For example, a trust with a large portion of the accounts contained therein tied into a co-brand partner will be scrutinized as to the remaining term of the agreement, disposition of cardholder accounts, relationships in the event the agreement is terminated or expires, and similar potential impacts upon the accounts which might negatively affect the trust's ability to pay investors their return. Agencies are looking for products and product structures which will likely undergo minimal adverse change over the life of the securities issued by the trust.

INTEREST RATE/TYPE

The level of interest charged as well as the manner in which the rate is applied to the credit card account will have an impact upon such performance variables as account attrition within the trust and usage patterns. Rating agencies look at the mix of fixed versus variable interest rate cards as well as the structure of the variable rates, including floors and ceilings in effect. They attempt to analyze the likely impact these different prices and structures will have upon the revenue generation capability of the accounts over the life of the trust.

CARD USAGE PATTERNS

How cardholders use their credit card accounts, as a payment device versus a lending vehicle, will have a substantial impact upon the revenue a credit card trust will generate. Agencies look carefully at the patterns of the accounts contained within the trust. They evaluate the amount of interchange and interest income the portfolio is likely to generate over the life of the trust to determine if it is sufficient to ensure payment of the return to investors.

FEES

Annual fees, late payment fees, overlimit fees, cash advance fees, and the myriad of other fees issuers charge are an integral part of the profitability of the credit card issuing business. Rating agencies analyze the amount of fee income generated by accounts sold to a trust along with the source of that income in order to assess the likelihood of this important revenue stream either increasing or decreasing over the life of the trust. In addition, they evaluate what the makeup of the mix of fees collected is telling them about the overall quality of the accounts placed within the trust. For example, a strong fee income revenue stream made up primarily of cash advance fees, late fees, and overlimit fees might indicate a poor quality portfolio which is likely to experience higher chargeoff rates over the life of the trust than say a portfolio with an equivalent fee income stream, but which comes primarily from annual fees.

REPRICING FLEXIBILITY

Rating agencies concern themselves with cardholder agreements to determine the flexibility trust originators have in repricing accounts over the life of the securities issued, especially with respect to fixed rate accounts which are subject to more risk from an interest rate volatility point of view. They look for terms which enable issuers to reprice accounts with minimal customer notice periods and without the need to maintain existing balances at current rates should cardholders decide they do not wish to accept the repricing as is their right in some markets.

Risk considerations

CREDIT UNDERWRITING

A critical element in determining if a trust will perform as required over time is the nature of the trust originator's new account underwriting process. Rating agencies investigate this aspect of the card-issuance process thoroughly in order to determine if the originator is utilizing appropriate techniques and judgment. They will see if credit application scorecards are utilized and, if so, if they are up-to-date, valid and applied correctly. They will also review the bank's credit policies and exceptions, as well as scorecard override parameters and levels of overrides made, both high and low side. All of this analysis will be used to make a judgment as to whether or not the credit quality of the trust accounts is likely to improve, decline or stay essentially the same over the life of the trust. This is a critical judgment as loss rates will have a dramatic effect upon the trust's ability to pay the return to investors as promised.

CREDIT SCORE DISTRIBUTION

Another key element in assessing risk within a securitization trust is the analysis of the credit score distribution of the accounts. In markets with a credit bureau, credit scores offer one of the most objective forms of assessing credit risk available. Rating agencies will look at current score distributions as well as historical patterns of movement in the trust accounts' credit scores in order to render a judgment as to the likelihood of the trust showing an increasing, decreasing, or stable trend relative to account-level credit risk over the life of the securities issued.

GEOGRAPHIC AND DEMOGRAPHIC DIVERSITY

Agencies look for a reasonable distribution of accounts across geographic as well as demographic parameters to ensure there are no concentrations of risk within the portfolio of trust accounts. If, for example a trust exhibits a concentration of accounts in a geographic region with one or two primary employers, then the risk of the portfolio experiencing credit problems over the life of the trust is greater than if accounts are spread more evenly throughout a broader geographic area due to the employment concentration issue. Similarly, portfolios with demographic concentrations around age, income, residence type, and similar variables will exhibit more risk than portfolios with a broader distribution of customer types.

ACCOUNT SEASONING

One of the most important elements rating-agency analysts evaluate in looking at a credit card securitization trust is the distribution of accounts by age. There is a very high correlation between the length of time an account has been on an issuer's books and the predictability of that account's future performance based upon past history. Trusts which have a distribution of accounts around a median age of three or four years are far more likely to exhibit predictable behavior over the life of the trust than are ones with a distribution around a median of one or two years. This age distribution, or seasoning, of accounts is a major factor in determining the price at which an issuer can sell securities backed by their trust accounts.

COMPETITION

Another element factored into the rating agencies' analysis of credit card securitization trusts is the impact that competition is likely to have upon the trust accounts' performance over time. This entails comparing the trust accounts' pricing and benefits structure to other options available to consumers in the marketplace and making a judgment as to whether or not that means account attrition is likely to be high or low over the life of the trust. In addition, agency analysts evaluate the likelihood of new competitors entering the marketplace over the life of the trust and the potential impact such new entrants might have upon trust account performance.

MANAGEMENT

Part of the rating agencies' evaluation of likely trust performance entails in-depth interviews with the management team of the originator of the trust. This is done to assess management's capability to identify and adapt to changes in the marketplace over the life of the trust. Originators with a strong history of successful card issuance and a stable management group will be able to obtain better pricing of their securitization securities in the marketplace than will relatively new or inexperienced issuer management teams.

Trust and securities structure considerations

MASTER VS. STANDALONE TRUST

Rating agencies will opine as to the benefits and risks associated with each type of trust structure and its impact upon account performance over the life of the trust. In general, master trust structures are preferred because they provide more flexibility in managing the trust and the related securities issued over time. For example, in a master trust, if attrition is greater than anticipated and is adversely affecting revenues within the trust, accounts can be added relatively easily versus a standalone trust.

FIXED VS. FLOATING RATE SECURITIES

Rating agencies evaluate the risks associated with likely attainment of the returns promised by issuers on their card-backed securities based upon the structure of the return itself. Fixed rate structures have different risk characteristics than do variable rate ones. Depending upon which way interest rates are likely to go over the duration of the trust, fixed rate securities may be preferred over variable rate ones or viewed as riskier than variable rate alternatives. Variable rate structures have the built-in benefit of mitigating interest rate risk to a degree, but they also eliminate the opportunity for the trust to build up excess spread during periods of low interest rates in the marketplace. Rating agency analysts will render a judgment as to how the structure of the security itself is likely to impact the ability of the trust to pay the return promised over the period for which it is offered.

Now that each aspect of a securitization structure is understood, from the originator (the bank issuing credit cards) to the trust to credit enhancement to the rating agencies, how does it all come together? Figure 15.1 shows the basic elements and how they fit together over the life of a securitization trust.

The exhibit shows the bank which issues the credit card accounts selling them to the trust in exchange for cash and certificates pledging credit card assets. The trust, in turn, via the independent trustee, issues securities, or notes, which are sold to investors. The bank services the credit card accounts it sold to the trust for the duration of the securities issued and receives the excess spread account from the trust throughout the life of the process.

Understanding securitizations is one thing, but why do bankcard issuers go to all the trouble and expense of creating securitization trusts and selling securities backed by the future revenue streams of their bankcard accounts? Why not just use the traditional sources

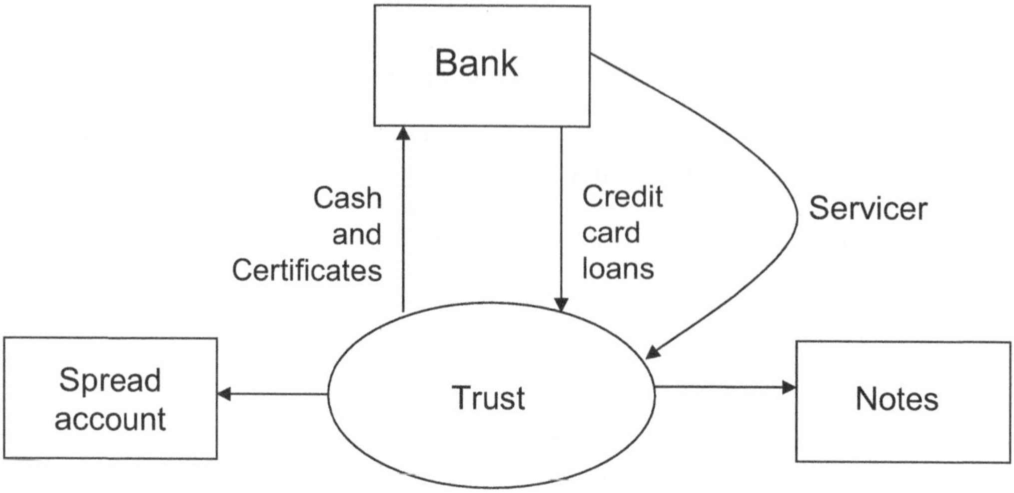

Figure 15.1 Structure of a card-backed securitization

of portfolio funding such as deposit account balances, loans from other banks and commercial paper issuance?

Securitization benefits

There are a number of benefits for issuers for securitizing card receivables depending upon their skill and expertise in operating their card-issuing business. Some will relate specifically to the issuer of the securities while others accrue to all parties involved in the process. All asset-backed securitizations achieve several general advantages for their practitioners.

BROADENING THE MARKET OF FUNDING SOURCES

Securities backed by financial assets are very liquid and are traded the world over. This opens up new sources of funding for these assets to their originators. It also opens up new avenues for supporting rapid growth in receivables as they can be funded on a short-term basis while the growth is occurring, then converted to a longer-term funding mechanism via securitization once growth has slowed. This liquidity benefit makes the funding of new bankcard assets easier for issuers.

REDUCING FUNDING COSTS

Securitizations have a tendency to reduce the originator's costs associated with the funding of securitized receivables as the process eliminates intermediaries from the funding process such as other banks and related entities, thus lowering the cost of obtaining the required funds. As originators securitize more and more of their assets, their cost of structuring each securitization is reduced through efficiency gains, thus further reducing the cost of the funds generated.

RISK DIVERSIFICATION

Securitized assets transfer the risk of ongoing performance and catastrophic loss from the originator to the investors. This lowers these risks for the originator, thus assisting in reducing the capital originators are required to keep against securitized assets. This enables them to deploy this capital in other ways, thus allowing for expansion of the bank's business in areas beyond bankcards.

In addition, specific banks may also gain other benefits via securitization depending upon their individual circumstances. For instance, the global market of traders in securitized assets may enable an issuer in one market to gain access to capital from another via the sale of its securities backed by its securitization trust in a foreign market. This may also assist issuers in lowering their funding costs depending upon the interest rate environment in the issuer's home market versus rates in others around the globe now accessible via the securitization market. The global securitization marketplace allows issuers in one market, say the US, to sell their asset-backed securities in another market, say Germany, thus taking advantage of interest rate differentials between the two markets.

The benefit regarding reduction in capital required in support of securitized assets is very specific to individual markets. From an accounting perspective, most securitization trusts are established such that assets sold by the originator to the trust are considered a true sale as that term is understood to be in the accounting world. This means that the trust and investors in the trust's securities ultimately are the owners of the future cash flows generated by the credit card assets securitized, thus freeing the originator from the need to have capital backing of these assets even though they remain the servicer of the accounts for the duration of the trust. From a regulatory capital adequacy viewpoint, however, different markets will have very different interpretations of what the originating bank is required to maintain in terms of capital against these 'sold' assets. In many countries, banking regulations regarding capital adequacy and safety and soundness of the banking system will supersede any accounting treatments regarding capital requirements for securitized assets. It is crucial that banks engaging in the securitization of a portion of their bankcard portfolio understand the capital adequacy rules which will govern a transaction in their market.

Similar to capital reduction benefits, issuers who securitize a portion of their bankcard assets may also benefit from a reduction in the loan loss reserves they are required to keep against their bankcard business. The sale of assets to a trust results in a lower level of assets outstanding on the originating bank's books after the transaction. Again, depending upon local banking regulations, this may entitle the issuer to reduce the loan loss reserve it carries on its books for its card business. As loan loss reserves, when reversed, become income, this can be a major benefit to issuers who can use the loss reserve reduction as a gain in income for the quarter in which a securitization transaction is implemented. This will ultimately be determined by the banking and accounting regulations in the market where the originating bank operates.

Finally, by transferring ownership interest in the bankcard assets to the trust and on to investors, the originating bank reduces its exposure to both credit and interest rate risk. This is now the concern of the investors in the trust's securities and it is their responsibility to research and be comfortable with the level of these risks contained in the assets which serve as collateral for the securities they purchase. The rating agencies certainly investigate these risks when evaluating a securitization trust and their report usually contains a specific commentary regarding the credit and interest rate risk they believe are inherent in the assets serving as collateral in the trust.

So do these potential benefits of securitization for bankcard issuers justify the cost and resource required to complete a securitization? Well, in most instances the answer is a resounding yes. Issuers must devote a fair amount of resource to the development and implementation of a securitization. First, they must create the entire historical trend-reporting on the group of accounts to be securitized so that a prospectus for the trust can be developed and so that the rating agencies can conduct their analysis. Then, issuers must retain outside counsel and investment banking advisors to assist in the creation of the trust and securities to be issued from the trust. Finally, issuers must provide the daily, weekly, and monthly reporting required by the trustee of the trust as the issuer remains the servicer of the securitized accounts. This reporting includes the tracking of payments by securitized accounts and the breakdown of those payments into principal, interest, and fees. All of this data and reporting development usually requires systems enhancements to accommodate. As a result, the creation of a securitization trust and the ongoing support requirements thereafter can cost issuers between $2 and $3 million to implement.

Is this cost justified by the potential benefits? Suppose an issuer wishes to securitize $500 million worth of bankcard assets and the initial cost to do so is $2.5 million. This represents one-half of one percent, or 50 basis points of the $500 million portfolio. So long as the benefit related to the reduction in cost of funds exceeds 50 basis points *over the life of the securitization trust* then the initial cost is justified. Most securitization securities are issued for a three to five year term, thus making the 50 basis point threshold quite easy to achieve. Essentially it means that the reduction in cost of funds for the issuer must be around 10 basis points a year over a five-year trust. Most securitizations provide substantially greater reductions in funding costs vis-à-vis alternatives. And, of course, this is before taking into account any of the other financial benefits of securitization such as reductions in capital deployed against the card business which raise the return on equity of the portfolio or the reduction in loss reserves required which can result in an immediate increase in current period earnings.

So, as demonstrated by the example, securitizing a portion of the bankcard portfolio almost certainly will result in financial gain for the issuer in almost any circumstance. Individual issuers choosing to securitize a portion of their bankcard assets must research the legal, regulatory, and accounting issues specific to their market and trust structure to ensure that they attain all of the benefits they seek from the process, but at a minimum, any issuer will gain lower funding costs and some amount of capital release by securitizing.

Other important concepts in securitization

The past few pages have described the basic concept and structure of asset-backed securitizations, but this does not begin to scratch the surface of the complex nature and multiple structure options inherent in any trust. Without attempting to address all of the complexities securitization trusts contain, there are several additional elements which need to be understood in order to fully grasp how securitizations work and their impact upon the financial markets of the world.

Previously, the two primary types of trusts, standalone and master, were described and their relative merits discussed. These trusts can be created to serve one of two markets, either public or private. The basic structure of the trust does not change depending upon which market is being addressed, but there may be terms and conditions regarding the securities issued against the assets contained within the trust which will vary depending upon the purchaser.

Privately placed securitization trusts function much the same as previously described, but with one caveat – their performance data is not made known to the general public as no securities are sold to the general public. Instead, a private securitization is a transaction between an issuer and an individual or corporate entity whereby no additional parties are privy to the terms and conditions of the transaction. As a result, the terms of private securitizations tend to be much more in favor of the investor and less favorable to the issuer. Why do a private securitization? In many cases it is because the issuer would have a great deal of difficulty bringing a public securitization to market. This could be due to the seasoning of the accounts in the trust, meaning they are too recently acquired to have a meaningful performance record, or it could be because the issuer specializes in granting credit to less creditworthy individuals, the subprime market, thus making the creation of a public trust more costly due to the credit enhancement components required to make the securities to be issued investment grade. Regardless of the reason for avoiding the public markets, privately placed securitizations can still deliver the benefits associated with securitizations in general, including an overall reduction in funding costs for the issuer and potential capital and loan loss reserve benefits as well.

Publicly sold securities are issued by securitization trusts and sold to corporate or individual investors via brokerage firms just like stocks or bonds. And like any publicly traded instrument, there are a plethora of firms which track and analyze the performance of the securities issued and sold on a monthly basis. All securitizations which are publicly traded must make their financial performance transparent. This means all key performance indicators such as trust portfolio yield, delinquencies, loss rates and payment rates must be reported to the trustee each and every month and the trustee, in turn, makes this data available to anyone wishing to view it in order to gauge whether or not they wish to invest. Every publicly issued securitization trust has its performance available via the Internet, Bloomberg terminals, or analyst reports on a monthly and quarterly basis. There are websites that track and report on every deal in every asset class in almost every market in the world. Access to this information is free and available to anyone who wishes to take the time to review the data offered.

Major brokerage houses and analyst firms also track and report on the securitization market regularly. Firms such as Morgan Stanley Dean Witter, Banc One Capital Markets Inc., and Credit Suisse First Boston have dedicated analysts who do nothing but review, analyze, and comment on securitization trust data. In addition, the three major rating agencies – Fitch, S & P, and Moody's – also track and report upon public securitization trust data.

Why is this transparency in the performance of securitization trusts so important? Why are simple statistics such as the ones shown below so critical to the efficient operation of the market?

US PUBLIC CREDIT CARD SECURITIZATION TRUST PERFORMANCE DATA

2Q 2004

- Yield: 17.3 per cent
- Delinquencies: 4.3 per cent

- Losses: 6.6 per cent
- Payment Rate: 17.6 per cent
  (*Source*: Standard & Poor's *US Credit Card Quality Index*, 'Performance data results continue positive trend': July 29, 2004)

Basic averages summarizing the performance of all trusts in a marketplace such as the data displayed above provide a ready benchmark against which any individual card issuer's trust performance can be easily measured and assessed. Investors have access to detailed information regarding the performance of each individual trust, thus enabling informed investment decisions. Utilizing the information readily available, investors can decide if they wish to purchase securities with a higher rate of return, but a corresponding increase in the level of risk associated with obtaining that return, or if a lower yielding, but more stable investment makes more sense. The availability of detailed performance data creates an informed investor community which leads to a rational market.

Transparency of performance data and trends forces credit card management teams to ensure that their portfolios deliver the results necessary within the competitive framework of the marketplace. Failure to do so will result in poor performing bankcard portfolios being unable to raise funds on a cost-effective basis as investors will place their money with portfolios which are performing better. The requirement to report all performance data every month serves as a mechanism to force bankcard managers to meet or exceed established standards, or suffer the consequences in terms of higher costs, slower growth rates, and limited access to public markets for capital and funding. In addition, a bankcard issuer which underperforms the market will have difficulty the next time it wishes to raise funds via the securitization marketplace based upon its past performance. It will be forced to pay a higher return to investors and add more costly credit enhancements to its trust in order to attract investors to its securities. Within the framework of the publicly traded credit-card-backed securities market, readily available performance data acts as a 'self-cleaning oven', forcing out the weaker players, thus ensuring long-term viability and liquidity of the securities accepted by the market.

Beyond the trust structure and the public/private delineation of securitization trusts, how a trust actually operates is also important to understand. Every trust, regardless of structure or market, once created, operates the same way on an ongoing basis. Upon issuing securities which are sold, the trust begins to operate in a manner which ensures that investors are paid the rate of return promised on the securities they purchased as well as receiving back their original invested principal upon the ending of the term of the security. This is accomplished in two distinct phases of the trust's operation; the revolving period and the amortization period.

REVOLVING PERIOD

Every securitization trust sells securities to investors backed by the revenues generated by the credit card accounts held within the trust. These securities have three key components: a principal amount, term, and stated rate of return, which can be on either a fixed or floating basis. Most trusts issue securities with varying terms, usually from three to five years, with a corresponding rate of return for each term. Asset-backed securities are usually denominated in amounts no less than US $100 000 given that the size of most trusts is in the hundreds of millions of dollars.

Once issued, the first period of time after issuance is called the revolving period. During this period, the investor receives only the interest associated with principal amount of the security they purchased. For example, if an investor purchased $100 000 in principal at a 5 per cent annualized rate of return, they would receive one-twelfth of $5000 each month, or $416.67. This would continue throughout the revolving period.

AMORTIZATION PERIOD

At some point between the start of the revolving period and the end of the term of the security, the trust will transition from the revolving period to the amortization period. During the amortization period investors are paid the rate of return promised on the security they purchased plus a portion of their principal investment amount each month with the payments calibrated such that the last payment, which will coincide with the final month of the term of the security, will result in the full repayment of the principal amount invested plus all interest promised. In most instances, the trust transitions from the revolving period to the amortization period somewhere around the halfway point of the term of the security issued.

Through this standard operating process, securitization trusts are able to raise funds and repay them in an orderly and timely fashion assuming the trust performs as anticipated. But what if the trust does not perform as anticipated? What if losses are higher, or revolve rates are lower, or attrition exceeds expectations, or some other performance variable is less than desirable? How do investors receive all of their principal and interest? How are they protected?

If a securitization trust encounters performance difficulties such that the revenue coming into the trust each month is insufficient to meet its operating expense, and principal and interest payment requirements, then the trust is said to be entering an 'early amortization' event. Early amortization means that protective covenants contained within the structure of the trust are triggered and the manner in which the cash generated by the trust is redistributed in order to ensure protection of the investors' principal invested amount. Usually early amortization events result in the originator of the trust, the bank issuing the credit cards and serving as the servicer of the trust, having to make up the shortfall, either through the addition of cash and/or additional credit card accounts into the trust as collateral or via the forgoing of its monthly servicing fees and excess spread revenues.

All securitization trusts contain provisions, or triggers, describing what actions will take place should an early amortization event occur. These triggers are usually performance metrics such as loss rate, yield, and payment rate expressed as either a point-in-time threshold or a three- or six-month rolling average. For example, a trust may state that in the event the loss rate on a rolling three-month average exceeds 7 per cent, then certain actions will occur to ensure the principal and interest payments to the investors remain uninterrupted.

Early amortization events are serious issues within the asset-backed securities marketplace. Certainty regarding the payment of interest and principal to investors is necessary to ensure the liquidity of the market and that future accessibility for new trusts is maintained. The combination of trust structure, credit enhancement, and early amortization triggers coupled with the transparent nature of trust performance data ensure a readily available and efficient securitization market.

WHY IS SECURITIZATION IMPORTANT?

After reviewing the contents of this chapter thus far, it is easy to see why bankcard professionals need to understand securitization and its impact upon the cards business. But why should anyone else outside of the bankcard business care about such a specialized and arcane financial process? How does it impact people not actively involved in the bankcard industry? Do lorry drivers and till clerks really need an in-depth knowledge of securitizations to go about their daily lives?

The answer is of course no, but an understanding of asset-backed securitizations and their impact upon global markets may help make them better consumers and better investors. As capital increasingly flows beyond borders in search of the best and safest returns, financial instruments such as securities backed by credit card assets become more attractive to a number of potential investors, and this demand for them helps to ensure that consumers the world over will receive the credit they seek in the most convenient form available...the credit card.

Index